HERBS

From Cultivation to Cooking

HERBS
From Cultivation
to Cooking

Compiled by
HERB SOCIETY OF CINCINNATI

PELICAN PUBLISHING COMPANY

GRETNA 1987

First printing, 1979
Second printing, October 1980
Third printing, September 1982
Fourth printing, November 1987

Library of Congress Cataloging in Publication Data
Main entry under title:

Herbs, from cultivation to cooking.

Includes index.
1. Cookery (Herbs) 2. Herb gardening. I. Herb
Society of Greater Cincinnati.
TX819. H4H464 1982   641.3'57   82-13229
ISBN: 0-88289-685-7

COMMITTEE

Margaret Minster, Editor and Cookbook Coordinator
Marge Haller, Assistant Cookbook Coordinator
Rosemarie Culver
Venus Derrick
Helen Kovach
Lois Nebergall
Williamette von Hedemann

Cover Photography
W. F. Schildman

Illustrations
Nina Ransohoff

Manufactured in the United States of America
Published by Pelican Publishing Company, Inc.
1101 Monroe Street, Gretna, Louisiana 70053

CONTENTS

CONTRIBUTING RESTAURANTS

Charley's Crab
9769 Montgomery Rd., Montgomery, Ohio 45242

Chester's Roadhouse
9678 Montgomery Rd., Montgomery, Ohio 45242

China Gourmet
3340 Erie Ave., Cincinnati, Ohio 45208

Coach House
855 S. Broadway, Lexington, Ky. 40504

Golden Lamb
Lebanon, Ohio 45036

Gourmet Room
Terrace Hilton, Cincinnati, Ohio 45202

Heritage
7664 Wooster Pike, Cincinnati, Ohio 45227

London Chop House
155 W. Congress, Detroit, Mich. 48226

Longwharf Restaurant
Water Front Bay St., Sag Harbor, L.I., N.Y.

Maisonette
114 East 6th St., Cincinnati, Ohio 45202

Pigall's
127 West 4th St., Cincinnati, Ohio 45202

Pogue's
4th St. Market, Cincinnati, Ohio 45202

Shakertown
Pleasant Hill, Kentucky

Shillito's Dining Room
Race Street, Cincinnati, Ohio 45202

"21" Club
21 West 52nd St., N.Y., N.Y. 10019

CONTRIBUTING PROFESSIONALS CHEFS, TEACHERS, AUTHORS, LECTURERS

DORA ANG
Teacher, caterer. Chinese, Indonesian and Dutch cuisine

MELANIE BARNARD
Teacher, free-lance food columnist

BILL BARUM
Caterer and teacher

MICHAEL BATTERBERRY
Editor in chief of the "International Review of Food & Wine"

SCOTT BERMAN
Chef, Longwharf restaurant, Sag Harbor Long Island, N.Y.

CHARLES BOLTON
Writer-in-residence, Xavier University, free-lance writer on foods

LEE CAIN
Garden columnist, Cincinnati Post

CHRIS CARSMAN
Co-owner, What's Cooking

STANLEY DEMOS
Author, executive chef and owner of Coach House, Lexington, Ky.

MARNY DILTS
Lecturer, owner of Chalet Lodge Herb Farm, Delaware, Ohio

JERRY EAST
Executive chef, Shillito's

GERTRUDE FOSTER
Author and editor "Herb Grower Magazine" Falls Village, Conn.

ALICE GALVIN
Teacher

CHEF JIM GREGORY
Executive chef, Cummins Manufacturing and teacher, Columbus, Ind.

CLAIRE GREGORY
Chef's assistant extraordinaire

MARILYN HARRIS
Teacher

RUTH HOWARD
Teacher

VIRGINIA LARSON
Teacher, owner of La Cooking school, Troy, Ohio

MRS. JO LOHMOLDER
Lecturer

ROSEMARY F. LOUDEN
Lecturer

ROSELLA MATHIEU
Author and renowned herbalist

JANE MILLER
Owner of Hurrah

LINDA MILLER
Teacher

BING MOY
Chef and owner of China Gourmet

JERRY NATOWITZ
1st Prize Cincinnati Post Cooking Contest

JULIE BROGRAN NORTHRUP
Home economist

MONA POYNTER
Dietitian and teacher

CHEF PULVER
Executive chef, Gourmet Restaurant Terrace Hilton, Cincinnati, Ohio

MARGY ROBSON
Former co-owner Panhandler

BARBARA REMINGTON
Owner, Dutch Mills Herb Farm, Forest Grove, Oregon

BARBARA ROSENBERG
Teacher

JOYCE ROSENCRANS
Food Editor, Cincinnati Post

ADELMA SIMMONS
Author, lecturer, owner, Caprilands Herb Farm, North Coventry, Conn.

DON WHITTLE
Owner, Pigall's

LEONA WOODRING SMITH
World famous lecturer and author

JOAN STADLER
Lecturer and herb enthusiast, Urbana, Ohio

DAISY STICKSEL
Herbalist and lecturer

FERN STORER
Former Food Editor Cincinnati Post, nationally syndicated
column on microwave cooking

INELDA TAJO
Teacher — Italian cuisine

LOIS YOUNG, OLGA EINFELT, JANE THOMPSON
Canadian cookbook editors

INTRODUCTION

Herbs have been used throughout the centuries for many purposes: in medicine, science, cooking, and just for their delightful fragrance.

As the Greater Cincinnati Herb Society's book developed, we began to realize the tremendous versatility of herbs. We discovered that one could use one's own imagination and creative ability, in the kitchen, in the garden, and in decorating around the house.

Herbs not only provide ordinary dishes with tantalizing new flavors, but they enhance gourmet dishes as well. They contribute endless and exciting variations to daily menu planning.

The world of herbs is a magic world. When you begin to experiment, trying first one, and then another, you will soon find yourself beckoned on to trying them all.

In this book, we have introduced you to the many diversified uses of herbs. We hope the book will inspire you "to do your own thing" with herbs.

Each herb has its own distinctive scent, pleasant, sometimes pungent, but always easily identifiable. This characteristic alone makes herbs a pleasure to use and enjoy.

You will find that your family and friends are going to appreciate the end results when you cook with herbs, but only you and you alone will have the almost sensuous pleasure of cutting fresh basil, oregano, parsley, thyme, and sniffing the aromatic quality of each individual herb as it is cut. That is one of the many fringe benefits of growing your own herbs.

Our cultivation, propagation, and preservation chart gives you the best methods for growing and drying herbs.

In our recipes, we suggest using fresh herbs whenever possible. There is no doubt that they are more flavorful than dried ones. However, remember that the rule of thumb equivalent of fresh vs dried is: USE TRIPLE THE AMOUNT OF FRESH HERBS TO DRIED HERBS. That is because dried herbs are much stronger in flavor. Dried herbs should not to stored in bright light and should not be kept for more than one year.

In this book, we also recommend your using freshly ground pepper because it does add more flavor to a recipe.

We were fortunate in receiving many recipes from professional chefs, teachers, and top restaurants in our Cincinnati area, as well as a few from farther afield. The names of the professionals will be listed with their recipes. All other recipes were contributed by members of the Herb Society and their friends.

We sincerely hope that you will enjoy our mouth-watering recipes, and we also hope this book will inspire you to do some experimenting on your own, both in the garden and in the kitchen.

Margaret Minster, Editor and Cookbook Coordinator

A special thanks to all the people, too numerous to mention, who have contributed their time to this book. It was indeed a labor of love for herbs that made it possible.

M.M.

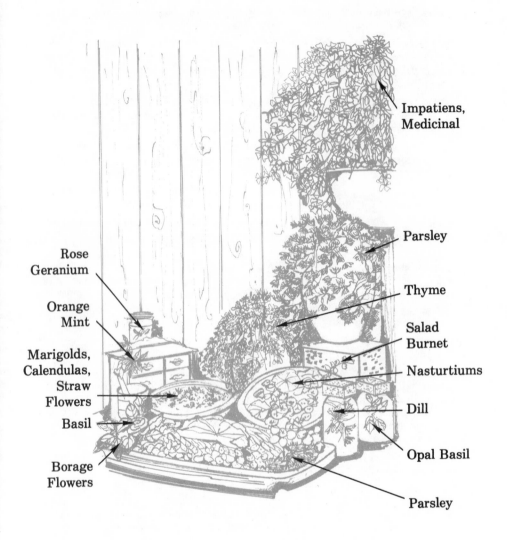

Impatiens,
Medicinal

Parsley

Thyme

Salad
Burnet

Nasturtiums

Dill

Opal Basil

Parsley

Rose
Geranium

Orange
Mint

Marigolds,
Calendulas,
Straw
Flowers

Basil

Borage
Flowers

I pray thee, give it me.
I know a bank where the *wild thyme* blows,
Where oxlips and the nodding violet grows;
Quite over-canopied with lush woodbine,
With sweet musk-roses, and with eglantine;

Shakespeare

A Midsummer Night's Dream

Appetizers

RAW VEGETABLES FOR DIPS

Raw vegetables, also referred to as crudites, which lend themselves to dips are listed below. Keep them crisp in the refrigerator until serving time. Very elegant to serve them on ice intermingled with cooked shrimp and assorted olives, garnished with fresh herbs.

Asparagus, young, tender, slim tops
Belgian endive leaves
Broccoli sprouts, young, broken into florets
Carrots, in strips
Cauliflower, young, broken into florets
Celery, in strips
Cherry tomatoes, whole
Cucumbers, young, in strips
Fennel root bulbs, (only Florence fennel), in strips
Green peppers, seeded and cut in strips
Radishes, whole, may be made into flowers
Scallions, young and tender, whole
Squash, yellow, summer, in strips
Zucchini, young and tender, in strips

Also excellent: Cooked artichokes, served whole. Individual leaves used for dip.

BAKED DIP

1 cup sharp Cheddar cheese, grated
1 small onion, grated
1 cup mayonnaise
½ teaspoon thyme, dried
½ teaspoon marjoram, dried

Mix well and bake in 350°F oven until hot. Serve with crackers.

Yield: 2 cups

CURRY DIP

1 cup mayonnaise
1 teaspoon tarragon, dried
1 teaspoon garlic salt

1 teaspoon instant minced onion
1 teaspoon curry powder

Mix all ingredients and allow to stand several hours or overnight to blend flavors. Serve with a variety of raw vegetables.

Yield: 1 cup

HERB-CURRY DIP

1½ teaspoons lemon juice
½ teaspoon Worcestershire sauce
1 tablespoon grated onion
1 cup mayonnaise
½ cup sour cream
¼ teaspoon salt
1 teaspoon crushed herbs — rosemary, sage, oregano, and other favorites (mixed)
⅛ teaspoon curry powder
1 tablespoon parsley

Blend in food processor or blender about 12 hours in advance; do not re-stir before serving. Serve with raw vegetables.

Yield: 1½ cups

MAYONNAISE NICOISE DIP

2 cloves garlic
12 anchovy fillets, drained
1 teaspoon capers
½ cup Greek olives, pitted
1 teaspoon fresh basil or tarragon
2 tablespoons chopped Italian parsley
2 cups mayonnaise, preferably homemade

Chop garlic, anchovies, capers, olives, basil, and parsley very fine and blend all, except 1 tablespoon parsley, with mayonnaise. Refrigerate overnight. Sprinkle 1 tablespoon parsley over top. Serve as a dip with raw vegetables.

Yield: 2 cups

MIXED HERB DIP FOR RAW VEGETABLES

1 cup mayonnaise
½ cup sour cream
1 teaspoon mixed herbs (thyme, basil, rosemary, chives, marjoram)
½ teaspoon Worcestershire sauce
½ teaspoon salt
⅛ teaspoon curry powder
1 tablespoon snipped parsley
1 tablespoon grated onion
1½ teaspoons lemon juice

Blend well. Refrigerate several hours. Serve with raw vegetables.

Yield: 1½ cups

SPINACH VEGETABLE DIP

1 cup mayonnaise and 1 cup sour cream
1 (10-oz.) package frozen chopped spinach, cooked and drained well
½ cup chopped green onions
½ cup chopped fresh parsley
1 teaspoon salt
½ to 1 teaspoon pepper
1 teaspoon Beau Monde

Mix in blender. Serve with raw vegetables.

Yield: 2½ cups

STUFFED MUSHROOMS

Shakertown

2 pts. mushrooms
2 tablespoons finely chopped onions
2 tablespoons butter
¼ cup soft bread crumbs
¼ cup toasted chopped almonds
2 teaspoons lemon juice
½ teaspoon salt
½ teaspoon Worcestershire sauce
½ cup cream
½ teaspoon thyme
½ cup grated cheese

Wash mushrooms and remove stems. Put caps in lemon juice. Chop stems and saute in butter for 5 minutes. Add onions, crumbs, thyme and cook a few minutes. Strain off lemon juice from caps and add to cooked mixture. Fill caps with mixture. Place in shallow baking dish. Pour cream around mushrooms and bake 15 minutes at 400°F. Top caps with the grated cheese and bake 10 minutes more. Serve hot.

Serves 8 to 10

TAPENADE

Melanie Barnard

1 (2-oz.) can anchovy fillet,
undrained
2 teaspoons capers
3 tablespoons red wine vinegar
2 tablespoons chives, minced
¼ cup fresh parsley, chopped
1½ cups mayonnaise
⅛ teaspoon freshly ground
black pepper

In a blender or processor, puree anchovies, capers, vinegar, chives, and parsley. Stir in mayonnaise and pepper. Chill well. Serve as a dip for raw vegetables.

Yield: 1¾ cups

14

BEER CHEESE

Shakertown

1 pound Old English sharp cheese
2 large cloves garlic
1½ teaspoons Frank's Red Hot Sauce
⅓ cup warm beer

Cut cheese into 1 inch squares and put in mixing bowl; let come to room temperature. (To hasten the softening, place mixing bowl in hot water.) Slice garlic and run through garlic press, adding to the cheese as you press it. Add Red Hot Sauce and beat at high speed for one minute. Add beer and beat again at high speed for two minutes. The mixture should spread easily; if not, add more beer. Store in crocks and refrigerate. To serve, let it come to room temperature. Serve with party rye bread sliced silver-dollar thin.

Yield: Approx. 1¼ lbs.

BOURSIN CHEESE I

The Heritage

1 (8-oz.) package whipped butter
2 (8-oz.) packages cream cheese
1 small package whipped cream cheese
2 cloves garlic, minced
¼ teaspoon ground cloves
1 teaspoon dill, dried
½ teaspoon marjoram, dried
½ teaspoon basil, dried
½ teaspoon chives

Let whipped butter, cream cheese, and whipped cream cheese soften. Add herbs and mix.

Yield: 1½ cups

BOURSIN CHEESE II

Virginia Larson

½ cup cottage cheese, large curd (you may substitute 8 ozs. cream cheese)
2 tablespoons unsalted butter
4 tablespoons chopped parsley
1 clove garlic, minced
Salt to taste
¼ teaspoon dried thyme or 1 or 2 teaspoons fresh thyme, chopped
Lemon juice to taste, about ½ lemon

Continued

Drain cheese well, if using cottage cheese. Work cheese and butter to smooth paste. Pound parsley, garlic, thyme, lemon juice and salt together and work into cheese paste with oiled hands. Shape into a round ball on flat oiled board. Sprinkle with chopped parsley or chives, if desired. Wrap in aluminum foil. Let ripen in refrigerator for 5 days.

Variation:
Partially hollow out ½-inch thick cucumber slices, which have been scored and allowed to drain overnight, refrigerated. Mound ripened boursin cheese in cucumber slices. Criss cross 2 strips of smoked salmon over cheese and garnish with a sprig of parsley and several capers.

Yield: ¾ cup

BOURSIN CHEESE III

Ruth Howard

1 clove garlic
8 ozs. unsalted whipped butter
16 ozs. cream cheese
½ teaspoon each: salt, basil, marjoram, chives, dried
¼ teaspoon thyme, dried
1 teaspoon dill
1 tablespoon parsley, fresh
¼ teaspoon freshly ground pepper

Can be done in food processor, blender, or by hand. Crush garlic first.
Add remaining ingredients and mix thoroughly. Serve on crackers or Melba toast.

Yield: Approx. 2 cups

CARAWAY CHEESE

Ruth Howard

1 lb. sharp Cheddar cheese, grated
3 ozs. cream cheese
¼ cup walnut oil or olive oil
1 teaspoon dry mustard
1 teaspoon caraway seed
2 tablespoons brandy

Combine cheeses. Add oil and mix until smooth. Blend in mustard, caraway, and brandy. Store in jar in refrigerator.

Yield: Approx. 2 cups

COMFREY-CHEESE ROLLS-UPS

"The Complete Herb Guide"
Rosella F. Mathieu

12 tender comfrey leaves
6 finger-sized pieces American or Cheddar cheese
¼ cup bread crumbs
3 eggs
Salt and pepper
2 tablespoons chopped parsley
1 clove garlic, minced
2 tablespoons Parmesan cheese

Sprinkle 6 clean dry comfrey leaves with bread crumbs, place the cheese fingers on them and roll up. Use the other 6 leaves to wrap the rolls in the opposite direction, covering the open ends of the rolls. Secure with toothpicks. Beat eggs and add the seasonings and cheese. Dip roll-ups into the mixture. Fry until golden in oil or lard. Note: Butter or margarine tends to make the rolls stick.

Yield: 6 roll-ups

CURRIED CHEESE BALL

11 ozs. cream cheese
8 ozs. sharp Cheddar cheese, grated
2 to 3 stuffed olives, chopped
3 cloves crushed garlic
1 tablespoon curry powder
1 tablespoon chives, minced
1 cup black walnuts, chopped coarsely or broken
Chopped parsley, for garnish

Blend cheeses, garlic, olives, curry powder. Add chives and walnuts and mix thoroughly. Form into ball or log. Refrigerate or freeze. Sprinkle with chopped parsley. Serve at room temperature with crackers.

HERBED CHEESE

Ruth Howard

1 lb. sharp Cheddar cheese, grated
3 ozs. cream cheese
¼ cup walnut oil or olive oil
1 teaspoon dry mustard
½ teaspoon each: marjoram and tarragon, dried
4 tablespoons dry sherry

Combine cheeses. Add oil and mix until smooth. Blend in mustard, herbs, and sherry. Store in jar in refrigerator.

Yield: Approx. 2 cups

HERBED CREAM CHEESE SPREAD

8 ozs. cream cheese
1 to 2 teaspoons horseradish (or to taste, depending on strength)
2 tablespoons chopped parsley
2 tablespoons chopped young salad burnet leaves
2 tablespoons minced chives
1 small onion, minced or grated

Soften cheese and blend all together. Refrigerate several days to allow flavors to blend. Serve on crackers or use for filling in rolled tea sandwiches, garnished with a sprig of salad burnet.

Yield: 1 cup

HERBED SPREAD

8 ounces Neufchatel* cheese
1 stick unsalted margarine, softened*
1 clove garlic, pressed
1 tablespoon oregano
½ to 1 teaspoon each: thyme, basil, marjoram, dill seed

*Cream cheese and sweet butter may be substituted. Combine all ingredients and mix well.

Serve with lightly salted crackers, or add salt to cheese and serve with unsalted crackers.

May make a few days ahead. Quantities given for fresh herbs; adjust downward, if using dried.

Yield 1½ cups

SARASOTA SESAME CREAM CHEESE

2 tablespoons sesame seeds
1 tablespoon olive oil
1 (8-oz.) package Philadelphia cream cheese
1 tablespoon soy sauce

Brown 2 tablespoons sesame seeds in olive oil.

Let seeds partially cool; drain. Press them over top and all sides of the Philadelphia cream cheese.
Pour soy sauce over cheese.
Refrigerate, but remove before serving to allow cheese to soften.
Serve with crackers or Melba toast.

Yield: 1 cup

MUSHROOM CHICKEN LIVER PATE

Civic Garden Center "Herb Cookery"

¼ cup butter
½ lb. fresh mushrooms
1 lb. chicken livers
1 tablespoon garlic salt
1 tablespoon paprika

⅓ cup finely chopped
green onions
⅓ cup white wine
1 teaspoon dill
3 drops Tabasco
½ cup soft butter
Salt and pepper to taste

Simmer mushrooms, chicken livers, garlic salt, paprika and onions in ¼ cup butter for 5 minutes. Add wine, dill, and Tabasco. Cover and cook slowly for 5 to 10 minutes more. Cool and mix well in processor or blender. Blend in soft butter, salt, and pepper. Turn into a greased bowl. Chill overnight. Unmold before serving and garnish with chopped parsley, thin lemon slices and 3 sprigs of fresh dill.

Yield: Approx. 1½ lbs.

PATE AUX HERBES

Alice Galvin

2 lbs. lean pork tenderloin
½ lb. chicken livers,
washed and dried
6 ozs. Canadian bacon
6 ozs. bacon
1 lb. spinach, washed well
2 medium onions, chopped
2 garlic cloves, chopped
2 eggs, beaten

1 teaspoon salt
½ teaspoon pepper
½ teaspoon rosemary
½ teaspoon basil
½ teaspoon marjoram
¼ teaspoon thyme
¼ teaspoon nutmeg
½ lb. thinly sliced bacon

Pre-heat oven to 325°F

Chop meats very fine in food processor.
Chop spinach stems and leaves in food processor.
Mix meats and onions very well by hand. Add spinach.
Add all other ingredients except bacon slices.
Line a pate pan with bacon slices and spoon in pate mixture, packing it firmly. Cover with bacon slices.
Put pan in a large baking dish and pour boiling water up to the edge of the pate mold.
Bake 1½ hours, adding more boiling water, if necessary.
Serve chilled and thinly sliced.

Yield: Approx. 2½ lbs.

PATE DE CAMPAGNE

Virginia Larson

1½ pounds sausage
1 teaspoon salt
½ teaspoon ground pepper
1 teaspoon thyme, dried
2 thin slices cooked ham
1 pound pork loin, cut ½-inch thick

Mix sausage, salt, pepper, and thyme well.
In a loaf pan, alternate ham and pork slices with sausage layer on top and bottom. Cover with foil.
Place in another pan containing hot water, half the depth of the pan and bake at 400°F for 2 hours.
Weight with heavy object, such as brick, until cool.
Serve with thin-sliced rye bread.

Yield: Approx. 1 lb.

PATE DE PROVENCE

Virginia Larson

1 cup cooked beef, coarsely chopped
6 anchovy fillets, drained, washed, and dried
¼ pound unsalted margarine
2 teaspoons grated onion
1 teaspoon lemon juice
½ teaspoon crushed thyme, dried
1 garlic clove, crushed
Black pepper, freshly ground

Puree all ingredients in blender or food processor.
Spoon into small earthenware crock.
Cover air-tight and refrigerate at least four hours.
Serve with Melba toast, French, or black bread.
Will keep three weeks, refrigerated.

Yield: Approx. 1 cup

"Rosemary for Remembrance"

Shakespeare

Remember:
Use triple the amount of fresh herbs to dried herbs!

20

PATE MAISON

Bill Matthews

2 pounds chicken livers
2 pounds calves' liver
2 pounds pork liver
2 pounds sausage
1 pound bacon, cut into bits
1 pound bacon, in slices
1 tablespoon each of basil, pepper, thyme, marjoram and rosemary
8 large eggs
1 cup good cognac

Finely chop all liver, or process in a food processor with steel blade. Beat eggs with cognac and seasonings and combine with chopped meats and cut up bacon. Test a small portion by frying in a frypan and then adjust seasoning. Do not taste raw because of the raw pork.

Line 2 or 3 pate pans or loaf pans with bacon slices and fill with liver mixture. Fold over ends of bacon and top with slices of bacon.

Place in flat pan with one-half inch of water coming up the sides of the pate pan and bake for three hours at 300°F. Remove from oven and weight down with bricks or canned food until cooled to room temperature. Store in refrigerator. Note: If using a loaf pan instead of a pate pan, cover pan with a triple layer of foil before baking.

Yield: 50 servings for a buffet, or enough for a large party as an hors d'oeuvre

SHRIMP APPETIZER

1½ lbs. fresh shrimp in shell
Juice of 1 large lime
1 teaspoon salt
3 tablespoons coriander leaves, minced
1½ tablespoons chives, minced
1½ tablespoons Italian parsley, minced
3 tablespoons olive oil
2 tablespoons butter
Lime halves for garnish

Peel and clean shrimp (leaving on tails). Place in a flat dish and sprinkle with lime juice and salt.

Combine minced herbs.

In a large heavy skillet, heat oil and butter. When hot, saute shrimp for a few minutes, stirring until they change color and look opaque. When they are pink, add the herbs, reduce heat to low, cook about 1 to 2 minutes.

To serve, place shrimp on plate, pour pan juices over, and garnish with fresh lime halves.

Serve with French bread.

Serves 6

FENNEL SHRIMP

1 pound cooked shrimp or 2 (4½ ozs.) cans shrimp
½ cup tarragon vinegar
½ cup olive oil
3 green onions, chopped (including greens)
1 clove garlic, chopped (or more to taste)
1 tablespoon chili sauce
1 teaspoon Dijon Mustard (or Mr. Mustard)
1 tablespoon chopped fresh fennel or dill
½ teaspoon paprika
½ teaspoon chopped parsley

Mix all but shrimp, paprika, and parsley; then pour over shrimp and allow to marinate overnight. When serving, sprinkle paprika and chopped parsley over all.

Serve 4 to 6

FRIKEDEL JAGUNG, SHRIMP (Indonesian)

Dora Ang

8 ozs. shrimp, chopped
5 to 6 large ears corn, grated
1 to 2 eggs
3 tablespoons flour
3 tablespoons green onion, chopped
¼ teaspoon pepper
1 teaspoon salt
1 tablespoon each grated garlic and onion
1 teaspoon coriander seeds, ground
3 cups vegetable oil

Chop shrimp fine. Add all ingredients and mix together well. Heat oil in pan, preferably in a wok, 325° or 350°F. Pour about 1 tablespoon of the mixture into frying pan for each fritter, making 4 to 5 fritters at a time. Fry for about 3 minutes or until golden brown.

Serve 8 to 10

HERB BUTTER-SAUCED SHRIMP

1 pound cooked shrimp
2 tablespoons butter
½ teaspoon paprika
Pinch each oregano, basil, marjoram
½ teaspoon Worcestershire sauce
Juice of ½ lemon
½ clove garlic, chopped fine
1 tablespoon chopped parsley

Melt butter; add all ingredients except shrimp. Heat sauce. When ready to serve, add shrimp. An electric skillet is excellent for this. Heat well and serve at once.

Serve 4 to 6

KEE KIAN (CHINESE)

(Pork and Shrimp Sticks)

Dora Ang

¾ pound ground pork or ham
¾ pound ground shrimp, raw
3 cloves garlic (1 teaspoon chopped)
2 teaspoons salt
1 teaspoon pepper
1 teaspoon sugar
⅛ teaspoon 5-spice powder
3 eggs
1 cup flour
3 cups vegetable oil

Dipping Sauce:
½ teaspoon Chinese chili sauce or Tabasco
2 tablespoons tomato catsup

In a bowl, mix ground pork, ground shrimp, garlic, and the spices. Add eggs and stir in flour. Transfer into a heat-proof bowl which has been sprayed with No-Stick spray.

Steam for 30 minutes by placing bowl in wok or similar pan, elevated, so water just steams. Let cool.

Transfer steamed Kee Kian (all ingredients except sauce) to a chopping block and cut in small pieces.

Heat vegetable oil in wok and deep fry in hot oil until brown and crisp (10 to 15 pieces at a time). Serve with dipping sauce.

Serves 8 to 10

MARINATED SHRIMP I

2 pounds cooked, cleaned shrimp (split, if large)
2 onions, sliced thin
1 cup salad or olive oil
1 cup white vinegar
¼ cup sugar
½ jar (10 ozs.) capers, plus juice
Salt and pepper to taste
½ teaspoon Dijon Mustard (or Mr. Mustard)
1 tablespoon Worcestershire sauce
Dash Tabasco
½ lemon, sliced thin
1 or more cloves garlic, chopped fine
2 bay leaves, broken
1 teaspoon horseradish
1 tablespoon chopped parsley and/or fresh dill for garnish

Mix all ingredients together except shrimp, parsley, dill.
Pour marinade over shrimp. Refrigerate for 24 hours, stirring occasionally.
When ready to serve, sprinkle with chopped parsley, and/or chopped dill.

Serves 8 to 10

MARINATED SHRIMP II

2½ lbs. uncooked shrimp
½ cup celery tops
3 teaspoons salt
¼ cup mixed pickling spices
2 cups thinly sliced onions
7 or 8 bay leaves
1¼ cups salad oil or olive oil
¾ cup white vinegar
1½ teaspoons salt
2½ teaspoons celery seed
2½ tablespoons capers and juice
Dash Tabasco

Cook shrimp your usual way, adding celery tops, 3 teaspoons salt and pickling spices in water. Drain and clean shrimp. Alternate shrimp with sliced onions in a shallow dish. Add bay leaves. Combine in separate bowl: salad oil, vinegar, salt, celery seed, capers and juice, and Tabasco. Mix well and pour over shrimp. Cover and store for 24 hours in refrigerator. When ready to serve place toothpicks on table or tray, so guests may spear shrimp and eat, or serve on individual cocktail plates.

Serves 10

ANTIPASTO

This dish is versatile both in ingredients and ways of serving. The list of ingredients may be varied. Antipasto may be used as an hors d'oeuvre, as a first course, as a salad with pasta, or as an entree. There are no quantities listed; this is a suggestion of various items that may be used.

The dressing should be basically your favorite Italian. The herb additions, basil, oregano, and marjoram, will add a great deal to the flavor.

Ingredients:
  Mushrooms, sliced, preferably fresh
  Garlic salami, sliced thin, halved or quartered
  Italian pepper, medium or hot (if you prefer spicy food)
  Italian red onion, sliced thin
  Green pepper, sliced thin
  Sardines
  Anchovies
  Capers
  Cherry tomatoes
  Salt and freshly ground pepper
  Baby shrimp, optional
  Provolone cheese, sliced thin, halved or quartered
  Olives, black, and green
  Tuna fish
  Mayonnaise

This dish is best if ingredients are marinated overnight, except for sardines, tuna, and tomatoes.

Arrange vegetables, herbs and other ingredients in a shallow pan, large enough to turn them occasionally and baste with Italian dressing.

When you are ready to serve, place a bed of lettuce in a serving bowl or platter. Ruby red lettuce is attractive for this. Drain marinated ingredients; keep marinade. Place tuna fish in center, mask with mayonnaise and garnish with capers. Arrange marinated ingredients around tuna fish. Place sardines around tuna as though they were swimming. Put remainder around edge of platter. Garnish with fresh basil, oregano, or salad burnet. Drizzle marinade over all but tuna.

ARTICHOKE HEART NIBBLES

2 jars (6 ozs.) artichoke hearts marinated in oil
1 small onion, finely minced
1 clove garlic, finely minced
4 eggs, beaten
¼ cup dry bread crumbs (Pepperidge Farm Herb Stuffing)
Salt, pepper to taste
1 teaspoon oregano
Dash Tabasco
½ cup shredded sharp Cheddar cheese
2 tablespoons parsley, chopped

Drain artichokes, reserving liquid from jar. Cook onion and garlic in this liquid until transparent. Put these and all other ingredients in blender or food processor. Mix well. Turn into a greased baking pan (7" x 11").

Bake at 325°F for about 30 minutes. Let cool. Cut in squares. Reheat when ready to serve. May be frozen and reheated after thawing and bringing to room temperature.

Yield: Approx. 30

CURRIED APPETIZER BALLS WITH CHICKEN

Mona Poynter (Mrs. Donald)

1 cup cooked, ground chicken or turkey (white meat preferred)
½ cup celery, finely diced
1 teaspoon curry powder
2 tablespoons mayonnaise
Salt to taste
½ cup almonds, toasted, finely chopped

Combine chicken, celery, curry powder, mayonnaise, and salt. Chill slightly and form into tiny balls, about ¾" in diameter. Roll in almonds. Chill thoroughly. Serve on toothpicks.

Chicken and celery may be ground together. Almonds can be finely chopped in blender.

Yield: 15 to 18 balls

EGGPLANT HORS D'OEUVRE OR SALAD

1 large eggplant
4 green onions, chopped
1 large tomato, peeled, seeded, and chopped
2 tablespoons parsley, chopped
1 clove garlic, minced
2 tablespoons white vinegar

Continued

26

¼ cup olive oil
½ teaspoon salt
½ teaspoon oregano, dried
Freshly ground pepper
8 to 10 Greek or Italian olives

Bake whole eggplant at 375°F for about 50 minutes or until soft. Dip in cold water. Peel off skin. Dice eggplant. Add rest of ingredients and chill for several hours.

Serves 6 to 8

FRESH PICKLED MUSHROOMS

Michael Batterberry

1½ lbs. firm white
mushrooms
1½ cups red wine vinegar
¾ cup brown sugar
1 cup water
6 to 8 large cloves garlic, peeled
and split lengthwise
2½ teaspoons kosher salt

6 bay leaves
14 peppercorns
2 cloves
1 tablespoon minced fresh
thyme or 1 teaspoon
dried
3 slices lemon
¼ cup olive oil, plus a few
extra teaspoons.

Wipe mushrooms clean with damp paper towel or cloth. Trim off tough bottom of stems. If mushrooms are large, cut them lengthwise into 2, 3 or 4 pieces, remembering that they will shrink in pickling to approximately half of their original volume. Simmer all other ingredients (with the exception of the extra spoons of oil) for 15 minutes in a wide enameled pot. Gently drop in the mushrooms and cook, stirring cautiously, so as to imbue all of them with the pungent juices without breaking them, for 3 or 4 minutes only. Remove pot from heat and allow mushrooms to cool in juices, turning them often with a spoon. Remove with a slotted spoon, let drain briefly, and toss before serving with just enough olive oil to coat them slightly. Decorate with fresh lemon wedges and bay leaves from the pot. Strain juices and keep for pickling next batch of mushrooms (liquid will keep in refrigerator at least 2 weeks).

Yield: Approx. 2½ cups

"Rosemary for Remembrance"
Shakespeare

Remember:
Use triple the amount of fresh herbs to dried herbs!

HERB CHEESE CRACKERS

For an hors d'oeuvre or serve with salads, soup, or iced tea (herbed, of course)

8 ozs. extra sharp Cheddar cheese
1 stick butter
1 cup flour
1 teaspoon thyme, dried
1 teaspoon marjoram, dried
Dash Tabasco
½ teaspoon Worcestershire sauce

Blend ingredients well. If you have a food processor, cut cheese and butter (softened) into 1 inch pieces, then add the rest of ingredients and blend.

This may be made ahead and put into a long roll for slicing or frozen in a ball, defrosted, and rolled flat like pie dough in wax paper. Then cut with cookie cutter. They may also be frozen after they have been baked.

Bake at 400°F about 15 minutes.

Yield: Approx. 36

OYSTER CRACKERS, HERBED

1 box oyster crackers
1 cup cooking oil or butter
Celery salt
Thyme, marjoram, or any of your favorite herbs to taste, sprinkled on crackers

Bake in a 250°F oven about 30 minutes or until oyster crackers are slightly browned.

This may be made in smaller quantities. Adjust ingredients accordingly.

HERB TART

Shakertown

1 (10-inch) pastry shell

Ingredients for herb filling:

4 eggs
½ cup heavy cream
½ cup milk
4 tablespoons Parmesan cheese
Salt to taste
Freshly ground black pepper
Freshly grated nutmeg
4 tablespoons onion, finely chopped

2 tablespoons butter
1 head iceberg lettuce, washed, cut in slivers
1 tablespoon chives, finely chopped
1 tablespoon fennel or dill, finely chopped (fresh)
2 tablespoons parsley, finely chopped
½ teaspoon rosemary, minced (fresh)

Continued

Method for filling:

Beat eggs together with cream and milk in a bowl. Beat in Parmesan; when well mixed, season to taste with salt, freshly ground black pepper, and freshly grated nutmeg.

Saute onion in butter in a skillet until just colored, add slivered lettuce and toss quickly (about ½ minute) just to heat lettuce through. Force through a fine sieve. Combine onion and lettuce mixture with herbs and add to egg mixture.

Method for tart:

Fill tart shell with herb mixture and bake in a 325°F oven for 30 to 40 minutes. Serve hot, lukewarm, or cold; cut in wedges.

Serves 6 to 8

HERBED VEGETABLES

Michael Batterberry

A welcome change from crudites. Choose the freshest specimens you can find crisp, tender and unblemished. Cauliflower, carrots, green beans and zucchini make an attractive combination, particularly when studded with freshly pickled mushrooms (see recipe) and Greek black olives.

Trim cauliflower into large bite-size florets, peeling stems with a small sharp knife. Drop into cold water to cover, acidulated with a tablespoon of lemon juice or white wine vinegar. Bring to a rapid boil; drain immediately; plunge florets into a bowl of cold water, and drain well once again. Marinate in a vinaigrette dressing of 1 part white wine vinegar to 4 parts olive oil, highly seasoned with dry mustard (dissolved in the vinegar), salt and white pepper.

Scrape and cut carrots into large bite-size chunks and boil 3 minutes. Drain and dress while still hot with a vinaigrette made of 1 part lemon juice, 3 parts olive oil, salt, pepper, a pinch of sugar, and either 2 tablespoons freshly chopped, or 1 tablespoon dried tarragon per ½ cup of dressing.

Boil trimmed green beans in generously salted water until tender but still crisp. Drain beans; plunge into cold water, drain again, and dry with paper towels. Marinate in the following dressing: high speed blend 1 cup olive oil, ¼ cup lemon juice, a dash of Tabasco, 4 inch squirt of anchovy paste, 2 heaping tablespoons of capers, a 2-inch strip of lemon zest, ½ teaspoon sugar, 2 handfuls of Italian parsley leaves. Correct for salt (when arranging to serve, excess marinade may be saved to dress a tomato salad).

Cut zucchini into chunky strips the size of little finger. Sprinkle rather heavily with coarse salt and let drain in a colander for an hour. Rinse, pat dry and saute for no more than 2 minutes in hot olive oil — about 2 tablespoons per pound. Drain again and marinate in a vinaigrette of 3 parts oil to 1 part lemon juice plus 2 tablespoons freshly chopped or 1 tablespoon dried basil per pound. Correct salt if necessary.

Chill vegetables separately, preferably overnight, in their marinades, giving them a toss or shake when it comes to mind. Arrange on a platter or in a bowl and dust with finely minced parsley. Have plenty of toothpicks at hand.

MARINATED CUCUMBERS

Peel 3 cucumbers and cut in long strips. Sprinkle with ½ teaspoon cream of tartar. Put in salted water with a sliced onion. Let stand several hours.

Bring the following mixture to a boil:
½ cup water
½ cup sugar
1½ cups white vinegar
2 teaspoons mustard seed
2 teaspoons celery seed
1 teaspoon pickling spices
1 tablespoon parsley or fresh dill for garnish

Pour over drained cucumbers. Let stand out 1 day, then refrigerate. Will keep for several days to a week.

May be garnished with fresh dill. Delicious as an hors d'oeuvre.

Serves 6 to 8

MARINATED SESAME RADISHES

Chef Scott Berman, Longwharf Restaurant, Sag Harbor, L.I., N.Y.

Crack radishes with a cleaver.

Pour 1 teaspoon salt over them and let stand 10 to 15 minutes.

Add:
1 teaspoon sesame seeds
1 tablespoon soy sauce
3 tablespoons cider vinegar
1½ tablespoons sugar
2 teaspoons sesame oil

Marinate ½ to 2 hours maximum.

MUSSELS, HERBED

1 (9-oz.) can mussels
¼ cup of the following herbs finely chopped and mixed: Italian parsley, marjoram, salad burnet, chervil, or a combination of dill and tarragon.
¼ cup or more mayonnaise, preferably homemade
¼ cup or more sour cream
½ teaspoon dry mustard
White pepper and salt to taste

Drain the mussels. Add the herbs. Add the mayonnaise, sour cream, and mustard which have been combined. Mix lightly. Chill and serve on beds of chilled lettuce.

Excellent for lunch or a first course.

Serves 3

SPICED PEANUT WAFERS — REMPEYEK KACANG (Indonesian)

Dora Ang

½ cup flour
½ cup tapioca flour or cornstarch
½ to 1 teaspoon baking powder
½ to 1 cup coconut milk
1 teaspoon salt
1 to 2 buds of garlic, chopped
Pinch of turmeric
Pinch of Kenchur (white ginger, optional)
1 cup shelled peanuts, raw
2 cups vegetable oil

Mix all ingredients (except the peanuts) together until smooth. Add the peanuts. Heat the oil, (preferably in a wok) and pour 1 tablespoon of the mixture into the hot oil (350°) — then add 4 or 5 pieces at a time for 1 to 2 minutes. Fry until golden brown on each side.

May be kept in an air-tight container or plastic bag for 1 to 2 days.

Yield: Approx. 3 doz.

TOMATO AND BASIL CANAPES

French bread, thinly sliced
Tomatoes, thinly sliced
Minced garlic
Salt and pepper
Anchovy fillet
Chopped basil
Olive oil

Place tomato slice on bread. Sprinkle with garlic, salt and pepper. Top with an anchovy fillet and a generous amount of chopped basil. Drizzle a little olive oil on each canape.

I cannot tarry: I knew a wench married in an afternoon as she went to the garden for *parsley* to stuff a rabbit; and so may you sir: and so, adieu, sir.

Shakespeare

"Taming of the Shrew"

Soups and
Salads

AUNT JESSIE'S 10-VEGETABLE STEW OR SOUP

(A very old recipe, updated)

Charles Bolton

Start with a large stew pot into which you have placed 1 gallon of distilled or spring water. In it, place 2 generous-sized short ribs, and simmer the ribs while you are preparing the vegetables.

Use 1 cup, coarsely-chopped (½ inch dice) but tightly packed, of each of 10 vegetables. The combination isn't important, although one should include the basic five: tomato, onion, celery, potato, and corn. Add string beans, chick peas, squash, broccoli, and okra, if available. Okra gives a very distinct edge to the stew, and is wonderful, but it should be dusted with two tablespoons of cornmeal after chopping. If you cannot get okra, use lima beans, carrots, anything that is handy. Of course, it doesn't need saying that this recipe is inexact. It's two hundred years old, and the original calls for a "big handful" of each vegetable, per "bucket of cold spring water."

When you are ready to add the vegetables, remove the meat from the pot and while it is cooling, bring the vegetables, without further seasonings, to a rolling boil. Remove the pot from the flame and stir in the meat, which you have removed from the bone and diced, and 1 tablespoon of each of the following condiments: salt, pepper, pressed garlic pulp, and crushed bay leaves. (Or, you may add 3 whole bay leaves.)

Then stir in one teaspoon of each of the following (crushed) dried herbs: basil, tarragon, rosemary, dill, and savory.

Return the stew to the flame, but reduce heat and simmer for at least 2 to 3 hours, stirring occasionally — you may find that you need to add more liquid. An 8-ounce can of V-8 vegetable juice, added about an hour before serving, is a very good 20th century improvement. Also, an hour before serving; or when you reheat the soup, if you make it ahead of time, stir in ½ cup of chopped fresh parsley, or three heaping tablespoons of dried parsley flakes.

Correct the seasonings to taste, and that's it.

Number of servings depend upon amount of vegetables used.

BEET FRUIT SOUP

Shakertown

8 new beets
2 cups water
¾ teaspoon powdered clove
Salt, pepper
Juice of 2 limes or lemons
Frozen grape juice concentrate
Grapefruit juice
Sugar to taste
1 cup dry red wine
Mint

Scrub beets very well, because the water they cook in is used in the soup (fresh beets are better but you can use good canned ones). Cut off stems, leaving at least one inch of stem, so they don't bleed. Cook in water until tender. Skin and slice them into blender. Add water and puree until smooth; add seasonings. Dilute grape juice with only 1½ cans of water, instead of usual 3. Add grape juice, grapefruit juice, sweetening and wine. If too thick, dilute with more grapefruit juice (should be consistency of thick cream). Keeps well in glass jars in refrigerator. Add chopped mint all over before serving. Can be served hot. Thicken with a little corn starch if you wish.

Yield: 2 quarts

CHARLEY'S CHOWDER

Charley's Crab Restaurant

¼ cup olive oil
2 garlic cloves, whole
3½ cups onions, finely chopped
1¼ cups celery, finely chopped
½ teaspoon oregano, dried
½ teaspoon basil, dried
¼ teaspoon thyme, dried
2½ cups tomatoes, (canned) diced and ground
3¼ quarts water and tomato juice, (half and half)
1½ lbs. fish fillets (pollock or turbot)
½ cup clam base
1¼ teaspoons salt (or to taste)

Heat oil until hot, add garlic and brown; then remove garlic. Add onions, celery, oregano, basil, thyme; cook until almost golden. Add tomatoes; cook 15 minutes, add remaining ingredients. Cook at a soft boil, approximately 1 hour, stirring frequently to break up the fish into small bits. Depending on the amount of water in the tomatoes, final cooking time may vary.

Serves 14 to 16

CHICKEN AND VEGETABLE SOUP

Soto Ayam (Indonesian)

Dora Ang

4 to 6 cups chicken broth
3 boneless chicken breasts
1 onion, chopped
2 buds garlic, chopped
2 teaspoons salt
Dash MSG (optional)
1 teaspoon coriander
1 inch long ginger root (medium size)
¼ teaspoon turmeric powder
¼ teaspoon pepper
3 tablespoons vegetable oil
1 tablespoon sweet soy sauce
1 ounce SU-UN or mungbean noodles
1 cup bean sprouts (optional)
2 cups cabbage, shredded
2 tablespoons celery leaves, chopped
2 hard-cooked eggs

Boil chicken breasts in chicken broth until tender and slice in 1-inch square pieces. Heat 3 tablespoons oil in pan or wok and fry the onion and garlic for 3 minutes.

Pour above into the chicken broth. Add salt, pepper, sweet soy sauce, ginger root, and the spices. Simmer on low heat for 30 minutes.

Prepare soup filling as follows: Boil SU-UN (noodles) cut into 4 to 5 inch strips. Immerse cabbage and bean sprouts in boiling water and drain.

To serve: Add SU-UN, bean sprouts, cabbage, celery leaves and sliced hard-cooked eggs to the soup, which has been ladled into individual soup bowls.

Serves 6 to 8

HERBAL HINT

Garnish cold cucumber soup with salad burnet.

COLD CELERY AND POTATO SOUP

3 cups celery, sliced
1 cup onion, sliced
2 tablespoons butter
3 cups chicken broth
2 cups water
1 teaspoon salt
½ teaspoon minced tarragon
½ teaspoon summer savory
½ teaspoon chervil
3 cups potatoes, peeled and diced
½ cup milk
Garnish: Minced fresh tarragon, if available, or parsley.

Cook celery and onion in butter in a saucepan over low heat for 10 minutes. Add chicken broth, water, salt, and herbs. Bring to boil, reduce heat, add potatoes and simmer for 25 minutes or until potatoes are soft. Transfer to a blender or food processor and puree in batches for 30 seconds. Strain into a bowl, stir in milk, and let cool. Chill in refrigerator for several hours or longer. Serve in chilled bowls, garnished with fresh tarragon or parsley.

Serves 6 to 8

COLD CUCUMBER SOUP

Golden Lamb Inn

2 green onions (or leeks), chopped
1 onion, chopped
1 teaspoon butter
½ cup celery, chopped
3 raw potatoes, peeled and diced
Dash thyme
4 cups chicken stock
Dash Tabasco
Salt to taste
2 cups sour cream
1 cucumber, finely grated (no seeds)

Saute onions in butter, add celery, potatoes, thyme, and stock. Cook until potatoes are soft. Force through food mill. Chill.

Add Tabasco, salt, sour cream, and cucumber. Mix well. Serve cold. Garnish with chopped chives, parsley, or small amount of fresh dill.

Serves 6 to 8

COLD GREEK LEMON SOUP

½ cup uncooked rice
1 tablespoon salt
3 quarts chicken broth
6 eggs
½ cup lemon juice

1 teaspoon white pepper
2 tablespoons granulated sugar
2 lemons, sliced paper thin
Fresh mint

Boil rice, salt, and broth 15 minutes; remove from heat, set aside. Beat eggs with an electric mixer until frothy; then beat in lemon juice, pepper, and sugar. Ladle 3 cups of broth into egg mixture, 1 cup at a time. Pour beaten egg mixture into rice mixture, stir well, and refrigerate.

Serve chilled in bowls garnished with lemon slices and chopped fresh mint.

Serves 10 to 12

COLD GREEN SUMMER SOUP

5 cups chicken stock or broth
2 cups chopped green beans
2 cups chopped Romaine lettuce
2 cups chopped zucchini
¼ cup chopped Italian parsley
Salt and pepper to taste
Garnishes, see below

Combine the chicken stock and vegetables in a saucepan. Simmer, partially covered, for about 15 minutes or until vegetables are tender. Put vegetables and liquid through a food mill, blender, or food processor. Season with salt and pepper. Chill thoroughly and garnish each serving as desired.

Garnishes: Sliced cucumber, hard-cooked egg, or sliced cucumber and/or chopped parsley.

Serves 6 to 8

"Rosemary for Remembrance"

Shakespeare

Remember:
Use triple the amount of fresh herbs to dried herbs!

COUNTRY SOUP

Shakertown

½ lb. lean sliced bacon, cut in small pieces
2 cans (11-¾ ozs.) condensed onion soup
1 can (1 lb. 13 ozs.) solid pack tomatoes
1 cup diced carrots
1 cup sliced celery
1 cup diced potatoes
½ lb. zucchini, diced
1 clove garlic, minced or mashed
1 bunch parsley, chopped
9 cups water
1 bay leaf, crumbled
Generous pinch each thyme, marjoram, and basil
Salt and pepper to taste
2 cups broken uncooked spaghetti
2 cans (1 lb. each) cooked dried lima beans
¼ cup grated Parmesan cheese

In a large kettle combine the bacon, soup, tomatoes, carrots, celery, potatoes, zucchini, garlic, parsley, water, and seasonings. Bring to a boil, then cover and simmer gently for 1 hour, stirring occasionally. Add spaghetti and continue cooking for 30 minutes longer, stirring frequently. Just before serving, add lima beans (including liquid) and cheese. Taste and season with more salt and pepper if necessary. Serve in heated bowls and pass additional grated Parmesan cheese.

Serves 10 to 12

CURRIED LIMA BEAN SOUP

1 (10-oz.) package frozen baby lima beans
2 tablespoons butter
⅓ cup sliced green onions
1 teaspoon curry powder
½ teaspoon salt
⅛ teaspoon pepper
½ teaspoon dried tarragon
4 sprigs parsley
½ cup heavy cream
1 can (13¼ ozs.) chicken broth
1 tablespoon chopped chives for garnish

Cook lima beans with butter, green onions, and curry powder until beans are soft (about 15 to 20 minutes). Empty into a blender or food processor. Add seasonings, herbs, and cream. Blend until smooth.

Pour into top of double boiler, add chicken broth, mix well, and heat over simmering water.

Serve each portion garnished with chopped chives. Herb toast, (see index) is a good accompaniment.

Serves 4 to 6

DILL SOUP

2 large onions, chopped
2 cloves garlic, chopped
4 tablespoons vegetable oil
2 lbs. tomatoes, fresh or canned
⅓ cup tomato paste
3 tablespoons cornstarch
3 cups beef consomme

½ cup finely chopped dill, fresh
1½ teaspoons salt
½ teaspoon pepper
2 cups milk or cream
½ cup whipped cream
More dill for garnish

Saute onions and garlic in oil, add tomatoes and saute 20 minutes. Meantime, mix cornstarch with tomato paste and consomme. Add this to onions, garlic, and tomatoes. Stir until boiling. Push through fine strainer; add chopped dill. Add salt and pepper, chill and add cream. Serve cold, garnished with whipped cream and dill (optional).

Serves 8 to 10

DILL POTATO SOUP, BERNESE OBERLAND

From the book, "Herbs and Spices Belong in Your Everyday Life"

Marny Dilts

(Served every Saturday night in the little Swiss village of Lauterbrunnen. As much a tradition as baked beans and brown bread in Boston.)

1 tablespoon margarine
1 medium onion, minced
3 teaspoons flour
4 large potatoes, cubed
1 teaspoon minced parsley
1 leek minced, if available
6 cups water
½ teaspoon dill seed
1 small sprig fresh dill
1 stalk celery, minced
1 teaspoon salt
⅛ teaspoon white pepper
Paprika

Melt margarine in large heavy saucepan, add onion, brown lightly; add flour, stirring constantly. Brown until a rich brown color. Add all ingredients. Cover, simmer gently 45 minutes. Remove dill sprig. Lower heat. Beat mixture with mixer until a creamy puree. Serve piping hot in preheated soup plates with Swiss cheese and muscat wine.

Serves 6 to 8

FRENCH SORREL SOUP

From the Book, "Herbs for Every Garden"

Gertrude Foster

2 handfuls sorrel leaves
4 tablespoons butter
2 shallots, minced
3 tablespoons flour
2 tablespoons fresh lovage

4 tablespoons fresh chervil
Salt, pepper to taste
2 cups chicken stock
2 egg yolks, beaten slightly
1 cup cream

Remove midribs of sorrel leaves by folding them and tearing the center rib from the top down. Chop finely and cook in butter in which minced shallots have been slightly browned. Stir constantly until the sorrel becomes a puree. Blend in sifted flour, minced fresh herbs, salt, pepper, and chicken stock. Bring to boil and pour some of the soup into the egg yolks. Return to the saucepan and add cream. Stir while cooking over lowest heat until thickened.

Serve hot with croutons, or cold with a dab of sour cream topped with chives. If you have a blender or food processor, the soup may be poured into the cream and egg yolks and whirled for one minute. This saves straining out any lumps or bits of stem.

Serves 4

FRENCH SPRING SOUP

1 pint water
1 head Romaine lettuce, crisp
1 cup spinach
1 tablespoon sorrel, optional
1 stick butter
1 lb. potatoes, peeled, diced
2 egg yolks, beaten
1 cup watercress leaves
2 tablespoons cream
1 pint milk
1 tablespoon tarragon
1 tablespoon chervil leaves
Salt and pepper to taste
Fresh parsley or watercress

Cook well washed lettuce, spinach, and sorrel in 2 tablespoons butter. Add diced potatoes, then 3 tablespoons of water. Cook slowly until potatoes are soft. Blend in food processor or mash well by hand. Add remainder of ingredients, including remainder of water; season with salt and pepper to taste. Cook gently about 10 minutes, stirring occasionally. When serving, garnish with parsley or watercress.

Serves 8 or more

GAZPACHO

(A cold soup or a loose salad)

The Heritage

Into a large bowl, empty: 1 (10-oz.) can chicken broth
1 (10-oz.) can tomato juice or V-8
2 tablespoons vinegar

Add:
2 tablespoons salad oil
1 clove garlic, minced
½ onion, cut up
½ green pepper, cut up
1 teaspoon sugar (optional)
½ teaspoon salt
½ teaspoon pepper
1 teaspoon oregano

Chill. At serving time add:
1 chopped tomato
1 grated cucumber

Add Tabasco, if you like it. Serve with garnish of chives or sour cream.

Serves 4 to 6

HERB SOUP

½ pt. finely shredded spinach
¼ pt. shredded sorrel
¼ blanched and sliced leek
Center leaves of head of lettuce, shredded
4 potatoes, medium size
3½ teaspoons salt
1 tablespoon chervil
4 tablespoons butter
2 quarts boiling water
2 egg yolks, optional
2 tablespoons milk, optional
5 slices bread, diced and fried in butter or browned in oven.

Put spinach, sorrel, leek, and lettuce in a stewpot with butter. Cook 15 minutes, being careful not to burn vegetables. Add potatoes, salt, and boiling water. Bring to rolling boil, reduce heat, and simmer 5 minutes. Soup may be pureed, returned to fire, brought to boil and combined with 2 egg yolks, which have been beaten with 2 tablespoons milk. Serve in soup tureen, garnished with crisp bread cubes.

Yield: 2 quarts, approximately

ICED CUCUMBER-MINT-YOGURT SOUP

2 cloves garlic, mashed
½ teaspoon salt
1 tablespoon olive oil
1 pint yogurt

8 ice cubes
1 large (or 2 small)
cucumbers, diced
2 (or more) tablespoons fresh
mint leaves, chopped

Crush garlic in salt, stir in olive oil, and let stand. Put yogurt in large bowl; add ice cubes and cucumber. Stir until cold. Discard cubes and add the garlic/oil mixture to ingredients in bowl. Add salt to taste.

Serves 4 to 6

MINESTRONE SOUP

Rosemary Louden

1 lb. plus 11 ozs. cooked red kidney beans
1 teaspoon salt
¼ teaspoon pepper
1 clove garlic, pressed
1 tablespoon oil
¼ cup chopped parsley
1 small zucchini, cut up
2 stalks celery, chopped
1 carrot, diced
4 or 5 leaves Swiss chard or spinach, chopped
3 tablespoons butter
1 (14½-oz.) can tomato sauce or stewed tomatoes
2½ cups water
½ cup sherry
½ cup uncooked elbow macaroni
2 bay leaves
1 teaspoon dried basil
Grated Parmesan cheese

Crush two-thirds of the kidney beans and leave the rest whole. Put everything in a large cooking kettle, except sherry, macaroni, cheese, and basil. Bring to boil and simmer for an hour or more, then add remainder of ingredients, except basil and cheese. The basil is added 15 minutes before time to serve with a dusting of grated Parmesan.

Serves 8 to 10

MINTED ZUCCHINI SOUP

(Victorian)

Charles Bolton

4 tablespoons butter
1 large onion, peeled and thinly sliced
4 cups sliced raw potatoes
4 cups (approximately) chicken stock
½ cup watercress leaves
½ cup fresh mint leaves, or 2 to 3 tablespoons dried
1 pound zucchini, sliced ¼ inch thick, unpared
½ teaspoon dried savory, crumbled
2 cups (approximately) Half and Half, or light cream
Salt and pepper, as desired

In a heavy skillet, melt butter and add the sliced onion; saute until transparent. Add the potatoes and enough chicken stock to cover. Bring to a full boil, then cover tightly, reducing heat. Simmer until potatoes are tender, about 30 minutes.

Add watercress leaves, mint leaves, and zucchini. Simmer 15 minutes longer. Add savory and allow to stand, covered, off heat, for about 30 minutes. Press the mixture through a food mill, or puree in batches in electric blender or food processor. Add Half and Half until desired consistency is reached, then season to taste with salt and freshly cracked pepper. Chill thoroughly. Serve cold.

Serves 4 to 6

OYSTER BISQUE

1 dozen (1 pint) shucked large raw oysters

1 cup oyster liquor   *1 bay leaf, in pieces*
3 cups milk   *⅓ cup melted butter*
1 cup heavy cream   *⅓ cup flour*
1 sliced onion   *1¼ teaspoons salt*
2 stalks celery, chopped   *½ teaspoon Tabasco sauce*
1 sprig parsley, chopped   *Chives for garnish*

Drain oysters, reserving 1 cup liquor. Dice oysters and place in a saucepan; add reserved liquor; slowly bring oysters to boiling point; remove from heat.

Scald milk and cream with onion, celery, parsley, bay leaf; remove vegetables and herbs.

In large saucepan, blend butter with flour, salt, and Tabasco sauce. Slowly stir in scalded milk and cream. Stir over low heat until thickened. Add oysters and cooking liquid. Pour into serving dishes and sprinkle with chopped chives.

Serves 6 to 8

PISTOU (BASIL SOUP)

From the book, "Herbs and Spices Belong in Your Everyday Life"

Marny Dilts

4 shallots, finely chopped and/or 3 large garlic cloves, crushed
3 tablespoons corn oil margarine
2 cans condensed tomato soup, or your own homemade
2 cups water
1 can cut green beans
2 teaspoons butter
2 tablespoons dried sweet basil
1½ cups cooked thin spaghetti
½ cup Parmesan cheese croutons
Fresh parsley for garnish

Saute shallots and garlic. Add soup and water. Saute beans in butter with basil. Add beans and spaghetti to soup. Simmer 5 minutes. Pour into hot soup bowls. Sprinkle with croutons and fresh parsley.

Serves 6 to 8

POTAGE TOUR D'ARGENT

(Kidney Bean Soup)

1 lb. kidney beans
½ lb. lentils
1 stalk celery, chopped
1 carrot, chopped
2 medium onions, chopped
4 sprigs parsley
2 cloves garlic, chopped fine
1 bay leaf, broken
1 teaspoon salt
¼ teaspoon butter
8 cups chicken stock
3 tablespoons butter
4 cups sorrel, finely shredded
(If sorrel is not available use curly endive plus 2 tablespoons lemon juice.)
5 tablespoons butter
½ cup parsley or chervil, minced
Freshly ground pepper to preferred taste

Soak kidney beans and lentils overnight in water to cover. Drain and put in a large soup kettle. Add celery, carrot, onions, parsley, garlic, bay leaf, salt, butter, and chicken stock. Bring to a boil; cover, and cook over a low heat for 1½ hours; or until beans are very tender. Put through blender, food processor, or Foley mill. Reheat, and correct seasoning with salt and pepper. There should be about 9 cups of puree.

Continued

Heat 3 tablespoons of butter; add sorrel, parsley, or chervil. Cook and stir until sorrel is wilted and loses color. Add this mixture to the bean puree. Stir in 2 more tablespoons of butter and serve very hot with a sprinkling of freshly ground pepper.

Serves 8 to 10

SAUSAGE SOUP

1 pound bulk sausage
2 (16-oz.) cans kidney beans
1 (1 lb., 13-ozs.) can tomatoes with juice
1 quart water, or use bean juice along with water
1 large onion, chopped
½ large or 1 medium green pepper, chopped
1 bay leaf
½ teaspoon thyme, dried
¼ teaspoon garlic powder
½ teaspoon pepper
1½ teaspoons seasoned salt
1 cup diced potatoes
1 dash Beau Monde seasoning

Brown sausage and pour off fat. Simmer everything except potatoes and green pepper in large covered kettle for one hour. Add potatoes and green pepper. Cook, covered, 15 to 20 minutes until potatoes are tender.

Serves 6 to 8

SEAFOOD AND FISH CHOWDER

Chef Gregory

2 to 3 tablespoons olive oil
½ cup green onions (white part), chopped
½ cup red or white onions, diced
½ cup green pepper, diced
1 cup white celery, diced
3 cloves garlic, minced
1½ to 2 lbs. firm fish, such as scrod, cod, swordfish, haddock; diced into 1-inch pieces
1 lb. raw shrimp, shelled
1 pint raw scallops, halved if large
1 teaspoon Maggi
1 drop Tabasco
Juice of one lemon
1 cup dry sherry
1 generous teaspoon Hungarian paprika

Continued

1 teaspoon chicken base
1 cup chicken stock
3 cups tomato juice
1 tablespoon fennel seeds
2 tablespoons chopped parsley
Salt to taste
1 teaspoon of additional sherry

Heat olive oil in heavy kettle. Add onions and green pepper and saute until onion is transparent. Add celery and saute a few minutes. Add garlic.

Add fish and cook over moderate heat until just opaque. Add shrimp and scallops. Add remaining ingredients. Stir and simmer a short time until flavors are blended and seafood is tender. Add additional sherry just before serving.

Note: If making ahead of time, combine all ingredients except fish and seafood. Simmer and combine flavors, cool, and refrigerate. Reheat, add fish and seafood when stock is hot, and simmer briefly until tender.

Serves 10 to 12

SEAFOOD SOUP

2 (10½-oz.) cans cream of tomato soup
2 (10½-oz.) cans cream of mushroom soup
1 quart fresh oysters (cut in half) and liquor
2 small cans minced clams and liquor
1 (8-oz.) can clam juice
1 quart milk
1 cup dry sherry
1 tube anchovy paste
1 to 2 tablespoons fennel seeds
Juice of 1 lemon
Pepper to taste

Marinate oysters and clams in fennel and lemon juice for several hours.

Heat soups, milk, and anchovy paste, but do not boil. Add oysters and clams with their liquor and marinade.

Serve hot but do not boil. You may add pepper, but no salt because of anchovy paste.

Serves 16 mugs

HERBAL HINT

Add chopped celery, thyme or marjoram to jellied beef bouillon with a drop of sour cream on top, for madrilene use basil and for chicken consomme, use tarragon. Serve in individual bowls.

SPICED TOMATO SOUP I

2 lbs. soup meat
6 cups tomato juice
1¼ cups tomato puree
2 cups water
2 or 3 tomatoes, peeled, seeded, and coarsely chopped
1 large onion, stuck with 6 whole cloves
2 bay leaves (fresh if you have them)
3 or 4 good-sized fresh basil leaves
2 tablespoons sugar
Salt and white pepper to taste

Place all ingredients in a large heavy kettle. Bring to a boil. Reduce heat, simmer covered until the meat is very tender. Remove herbs, onion, and meat before serving. Soup may be strained if desired; the meat may be diced and added to soup.

Serves 6

SPICED TOMATO SOUP II

1 can (1 lb., 12 ozs.) Italian pear-shaped tomatoes and liquid
4 cups beef broth
1½ cups grated celery root
1 clove minced garlic
2 tablespoons fresh minced parsley
1 teaspoon fresh chopped dill
¼ teaspoon thyme
¼ teaspoon ground celery seed
1 tablespoon fresh minced lovage
½ teaspoon sugar
⅛ teaspoon crushed red pepper
Salt and pepper
Sour cream and dill for garnish

Place all ingredients except garnishes into a large pot. Bring to a boil. Cover and simmer 1 hour, or until celery root is tender.

Puree in a blender and chill. Serve each bowl topped with a tablespoon of sour cream and sprinkled with dill.

Serves 6 to 8

"Rosemary for Remembrance"

Shakespeare

Remember:
Use triple the amount of fresh herbs to dried herbs!

VEAL RAGOUT SOUP

Bill Barum

(Light and creamy with fresh lemon fragrance)

1½ pounds cubed veal, medium diced (use a shoulder cut or economical veal breast)
1 large onion, chopped
2 tablespoons cooking oil
3 quarts stock, veal preferably, but chicken will do
1½ to 2 cups uncooked rice
A few bay leaves
½ to ¾ cup freshly chopped parsley
Juice of two large lemons
1½ cups whipping cream
Salt and lemon-flavored pepper to taste

Prepare veal cubes and set aside. In large soup pot, saute onion until transparent in slight amount of oil. Add veal and cook until liquid from meat is evaporated. Add stock and rice and simmer for about one and one-half hours with a few bay leaves.

To finish, add the chopped parsley, lemon juice, and cream. Heat gently; don't boil. Season to taste with salt and lemon pepper.

Serves 8 to 10

WHITE BEAN SOUP with HERBS

Shakertown

2 celery stalks, sliced
1 medium onion, sliced
1 medium leek, or another onion, sliced
3 tablespoons butter
6 cups liquid (chicken stock, or water or a combination)

1½ cups washed white beans or any type of flageolets
1 bay leaf
2 teaspoons salt
1 or more cloves garlic, peeled, optional

In an uncovered pressure cooker, or in a heavy 3 or 4 quart saucepan, saute the sliced vegetables in the butter 5 minutes until fairly limp, but not browned. Add the liquid, bring to a boil, then add the beans, bay leaf, salt, and optional garlic. Bring rapidly to a boil again, uncovered, and boil exactly 2 minutes. Remove from heat, cover pan, and set aside for 1 hour. Then bring to a boil again. Either pressure cook exactly 5 minutes at full pressure, then let pressure go down by itself– 15 to 20 minutes, or simmer slowly, partially covered, for 1½ to 2 hours, until beans are thoroughly tender. Add a little boiling water if liquid has evaporated below top level of beans.

Drain in a colander set over a glass bowl. Discard bay leaf. Squeeze contents of optional garlic cloves into beans; puree beans and other vegetables.

Reheat and Serve.

Serves 6

SOUP SEASONING BAGS

To be placed in cheesecloth bags (for 6 bags). Use 1 bag for each pot of vegetable soup.

2 teaspoons basil
4 teaspoons thyme
6 teaspoons sweet marjoram
4 tablespoons lovage (or 6 tablespoons celery leaves)
6 teaspoons dried Italian parsley
1 tablespoon savory, preferably summer
1 teaspoon peppercorns
1 teaspoon dried hot peppers, if desired

(Using your own fresh herbs, dried, will give added flavor to the bags.)

SALADS

AVOCADOS STUFFED WITH MARINATED VEGETABLES

4 large ripe tomatoes, skinned, seeded, and chopped
1 cucumber, peeled, seeded, and chopped
¼ cup red onion, chopped
¼ cup green pepper, chopped
1 small hot red pepper, finely chopped
3 tablespoons olive oil
2 teaspoons red wine vinegar
1 teaspoon salt
Freshly ground black pepper
1 clove garlic, minced
1 to 2 tablespoons fresh basil, chopped
3 avocados
Fresh lime or lemon juice
Salad greens

Mix tomatoes, cucumbers, green pepper, onion, red pepper, basil, olive oil, vinegar, salt, pepper, and garlic together well. Chill until cold.

Cut avocados in half, remove seed and peel. Sprinkle with lemon juice. Arrange each half on salad greens and fill with marinated vegetables.

Serves 6

BEETS 'N' BASIL

Cook whole beets, preferably fresh young ones, although canned may be used. Drain and marinate beets in your favorite salad dressing, seasoned with salt and pepper to taste and chopped opal or green basil. Toss well before serving and garnish with opal or green basil.

MINTED BEET AND YOGURT SALAD

2 cups medium fresh or canned beets, cooked, peeled, cubed, or sliced.
1½ cups yogurt
½ cup chopped fresh mint

Set aside ⅓ of mint as garnish. Combine ingredients. Refrigerate overnight to blend flavors. Serve cold.

Serves 4

CALICO BEAN SALAD

1 (10½-oz.) can cut green beans
1 (10½-oz.) jar sliced carrots
1 (12-oz) can whole kernel
sweet corn

2 tablespoons chopped onions
Celery seed dressing
Salad greens

Drain and combine vegetables. Toss with dressing. Cover, chill, and serve on salad greens.

Celery Seed Dressing:
½ cup brown sugar
⅓ cup basil vinegar
½ tablespoon salt

2 tablespoons celery seed
½ teaspoon ground turmeric
Dash pepper

Combine all ingredients. Dressing may be made ahead.

Serves 4 to 6

DILLED GREEN BEAN SALAD

Fern H. Storer

At hot day's end, when you've barely enough strength to open the refrigerator door, the sight of a cold salad to serve with cold chicken or other sliced meats makes it worth living through another 90-90 (temperature-humidity) summer day. Use tender snap beans for this salad, not the large sturdy pole beans which require long cooking. Use a sweet Italian onion or, if using so-called sweet white onion, soak the cut onion rings in ice water for an hour before using.

1 pound tender green beans
¼ cup chopped sweet onion
About half of a half-pint jar of slaw dressing
⅓ cup sour cream
1 teaspoon sugar
1 teaspoon vinegar
Salt and freshly ground pepper
Generous handful of fresh dill fronds, snipped, or a teaspoon of dried dill weed (not seeds)

Use: Refrigerator container with cover (1 qt.)

Rinse beans, remove strings, if any, cut off ends, then cut into inch lengths. Cook in boiling water until barely tender — probably about five minutes, but beans vary widely. Immediately drain and chill in ice water. Meanwhile combine slaw dressing, sour cream, sugar, and vinegar. Drain beans well; combine in refrigerator container with the chopped onion; gently stir in dressing. Season generously with salt and pepper, then mix in the snipped dill fronds or dill weed. Taste for seasonings — do not be skimpy with the salt and pepper. Cover tightly and refrigerate for a few hours before serving. Turn into salad bowl and garnish with a few red onion rings and feathery dill fronds.

Serves 6 to 8

GREEN BEAN AND MUSHROOM SALAD

Virginia Larson

1 lb. fresh young green beans
¼ lb. mushrooms, washed, dried, and sliced
Drizzle lemon juice over mushrooms
¼ cup your favorite vinaigrette dressing with
1 teaspoon Dijon mustard added and
1 teaspoon dried marjoram
5 or 6 crisp lettuce leaves
1 medium carrot, grated
1 tablespoon minced chives

Wash and snip off ends of beans. Bring a large pot of salted water to a rolling boil. Add beans and cook until crisply tender. Drain at once in a colander and run cold water over to stop cooking process.

Toss beans with part of the vinaigrette dressing and refrigerate.

Just before serving, drizzle vinaigrette over mushroom slices.

Arrange lettuce leaves on a chilled serving platter, mound beans in center. Surround with mushrooms, sprinkle grated carrot over mushrooms and chives over beans. Serve at once.

Serves 4

LIMA BEAN SALAD

1 package frozen baby lima beans
1 teaspoon dill seed
Salt and pepper to taste
¼ cup Italian dressing (your own or bottled)
½ (6½ oz.) can water chestnuts, drained and sliced

Cook lima beans briefly. Marinate while warm in dressing with salt, pepper and dill seed. Add water chestnuts just before serving and toss well.

Serves 4

STRING BEAN SALAD

Shakertown

2 cups cooked string beans
2 cups shredded lettuce
2 cups minced green onions (with tops)
2 sprigs summer savory, minced
6 nasturtium leaves (or spinach leaves)
Salt and pepper to taste
Dressing of your choice

Mix cold beans with shredded lettuce, toss onions over beans, add savory, nasturtium or spinach leaves. Season lightly with favorite dressing.

Serves 4 to 6

PARSLIED WHITE BEAN SALAD

1 lb. dried large white beans

Dressing:
⅔ cup olive oil
½ cup lemon juice
3 to 4 tablespoons wine vinegar
1 onion, chopped
½ cup parsley, chopped
Salt and pepper to taste

Cook and drain beans. While still hot, add dressing. Mix well and chill overnight. Serve with lemon wedges.

Serves 4 to 6

CHICKEN RICE SALAD

1½ cups cooked rice (keep warm)

Mix and pour over warm rice:

¼ cup green onion, minced
1 scant teaspoon curry powder
1 teaspoon Beau Monde Seasoning
Blend well with rice

Mix together:
2 tablespoons vegetable oil
2 tablespoons white wine vinegar
Blend well, add to above mixture and let stand overnight.

Next day add:
2 cups cooked diced chicken
1 cup diced green pepper
¾ cup mayonnaise
¼ to ½ cup almond slivers, toasted

Combine with rice mixture, adding chicken and almonds last. Blend well.

Serves 6 to 8

COTTAGE CHEESE WITH HERBS

1 tablespoon chives, chopped fine
1 tablespoon tarragon, chopped fine
1 tablespoon basil, chopped fine
1 tablespoon dill, chopped fine
1 tablespoon parsley, chopped fine
1 (16 oz.) carton cottage cheese
1 tablespoon sour cream (optional)
3 green onions, chopped

Continued

1 small cucumber, chopped, peeled; if small and tender, leave skin on
Pinch sugar
Salt and pepper
Paprika

Mix all ingredients thoroughly, except paprika. Put in serving bowl and sprinkle lightly with paprika.

Serves 4 to 6

HERBED SOUR CREAM CUCUMBERS

Rosella F. Mathieu

5 sprigs thyme
5 stems oriental garlic
Small handful chives
3 sprigs sweet marjoram
1 small sprig sweet marigold (Tagetes lucida)
2 leaves lovage
1 pint sour cream
½ cup yogurt
Milk to thin
2 tablespoons herb vinegar
Generous sprinkling of herb salt
1 large cucumber, sliced thin
½ teaspoon onion, minced (optional)

Mince herbs. Combine 3 scant tablespoons of herbs with other ingredients. Toss and serve.

Serves 4 to 6

MARINATED CUCUMBERS

2 cucumbers, peeled, seeded, sliced thin
½ cup vegetable oil
½ cup sugar
¼ cup white vinegar
Bunch fresh dill, chopped (about 1 tablespoon)
Handful chopped chives

Let cucumbers stand in large amount of cold, heavily salted water for several hours until softened. May add a few drops of green food coloring to the water for a prettier color. Drain, rinse in cold water, and drain well.

Combine oil, vinegar, sugar, and herbs in large jar, shaking to mix thoroughly. Add cucumbers and let marinate in refrigerator several days, shaking and turning upside down from time to time.

Serves 4 to 6

CUCUMBER AND NASTURTIUM LEAF SALAD

2 cucumbers
36 small nasturtium leaves
1 teaspoon Dijon mustard
2 tablespoons wine vinegar
6 tablespoons olive oil
Salt, freshly ground pepper
2 tablespoons fresh tarragon, finely chopped
6 nasturtium flowers

Peel and slice cucumbers thinly. Wash nasturtium leaves; remove stems and drain.

Combine mustard and vinegar in a bowl and stir until well blended. Add olive oil, salt and pepper to taste. Blend well. Stir in tarragon.

When ready to serve, combine cucumbers and nasturtium leaves in a bowl; add vinaigrette dressing and toss well. Garnish with nasturtium flowers and leaves. Salad burnet, with its cucumber flavor, is also a nice garnish.

Serves 4 to 6

PRESSED CUCUMBERS

"21" Restaurant

6 cucumbers
2 tablespoons mayonnaise
1 tablespoon lemon juice
Pinch nutmeg
Pepper to taste

Peel and halve the cucumbers lengthwise, removing the seeds. Slice each half-cucumber into ⅛-inch slices. Place the slices in a large sieve, sprinkle with salt, and cover with a weight; set the sieve over a bowl and allow the cucumbers to drain for several hours. When ready to serve, toss the slices with the mayonnaise, lemon juice, nutmeg, and pepper. (Garnish with herb of your choice)

Serves 10 to 12

SWEDISH CUCUMBER SALAD

1 large "burpless" cucumber, or 2 regular
1 tablespoon cider vinegar
2 tablespoons water
3 tablespoons oil
1 pinch of sugar
¼ teaspoon oregano

Continued

56

¼ teaspoon dill weed
2 tablespoons chopped parsley
1 dash garlic powder
Salt and pepper to taste

Slice cucumber very thin, if regular ones are used, soak them in cold water for a few minutes, then press water out. Mix all other ingredients. Pour over cucumber and let marinate in refrigerator for 1 hour or so.

Serves 4 to 6

DANDELION SALAD GOURMET

From the book, "The Forgotten Art Of Flower Cookery"

Leona Woodring Smith

1 garlic clove
3 to 4 cups raw dandelion leaves (young and tender ones)
16 to 24 dandelion buds
3 tablespoons oil
1 tablespoon lemon juice

1½ tablespoons vinegar
Salt and pepper
½ teaspoon chopped tarragon
½ teaspoon chopped chervil
6 ripe olives, sliced (optional)

Rub a salad bowl with a clove of garlic. Tear the dandelion leaves into bite size pieces. Add the buds in a separate bowl and combine the oil, lemon juice, vinegar, salt and pepper. Pour over the salad and add the tarragon and chervil. Toss gently. Sliced ripe olives may be added, if desired.

Serves 4

GREEK SALAD

Chef Gregory

1 quart water
½ cup red wine or cider vinegar
1 tablespoon olive oil
1 tablespoon dill weed
1 to 2 bay leaves
1 teaspoon garlic salt
1 teaspoon Maggi
1 drop Tabasco
1 medium onion, chopped
Generous amount of salt

Continued

Juice and rind of 2 lemons
6 to 8 small zucchinis, lightly peeled with ends trimmed
1 head cauliflower, washed and trimmed
½ cup milk

Dressing:
¼ cup chopped red onion
¼ cup capers with some of their juice
Juice of 2 to 3 lemons
1 teaspoon garlic salt
1 teaspoon Maggi
1 drop Tabasco
1 tablespoon dill weed or oregano, fresh
½ cup olive oil
Pinch of salt
Pinch of freshly ground black pepper
2 to 3 tomatoes, peeled, cut into wedges
Chopped parsley
Ripe Greek olives
Feta cheese

Combine all ingredients (minus dressing) except zucchini and cauliflower and milk in a heavy saucepan; bring to a boil and simmer 5 to 10 minutes.

Cut zucchini in quarters lengthwise, then in half. After stock has simmered, add zucchini and cook 4 to 5 minutes, just long enough to heat through. Drain.

Put cauliflower in a large saucepan, cover with cold water, salt generously, add ½ cup milk. Bring to a boil and simmer 8 to 12 minutes till tender, but do not overcook. Drain well and cut into florets.

Combine dressing ingredients. Place drained cauliflower and zucchini in a shallow salad bowl, pour dressing over while vegetables are still hot. Let cool. Add tomatoes and toss all together. Sprinkle with chopped parsley. Scatter olives and cheese over top.

Serves 10 to 12

ORANGE APPLE SALAD

4 large navel oranges, peeled, white membrane removed, thinly sliced
2 red or golden delicious apples, unpeeled, cored, thinly sliced

Combine fruits and add dressing made of:
½ cup chopped scallions
1 to 2 teaspoons fresh basil, chopped, or 1 teaspoon dried, crushed basil
¾ teaspoon sugar
½ teaspoon salt
3 tablespoons wine vinegar, preferably dill wine vinegar
6 tablespoons salad oil

Serves 4 to 6

PEAR OR PEACH SALAD

3 fresh or canned pears
or peaches, halved
1 pkg. (8-oz.) cream cheese
1 teaspoon cream

¼ teaspoon rosemary
¼ teaspoon marjoram,
powdered, if dried
2 tablespoons chopped pecans
or walnuts (unsalted)
Fresh mint sprigs

Soften cream cheese with cream, add rosemary and marjoram. Mix well in blender or by hand. Make walnut-size balls of cheese and roll in chopped nuts. Place balls in center of each fruit half. Garnish with fresh mint. Serve with your favorite fruit salad dressing.

Serves 4 to 6

HORSERADISH RELISH MOLDS

1 package lemon-flavored gelatin
¾ teaspoon salt
1 cup boiling water
1 tablespoon tarragon vinegar
Dash of white pepper
1 cup sour cream
1 teaspoon onion, finely grated
¼ cup horseradish

Add salt to boiling water, dissolve gelatin. Add vinegar and pepper. Chill until slightly thickened. Combine sour cream, onion, and horseradish with gelatin mixture. Mix well and pour into individual molds. Chill until firm. Unmold.

If using for a picnic, use individual plastic glasses. Do not unmold. Easy to transport. Excellent with cold meat dish.

Serves 4 to 6

ONION SALAD

Virginia Larson

This recipe must be prepared at least 2 hours ahead of serving time.

Thinly slice small red onions. Sprinkle with red wine vinegar or tarragon vinegar just to moisten; add a goodly amount of kosher salt. Add a cut up sprig of tarragon. Cover tightly with plastic wrap. Toss well before serving.

Allow 1 onion per serving

PIZZA SALAD

Pogue's 4th St. Market

1 (8-oz.) can tomato sauce
½ cup salad oil
¼ cup white wine vinegar
1 teaspoon sugar
1 teaspoon salt
1 teaspoon dried oregano, crushed
¼ teaspoon garlic powder
⅛ teaspoon pepper

1 medium head lettuce, torn (6 cups)
8 oz. sliced salami, cut in 1½" strips
1 cup shredded mozzarella cheese
1 cup shredded provolone cheese
2 medium tomatoes, chopped
½ cup pitted ripe olives, halved
1 tablespoon snipped chives
Whole black olives for garnish

Combine tomato sauce, oil, wine vinegar, sugar, salt, oregano, garlic powder, and pepper. Blend well in food processor or blender. Combine lettuce, salami, cheeses, tomatoes, olives, and chives. Pour dressing over salad and toss. Garnish with whole black ripe olives.

Serves 4 to 6

DILLED POTATO SALAD

3 lbs. potatoes, boiled, peeled, and cubed while warm.
1 cup olive oil or ½ cup olive, ½ cup salad oil
6 scallions, chopped
2 medium onions, thinly sliced
¼ cup minced parsley
¼ cup minced mint leaves
2 tablespoons snipped dill
Salt and pepper to taste
3 tablespoons lemon juice

Combine ingredients in large bowl. Sprinkle with lemon juice and toss.
May be made ahead.

Serves 4 to 6

FESTIVE POTATO SALAD

4½ cups boiled potatoes, cubed
6 eggs, hard-cooked
½ medium onion, chopped, or ½ cup chives, chopped
1 cup mayonnaise
1 teaspoon mixed dried herbs
½ teaspoon dill seed
¼ cup salad burnet, chopped
1 small clove garlic, minced
1 teaspoon tarragon vinegar
½ teaspoon salt, pepper, to taste
½ cup stuffed olives, sliced
3 dill pickles, about 2" long, sliced

Continued

Mix together potatoes, eggs, and onion or chives. In a separate bowl, combine mayonnaise with dried herbs, dill seed, salad burnet, garlic, vinegar, salt, and pepper.

Pour the dressing over potatoes. Stir in half of the olives and pickles, reserving the rest for garnish. Refrigerate for several hours.

Serves 6 to 8

HERBED NEW POTATO SALAD

2½ cups small new potatoes
1 teaspoon sugar
1 teaspoon white vinegar
½ cup finely chopped onion
Salt and freshly ground pepper to taste
¾ cup mayonnaise
Large bunch fresh dill weed, finely chopped (about 3 tablespoons)
2 to 3 tablespoons parsley, chopped
2 to 3 tablespoons chives, chopped

Cook potatoes in their jackets; peel and slice while warm. Sprinkle immediately with sugar and vinegar. Add onion, salt, pepper, and mayonnaise. Toss gently. Fold in herbs. Best made in advance and refrigerated. There should be enough herbs to make the salad slightly green in color. Garnish with a bouquet of dill or parsley, and sliced hard-cooked eggs, if desired.

Serves 4 to 6

FRENCH KRAUT SALAD

Mona Poynter (Mrs. Donald)

Grate together:
1 head cabbage or 1 quart
1 green pepper
1 Bermuda onion or 2 small onions

Mix and pour over cabbage:
⅓ cup vinegar
½ cup granulated sugar
½ teaspoon celery seed
½ teaspoon salt
¼ teaspoon mustard seed
¼ teaspoon turmeric

Put into jar. It's better second day. This may be used as a relish or salad.

Makes 1 quart

SAUERKRAUT SALAD

1 large can (#2½) sauerkraut, drained
1 cup celery, chopped (3 to 4 stalks)
1 onion, chopped
1 medium green pepper, chopped
1 chopped red pepper or pimiento

Syrup:
¾ cup tarragon vinegar
½ cup sugar (or to taste)
¼ teaspoon celery seeds (optional)
1 teaspoon dill weed

After draining kraut, cut fine with scissors. Mix all vegetables together.

Pour syrup over vegetables. Cover and refrigerate 24 hours. Will keep indefinitely, refrigerated. Mix well before serving.

Serves 4 to 6

HERRING SALAD

From the book, "Across Canada with Herbs"

8 oz. jar pickled herring, sliced
2 hard-cooked eggs, sliced
2 apples, cored and diced
2 tablespoons snipped chives

2 potatoes, boiled and sliced
1 tablespoon chopped fresh dill
3 tablespoons chopped parsley
½ cup sour cream

Combine all ingredients in a salad bowl, adding sour cream last. Mix well, cover, and chill at least 3 hours. If you wish, sprinkle extra parsley on top. Also excellent for hors d'oeuvres.

Serves 4

HOT SEAFOOD SALAD

Joyce Rosencrans

10 to 12 ounces of seafood
(May be a combination of frozen or canned crabmeat, frozen or canned shrimp)
4 hard-cooked eggs, chopped
½ cup chopped celery
½ cup sliced ripe olives
1 tablespoon instant minced onion
1 cup bread crumbs (whirl pieces of stale bread in blender or food processor)

Continued

1 cup sour cream
¾ cup mayonnaise
Scant ¾ teaspoon salt
¼ teaspoon dry mustard
Grinding of black pepper
¼ teaspoon dried tarragon, crumbled
¼ cup additional soft bread crumbs, tossed with melted butter
Parsley sprigs; lemon wedges for garnish

Use: Eight individual baking shells

If using canned crabmeat or shrimp, refresh with ice water and drain well. Remove bits of cartilage from crab, or defrost and drain frozen seafood. Combine with the hard-cooked eggs, celery, ripe olives, onion, bread crumbs, sour cream, mayonnaise, salt, dry mustard, pepper, and tarragon. Blend thoroughly and chill until ready to bake.

Grease baking shells. Have oven preheating to 350°F. Divide seafood mixture among baking shells; sprinkle buttered crumbs on top. Bake about 25 minutes or until hot throughout. Garnish with parsley and lemon wedges. Serve hot.

Shells may be set on saucers partially filled with heated rock salt.

Serves 8

CURRIED SPINACH SALAD

3 tablespoons sesame seeds
1 lb. spinach, washed
2 cups cherry tomatoes
¼ lb. bean sprouts (optional)

Curry Vinaigrette Dressing:
3 tablespoons white wine vinegar
2 teaspoons lemon juice
6 tablespoons olive oil
1 teaspoon salt
1 teaspoon curry powder
½ teaspoon dry mustard
½ teaspoon Dijon mustard
½ teaspoon ginger
¼ teaspoon turmeric
Dash hot pepper seasoning (optional)

Brown sesame seeds in a 300°F oven for 10 minutes. Remove heavy stems from spinach and tear leaves in strips. Place spinach, tomatoes, bean sprouts, and sesame seeds in salad bowl. Toss with curry vinaigrette dressing.

Serves 6

63

NEIL'S SPINACH SALAD

1 lb. fresh, crisp spinach, thoroughly rinsed (remove tough stem ends)
2 hard-cooked eggs, chopped coarsely
4 slices bacon, fried crisp and crumbled
½ cup crisp croutons
1½ teaspoons fresh tarragon
2 oz. Pernod, optional

Toss with your favorite salad dressing, preferably with tarragon vinegar.
Heat 2 oz. Pernod, ignite and flame at the table, pour over salad.
The Pernod adds a dramatic touch and an unusual flavor.

Serves 4 to 6

BASIL TOMATOES

Fern H. Storer

About an hour before serving, peel two fully ripe large tomatoes and cut each in two or three thick slices, then cut each slice in half (for easy serving). Place side by side (not stacked) in attractive shallow serving dish; tuck a few pieces of torn fresh basil leaf in seedy section of each; cover and refrigerate.

In a small cup combine two tablespoons sugar, one-half teaspoon salt, a generous grinding of black peppercorns, two tablespoons vinegar (cider or red wine), and two or three fresh basil leaves torn in small bits. Mix well, bruising basil leaves with back of a spoon to release flavor; cover and refrigerate. At serving time, dribble over tomatoes; garnish dish with a few whole fresh basil leaves.

Serves 2

Note: Peel tomatoes for the above dish with a thin, sharp paring knife — not by dipping into boiling water, which will make them mushy. Add dressing IMMEDIATELY before serving, not ahead of time; otherwise it will make the tomatoes soupy.

HERBAL HINT
Opal Basil makes a delightful vinegar with a deep burgundy color.

TOMATO CUCUMBER COMBO

2 medium-sized tomatoes, diced
1 medium cucumber, pared, cut in half and sliced

Dressing:
1 tablespoon sugar
1 tablespoon salad oil
2 tablespoons vinegar
1 teaspoon salt
¼ teaspoon dill weed

Pour dressing over vegetables. Toss lightly. Chill one hour or more. Drain. Keeps several days.

Serves 4 to 6

FRESH TOMATOES AU SAROSSE

Alice Galvin

6 tomatoes
½ lb. cottage cheese
½ cup sour cream
¼ cup heavy cream (whipping)
½ teaspoon salt,
kosher preferred
1 shallot, minced

1½ teaspoons chervil, fresh
1½ teaspoons chives, fresh
1½ teaspoons parsley, fresh
¾ teaspoon tarragon, fresh
¼ teaspoon white pepper

Blend cottage cheese and sour cream in food processor until smooth. Remove to mixing bowl.
Beat cream until stiff and fold into above mixture. Add salt.
Line an enamel colander with cheesecloth. Pour in mixture. Place on top of a bowl and refrigerate for 24 hours. It will drip.
After 24 hours, put mixture in a mixing bowl and add shallots and ¾ of all the herbs plus the pepper.
Cut off the top of six beautiful tomatoes. Scoop out the insides with a spoon or grapefruit knife.
Fill tomatoes with cheese herb mixture and sprinkle on remaining herbs for garnish.
Serve each tomato on a leaf of Boston lettuce.

Serves 6

INSALATA DI POMADORI

Melanie Barnard

Romaine lettuce leaves
6 large tomatoes, sliced thin
1 large red onion, sliced thin
8 anchovy fillets, chopped
¼ cup fresh basil leaves, chopped
1 clove garlic, minced
½ cup olive oil
¼ cup red wine vinegar

Arrange lettuce on a large, shallow platter. Arrange tomatoes in a circular overlapping pattern. Separate onion into rings and sprinkle atop tomatoes. Sprinkle anchovies over all. Sprinkle basil leaves over anchovies. In a jar combine oil, vinegar and garlic, shaking to mix well. Drizzle over salad. Let stand 10 minutes at room temperature before serving.

Serves 8

OREGANO TOMATOES

4 medium tomatoes, sliced
Salt, pepper to taste
1 tablespoon wine vinegar
1 tablespoon fresh oregano, minced
1 tablespoon onion, minced
4 tablespoons oil

Arrange tomatoes on platter and sprinkle with other ingredients.

Serves 4

SLICED TOMATOES OFF THE VINE OR WHOLE ONES OUT OF A CAN WITH BASIL

Plan one tomato per person.

Slice tomatoes ⅛" thick and sprinkle lightly with dry mustard, pinch of sugar, salt and freshly ground pepper, chopped fresh basil. Pour red wine vinegar over all. Let marinate. Turn occasionally. Do not refrigerate. When ready to serve, place on rimmed plate and drizzle marinade over tomatoes. Sliced red onions are a nice addition.

This recipe is excellent in the winter with canned whole tomatoes using their juice, dried basil, salt, and pepper. Eliminate other ingredients.

STUFFED TOMATOES

12 ripe tomatoes, peeled
4 avocados, peeled and diced, sprinkled with lemon juice
1 clove garlic, minced
Freshly ground pepper
Salt to taste
1 cup crisp celery, finely diced
Juice of one lemon
1 sprig tarragon, chopped
1 to 2 tablespoons chopped chives
1 cup vinaigrette dressing
¼ cup chopped parsley

Cut a thick slice off round end of tomato and scoop out seeds. Replace removed slice and refrigerate, covered with plastic wrap.

Mix avocado, garlic, pepper, salt, celery, lemon juice, tarragon and chives. Fill tomato halves with avocado mixture. Cover with tomato lids. Arrange on salad greens. Pour vinaigrette over and sprinkle with chopped parsley.

Serves 12

TOMATOES STUFFED WITH CRABMEAT

Chef Gregory

Sauce:
1 peeled, seeded cucumber, finely chopped
⅔ cup mayonnaise
½ cup sour cream
1 teaspoon Maggi
1 drop Tabasco
1 teaspoon garlic salt
White pepper to taste
1 tablespoon dill weed, fresh
2 tablespoons parsley, chopped
Juice of 1 lemon
2 tablespoons unflavored gelatin
¼ cup cold water

Remaining Ingredients:
½ to 1 lb. crabmeat, lobster, or shrimp
8 peeled tomatoes
Lettuce or Belgian endive
2 bunches asparagus, poached
1 lb. mushrooms
¼ cup olive oil
1 medium onion, chopped
¼ cup additional olive oil

Continued

Juice of 2 lemons
¼ cup wine vinegar
1 teaspoon garlic salt
1 teaspoon Maggi
1 drop Tabasco
Hearts of palm for garnish
Chopped parsley
Bunch of watercress for garnish

Salt chopped cucumber generously, let remain a minute, then place in a dishtowel, wash under cold water, wring out. Combine mayonnaise and sour cream in bowl. Add Maggi, Tabasco, garlic salt, white pepper, dill weed, parsley, and lemon juice. Stir together well.

Put gelatin in a separate bowl and soften in ¼ cup cold water; then heat over hot water until gelatin liquefies. Add to mayonnaise mixture. Add cucumber to mixture, stir, and chill until set. Add seafood; chill again until set.

Scoop out peeled tomatoes. Cut off top and fill tomatoes with seafood mixture and replace tomato caps.

Place lettuce or endive around rim of large platter. Place a bunch of poached asparagus at either end and tomatoes in middle.

Braise mushrooms in ¼ cup olive oil with onion. Bring up to boiling point and chill. Marinate in additional ¼ cup olive oil, lemon juice, vinegar, garlic salt, Maggi, and Tabasco. Place mushrooms over asparagus stems and pour marinade over asparagus. Garnish with hearts of palm. Sprinkle chopped parsley over tomatoes. Place a bunch of watercress in center.

Serves 8

SUMMER SALAD

Linda Miller

4 ripe tomatoes, quartered
1 sliced red onion
1 slivered green pepper, small
2 tablespoons chopped basil

Salt and pepper to taste
1 tablespoon wine vinegar
¼ cup olive oil

Toss all ingredients and refrigerate for ½ hour to let flavors blend.

Serves 4 to 6

TABBOULEH (LEBANESE SALAD)

Virginia Larson

⅔ *cup cracked wheat*
½ *cup chopped fresh mint*
2 cups chopped parsley
1 cup chopped tomatoes
¾ *cup olive oil*
½ *cup lemon juice*
Salt and pepper to taste
½ *cup chopped onions*

Cover cracked wheat with water and soak for two hours. Drain well. Mix all ingredients with the wheat and serve on crisp lettuce. Serve with small pita bread for hors d'oeuvres.

Serves 4 to 6

MARINATED VEGETABLE PLATTER

1 lb. mushroom caps
1 can Belgian carrots, drained or fresh miniature carrots
20 tiny potato balls, cut from large red potatoes with a small melon scoop
1 lb. whole green beans
Your favorite vinaigrette dressing
1 or 2 hard-cooked eggs, quartered
6 to 8 medium-sized tomatoes
8 artichoke bottoms stuffed with crabmeat salad, optional
Ruby, bibb, or Boston lettuce to line platter
Garnish: Basil leaves, borage flowers, 2 to 3 fluted mushroom caps, tomato rose or tomato basket filled with parsley

If using fresh carrots, steam until just tender.
Cook potato balls until just tender and drain immediately.
To cook green beans, bring a large pot of salted water to a rolling boil, add the beans all at once, and continue to boil until they are just crisply tender. Drain immediately, refresh with cold water, and drain again.

Poach mushroom caps in vinaigrette dressing a few minutes until just tender. Drain off ¾ of the dressing and marinate the carrots, potato balls, and green beans separately in this dressing. It is preferable to marinate the carrots and potato balls while they are still warm. The green beans will retain their green color if they are marinated shortly before serving.

Cut several tomatoes into large wedges, and make a slit in each wedge through the skin. Insert egg quarter into the slit with white side up. Slice the rest of the tomatoes.

Continued

Use either a round or rectangular platter. Drain the marinated vegetables. Edge the platter with lettuce leaves. Mound the carrots in the center, and place green beans on each side of the carrots, diagonally. Place the potato balls and the mushroom caps opposite each other, between the green beans and the carrots.

Place the egg-stuffed tomatoes at either end of the platter and the sliced tomatoes and crab-stuffed artichoke bottoms, if the latter are used, around the perimeter.

Garnish with basil leaves, borage flowers, tomato rose or tomato basket, and fluted mushroom caps. Artichoke bottoms with crab may be garnished with pimiento strips, tiny black olives, and a sprig of parsley, salad burnet, or dill.

Serves 10 to 12

CRUNCHY VEGETABLE SALAD

Vegetables:
2½ cups thinly sliced radishes
4½ cups thinly sliced celery
½ lb. sliced fresh mushrooms
2 scallions, thinly sliced
6 oz. can artichoke hearts (if marinated, cut back on amount of dressing used; if not, marinate in dressing before combining with other vegetables.)

Dressing:
¼ cup olive oil
¼ cup wine vinegar
1 teaspoon dried, crushed basil
1 teaspoon dried, crushed oregano
2 cloves garlic, crushed
1 teaspoon salt
1 teaspoon sugar

Vegetables and dressing may be prepared ahead, covered, and kept chilled. They may be combined up to one hour before serving.

Serves 6 to 8

Vegetables

GREEN BEANS IN CREAM AND MINT

Chef Scott Berman
Longwharf Restaurant
Sag Harbor, L.I., N.Y.

3 lbs. French cut green beans
2 tablespoons melted butter
1 cup heavy cream
1 tablespoon chopped fresh mint leaves, or ½ tablespoon dried mint.

Steam beans to desired tenderness. Add cream, butter and mint leaves. Stir well and serve.

Serves 6 to 8

GREEN BEANS WITH FRENCH-FRIED PARSLEY

1 lb. whole young green beans
1 cup cooking oil
2 tablespoons butter

1 cup washed fresh parsley, no stems, dried well
salt & pepper to taste

Cook green beans in water, until just crisp, and drain. Season with butter, salt & pepper. Keep warm. Deep fat fry (390°F) parsley in basket for a few seconds or until it rises to surface and is crisp. Drain on paper towel, add a slight amount of salt and sprinkle over green beans. Other herbs can be deep fried with this same method.

Serves 4

BAKED KIDNEY BEANS

2 (15½-oz.) cans red kidney beans
2 tablespoons bacon fat
1 large clove minced garlic
1 pinch English thyme
1 pinch rosemary
1 bay leaf
2 whole cloves
1 teaspoon salt
2 teaspoons dry mustard
¼ teaspoon cayenne pepper
2 tablespoons strong cider or wine vinegar
½ cup juice of pickled peaches
1 onion, minced
¼ cup strong black coffee
1 tablespoon Worcestershire sauce
1 jigger brandy
4 slices bacon (optional)
Italian smoked sausage, optional

Continued

Put beans in beanpot (pottery preferred.)
Add all ingredients to the beans except bacon, Worcestershire, coffee and brandy. Bake in a 325°F oven for one hour. Add the coffee, Worcestershire, and brandy. Top with bacon. Bake in 375°F oven about ½ hour until bacon is crisp. Small slices of Italian smoked sausage may also be added.

Serves 6 to 8

LIMA BEAN CASSEROLE

2 (10-oz.) boxes frozen Fordhook lima beans
3 slices bacon, cooked, crumbled, drained on paper towel
¼ cup chopped onion
¼ cup chopped celery
1 teaspoon summer savory
Salt and pepper to taste
1 (8-oz.) carton sour cream
1 teaspoon chopped pimiento
1 tablespoon chopped parsley
½ teaspoon paprika

Cook lima beans according to directions. Do not overcook. Set aside. Saute onions and celery in bacon drippings until onions are transparent. Place lima beans in casserole and mix in all ingredients except parsley and paprika. Bake in 350°F oven until bubbling. Sprinkle parsley and paprika over top of casserole. Serve at once.

Serves 6 to 8

BROCCOLI CASSEROLE

From the book, "Herb Gardening in 5 Seasons"
Adelma G. Simmons

2 (10-oz.) packages frozen broccoli spears, or 1 large head fresh broccoli
1 (10½-oz.) can cream of chicken soup
1 (10½-oz.) can cream of mushroom soup
1 cup cubed sharp cheese
1 onion, chopped
2 tablespoons chopped parsley
1 cup sliced cooked mushrooms (optional)
Salt and pepper to taste
Dash garlic powder

Cook broccoli in boiling water until tender; drain. Blend other ingredients together and add to broccoli. Place in a casserole and cover with topping.

Continued

Herb and cheese topping
2 cups bread crumbs
1 teaspoon ground sage or 1 teaspoon Capriland poultry seasoning
1 grated onion
1 tablespoon chopped parsley blended into ⅛ lb. butter (½ stick)
Grated cheese, chopped parsley and paprika for garnish

Brown bread crumbs; add sage, or poultry seasoning, onion and parsley butter mixture. Spread over broccoli casserole. Then sprinkle cheese, parsley and paprika over all. Bake in 350°F. oven until cheese melts and broccoli mixture bubbles, about 20 minutes.

Serves 6 to 8

Hint: For a complete dinner dish, mix 1 cup or so of chopped leftover chicken or turkey with broccoli mixture, or place slices of cooked poultry over broccoli before the topping is spread.

CABBAGE CURRY CASSEROLE

1 solid head cabbage, shredded
1 (10½-oz.) can beef consomme
1 bay leaf, broken
2 tablespoons butter
½ cup onion, chopped
1 clove garlic, chopped (optional)
1 tablespoon flour
1½ teaspoons curry or less to taste
Salt and freshly ground pepper
1½ cups sour cream
½ cup bread crumbs, finely ground

Shred cabbage and simmer in consomme with bay leaf for about 8 minutes. In skillet, melt butter and saute onion and garlic until onion is transparent. Blend in flour, curry powder, salt, pepper. Stir in sour cream. Do not boil. Add ½ cup of consomme that the cabbage was cooked in. Simmer until slightly thickened. Add drained cabbage to sauce. Stir and place in casserole. Sprinkle with bread crumbs and bake at 425°F for 15 to 20 minutes.

Serves 4 to 6

STUFFED CABBAGE

1 head of Savoy cabbage or regular
1 lb. ground beef
1 large onion, minced
1 large clove garlic, minced
2 sprigs thyme
2 sprigs marjoram
1 to 2 sage leaves, broken
Salt and pepper to taste
6 tablespoon raw rice, cooked until very soft
2 eggs, beaten

Continued

Strip leaves off fresh herbs, mince, and combine with rest of above ingredients, except cabbage. Mix thoroughly in food processor or blender. Cook cabbage in boiling water until leaves are wilted and can be cut easily from head, intact. May have to redip cabbage in boiling water several times. Cut out heavy veins from each leaf. Drain well. Place a small amount of filling in center of each leaf and roll up, folding ends in so you have a tight package.

Tomato sauce:
1 (16 oz) can tomato sauce
½ cup brown sugar
Juice of 2 lemons
Salt and pepper to taste
2 (14½-oz.) cans tomatoes (for top of casserole)
1 bay leaf

Combine above ingredients except canned tomatoes. Line an oven-proof casserole with any left over cabbage leaves. Place rolls seam-side down over leaves. Pour sauce over. Place canned tomatoes on top of sauce.

Bake at 350°F. for 1 hour covered, then 2 hours uncovered.

Serves 10

DILLED CARROTS

Fern H. Storer

Wait! Don't discard the spicy marinade, once you've used the carrots — recycle it. Add a can of drained and rinsed garbanzos and refrigerate a couple of days. After using the garbanzos, add a can of drained crinkle-sliced beets for a final spiced vegetable fling.

1 lb. carrots
1 cup cider vinegar
1 cup water
¾ cup sugar
1 teaspoon salt
1 tablespoon whole mustard seeds
1 tablespoon (or more) snipped fresh dill leaves (or one teaspoon dried dill weed)

Use: Refrigerator container with cover (1 qt.)

Peel carrots with slotted vegetable peeler; cut each cross-wise into three equal portions. Split bottom slender portions. Split the two upper portions, then cut each half lengthwise into strips about size of the split bottom portions. Combine in heavy saucepan with water to cover; bring to boiling and cook covered, only enough that one of thickest portions can be barely pierced with a sharp fork — perhaps six minutes. Drain immediately in a

Continued

colander and run cold water through them, then turn them into a bowl of ice water and chill thoroughly.

Meanwhile heat all remaining ingredients (except dill) to boiling (I do this in a quart glass measure in microwave oven). Turn the chilled carrot strips into refrigerator container; add the hot vinegar sauce. Gently stir in dill. Cool partially uncovered, then cover and refrigerate for at least eight hours before serving.

Serves 6 to 8

CARROTS IN TARRAGON BUTTER

Melanie Barnard

4 cups baby carrots, cleaned well
2 tablespoons water
3 tablespoons butter
1 tablespoon fresh tarragon, chopped, or 1 teaspoon dried tarragon
2 fresh parsley sprigs, minced

Place carrots, water, and butter in a medium saucepan. Bring to a boil, cover, and reduce heat to medium low. Cook about 15 minutes, until carrots are just tender. Stir in tarragon and parsley. Do not drain.

Serves 6

NEW ORLEANS CARROTS

4 medium sized carrots, scraped
1 can beef bouillon, or your own
Salt and pepper to taste
1 tablespoon butter

1 teaspoon fresh thyme, minced
1 teaspoon parsley
1 bay leaf

Simmer whole carrots in beef bouillon until tender.

Melt butter with seasonings in skillet. Place carrots in butter; serve hot with herb butter poured over them.

Serves 4

EGGPLANT AUX FINES HERBES

Bill Matthews

1 quart vegetable oil
4 small eggplants
1 cup flour
2 cups biscuit mix (such as Bisquick)
3 eggs
1 cup milk

½ cup grated Parmesan cheese
1 tablespoon caraway seed
3 tablespoons sesame seeds
1 teaspoon ground celery seed
Pepper to taste

Use: Heavy pan or electric deep fryer

Heat oil in heavy pan or electric deep fryer to 450°F. Peel and cube eggplants and make batter according to box directions, adding cheese, seeds and pepper to taste. Dip cubes in flour and then in batter and fry until golden crisp.

Serves 4 to 6

EGGPLANT ITALIANO

1 large or 2 small eggplants (peeled or not, as you prefer) into ¼ inch slices
1 egg beaten with teaspoon water
2 cups fine bread crumbs or Pepperidge Farm Herb Dressing
2 to 3 tablespoons olive oil
1 onion, chopped
1 or 2 garlic cloves, finely chopped
3 cups tomato sauce
1 tablespoon fresh basil, chopped
1 tablespoon fresh oregano, chopped
Freshly ground black pepper
2 tablespoons grated Parmesan or Romano cheese
6 slices mozzarella cheese
Chopped parsley

Salt and drain eggplant well on paper towels
Dip eggplant slices in beaten egg. Cover both sides with bread crumbs and saute in olive oil just long enough to brown slightly. Remove and drain while making sauce: saute 1 onion chopped, in olive oil, until transparent, adding finely chopped garlic cloves halfway through. Pour over this the tomato sauce and add basil, oregano and freshly ground black pepper to taste. Bring sauce to a boil. Simmer for 5 minutes, and pour ⅓ of sauce into shallow casserole. Place slices of eggplant in the sauce, sprinkle with Parmesan or Romano cheese and cover with 3 slices of mozzarella. Pour one half sauce over cheese and add more eggplant slices, Parmesan or Romano, and the remaining mozzarella cheese. Pour remaining sauce over, sprinkle with Parmesan and bake in 350°F oven for 30 minutes. Sprinkle with chopped parsley (if you wish) before serving.

This can be prepared ahead of time and reheated before serving.

Serves 6

BAKED STUFFED EGGPLANT I

1 large eggplant
2 tablespoons butter
1 cup chopped onions
1 cup chopped mushrooms
1½ teaspoons basil
¼ teaspoon pepper
1 lb. lean ground beef

½ teaspoon chervil
1 teaspoon salt
¼ cup tomato paste
¼ cup wheat germ
2 tablespoons parsley, fresh
chopped for garnish

Preheat oven 350°F.

Wash eggplant. Cut in half lengthwise. Carefully remove the pulp, leaving ½ inch outer shell. Dice pulp. Saute onion, mushrooms, seasoning and meat in butter or margarine. Stir in tomato paste, wheat germ, eggplant pulp. Cook until meat is slightly done. Spoon meat mixture into eggplant shell. Place in an oiled oven-proof dish. Bake 20 to 30 minutes in a 350°F oven. Garnish with parsley.

Serves 4

BAKED STUFFED EGGPLANT II

1 medium eggplant
1 onion, chopped
1 clove garlic, chopped
3 tablespoons olive oil
4 sprigs Italian parsley, chopped
1 teaspoon capers
4 anchovies, cut up
2 medium sized tomatoes, chopped
1 tablespoon green or black Greek olives, chopped
½ teaspoon oregano
½ teaspoon basil
¾ cup Pepperidge Farm Herb Dressing
Salt and pepper to taste
Heaping tablespoon grated Parmesan or Romano cheese

Preheat oven to 350°F. Scoop out eggplant pulp and chop fine. Saute onion and garlic in olive oil until light brown. Add eggplant, cook 2 minutes. Remove from heat and add chopped parsley, capers, anchovies, tomatoes, olives, oregano and basil, and half of crumbs. Blend well. Fill eggplant shells, top with remaining crumbs and grated cheese. Bake 30 minutes or until bubbling hot.

Serves 4

RATATOUILLE (FROM THE SUMMER GARDEN)

2 thinly sliced onions
2 seeded, sliced green peppers
1 peeled, sliced ¼-inch thick eggplant
3 peeled, sliced tomatoes
3 sliced zucchinis

Into a deep casserole, put a few drops of oil and a minced clove of garlic. Add by layers, the above fresh vegetables.

Repeat the layers until casserole is full. Season each layer with salt, freshly ground pepper, basil, and chopped parsley to your taste. Add a few drops of olive oil to top layer.

Bake at 350°F, 30 to 40 minutes, never stirring, but basting top as juices form. Don't overcook. Vegetables should just be "fork tender." Add last layer of parsley on top just before serving. Freezes beautifully.

Serves 6 to 8

RATATOUILLE WITH PITA BREAD

Pogue's 4th St. Market

2 tablespoons olive oil
1 large onion, chopped (cup)
2 cloves garlic, chopped very finely
1 green pepper, seeded and chopped
2 ripe tomatoes, quartered
2 zucchinis, trimmed and chopped
1 medium size unpeeled eggplant, chopped
½ teaspoon leaf basil, crumbled
1½ teaspoons leaf oregano, crumbled
1 cup tomato juice
¼ cup prepared Italian salad dressing
2 teaspoons salt
½ teaspoon pepper
12 medium pita bread, quartered
Chopped parsley

Heat oil in skillet; saute onion, garlic and green pepper until soft, about 5 minutes. Stir in tomato, zucchini, eggplant, basil, oregano, tomato juice, salad dressing, salt and pepper. Simmer, stirring occasionally, until mixture is thick and vegetables are soft, about 20 minutes. Cool. To serve, spoon ratatouille into pockets of pita bread. Garnish with parsley.

Serves 4 to 6

GLAZED ONIONS

"Across Canada with Herbs"

12 Firm white onions,
1" in diameter
4 tablespoons butter

2 tablespoons honey
½ teaspoon salt
1 teaspoon dried thyme

Trim and peel onions; arrange in buttered baking dish in one layer. Melt butter, add honey, salt, and thyme. Cook and stir until honey is liquid. Pour over onions to coat them. Bake in 400°F oven for about 35 to 40 minutes, until just tender. Baste from time to time so that onions will be golden brown. Serve at once.

Serves 4

FRENCH PEAS WITH MINT AND THYME

4 or 5 large leaves, iceberg lettuce
1 10-oz. box frozen peas
1 tablespoon butter
Salt and pepper to taste

1 small onion, quartered
1 teaspoon sugar
1 teaspoon thyme
1 tablespoon mint
leaves for garnish

Wash lettuce well. Line a pot with same. Put in peas and all other ingredients except mint. Cover. Cook as you would frozen peas alone, but about 10 minutes longer. Lettuce will be wilted and onion on the crisp side when ready to serve. Stir lettuce, onion, and peas lightly. Put in serving bowl and garnish with mint leaves (no stems).

Yield: 4

BASIL-BAKED POTATO

Bake potato your usual way. Mix 1 tablespoon butter, salt, pepper to taste and 2 teaspoons powdered basil. Cook over a low heat about 5 minutes. Split potato, make criss-cross slit across potato and pour herb butter mixture over all.

BAKED POTATOES WITH CURRY BUTTER

4 baking potatoes
¼ lb. butter, creamed
¼ teaspoon paprika
Dash freshly ground pepper

½ to 1 teaspoon curry powder
Few grains cayenne
Chopped parsley & chives

Whip butter and spices together. Use over baked potatoes, sprinkling chives and parsley on top.

CLAIRE'S POTATO DUMPLINGS

Claire Gregory

10 medium Idaho potatoes
½ lb. raw bacon, diced
1 medium onion, chopped
1 cup herb-seasoned croutons

1 large egg, beaten
½ cup parsley, chopped
1 tablespoon flour
Salt and pepper to taste
Fine herbed bread crumbs
1 cup melted butter

Continued

Boil potatoes uncovered in their jackets until tender. Drain, cool, and peel. Grate or rice them; do not mash. Fry bacon and onion. When onion is transparent, pour off excess fat. Add croutons to pan, then add riced potatoes, egg, parsley, flour, salt, and pepper to potato mixture. Fold ingredients together. Before handling potato mixture to make balls, run hands under cold water, dry them, dot with flour. Form golf ball sized-dumplings. Place in buttered casserole. Do not stack them. Refrigerate. This may be done a day in advance. Several hours before serving, bring dumplings to room temperature. Dust them with very fine herbed bread crumbs, drizzle butter over them. Bake in a 350°F oven about 30 to 40 minutes. These are excellent with pot roast or sauerbraten.

Serves 6 to 8

DILL-CREAMED POTATOES

Julie Brogan Northrop

1½ lbs. (about 15) tiny new potatoes
1 tablespoon butter or margarine
2 tablespoons flour
½ teaspoon salt
¼ teaspoon dried dill weed or 1 teaspoon snipped fresh dill weed
⅓ cup milk
¾ cup light cream

Cook potatoes in boiling, salted water about 15 to 20 minutes or until tender. Drain and peel.

Melt butter or margarine; blend in flour, salt, and dill weed. Stir in milk and cream. Cook and stir over medium heat until mixture thickens. Reduce heat, add potatoes, and heat through. Sprinkle with additional dill weed before serving.

Serves 4 to 5

NEW POTATOES WITH HERB BUTTER

Wash new red potatoes (do not peel), amount depending on number to be served.

8 to 10 new red potatoes. Boil until done but not mushy. Keep them firm. Drain, slice fan shape about ¼ inch slices. Pour herb butter sauce over them. Serve at once or reheat in oven at serving time.

Herb butter sauce:　　　　　　　*Chervil*
2 heaping tablespoons butter　　　*Tarragon*
*　or margarine — melt in skillet*　*Dill seed*
Add 1 teaspoon each:　　　　　　 *Dash of paprika*
Chopped chives　　　　　　　　　*Salt and pepper to taste*

Serves 4

NEW POTATOES WITH SOUR CREAM AND CARAWAY SEEDS

Cook new potatoes with jackets on. Warm sour cream slightly. Pour over potatoes and sprinkle with caraway seeds.

The very small new potatoes either red or white (when available) are excellent used as an hors d'oeuvre. Serve them cold with sour cream, caraway seed separately, to be used as a dip.

POTATOES PARISIENNE WITH ROSEMARY BUTTER

8 large red potatoes
1 stick unsalted butter
1 clove garlic, minced
Few drops lemon juice
1 to 2 teaspoons fresh rosemary, minced
Salt and pepper to taste
Chopped parsley for garnish

With a small, sharp melon scooper, scoop miniature potato balls out of red potatoes, either raw or slightly par-boiled. Drop into cold water as you cut them.

Blend rest of ingredients together; let marinate in refrigerator a few days.

Par-boil or steam potatoes until just barely tender. Drain and dry. Saute in rosemary butter, using as needed, until tender and lightly golden. Season with salt and freshly ground pepper. Sprinkle with chopped parsley before serving.

Yield 8 servings

POLKA DOT POTATO CAKE

"The Forgotten Art of Flower Cookery"

Leona Woodring Smith

4 tablespoons bacon drippings
3 medium baking potatoes
1 tablespoon chopped chive leaves
1 or 2 chive flowers (Pull petals from stems and check for strength. Young tender flowers are by far the best and should be thoroughly but gently washed and dried before using.)
Salt and pepper to taste

Place the bacon drippings in a skillet to melt. Peel and grate the potatoes and combine other ingredients with them. Spread evenly in the skillet and cook, covered, at medium heat until the bottom is nicely browned. Loosen around the edge carefully, turn over and brown the other side.

Serves 2 to 3

SAVORY ROAST POTATOES

½ cup butter or margarine
8 medium baking potatoes
1 teaspoon marjoram

Salt and pepper to taste
1 cup chicken broth
Parsley or fresh
marjoram for garnish

Preheat oven to 350°F.

Melt butter in casserole. Peel potatoes and roll them in butter. Sprinkle with marjoram, salt, and pepper. Bake uncovered for 1 hour. Turn and add chicken broth. Bake for another hour or until easily pierced with fork. Baste and serve. Garnish with chopped parsley or chopped fresh marjoram, if available.

Serves 8

STEAMED COMFREY WITH SPINACH

Rosella F. Mathieu

Although many people enjoy comfrey as a pot herb when cooked alone, I find it bland. So I cook it half and half with spinach, 1 lb. total. Stack young comfrey leaves on cutting board and cut in narrow strips. Mince the stems and add because they are high in nutrients. Cut spinach in strips but discard the stems.

Place greens in a pot with very little water and sprinkle with a mixed herb seasoning salt. Steam for 10 minutes. Add butter or margarine if desired. We, who are watching our weight, find it tasty enough without adding the extra calories.

For variety, mince an onion and place on top of the greens so they steam but do not cook in the liquid. Season with two ample pinches of basil, marjoram, and thyme to 4 cups of greens. After steaming, stir the mixture in the serving dish to mix and taste for seasoning. Plain or seasoning salt may be added, if necessary.

Serves 4 to 6

TARRAGON SPINACH TORTE

3 ozs. cream cheese, softened
1 cup Half and Half cream
½ cup soft bread cubes
2 eggs
½ cup Parmesan cheese, grated
1 cup cooked, chopped spinach,
drained

1 large onion, finely chopped
½ lb. mushrooms, finely chopped
4 tablespoons butter
1 tablespoon tarragon, fresh
¼ teaspoon nutmeg, freshly grated
¾ teaspoon salt
1 (9" to 10") pie shell

Mash cheese and blend in cream. Add bread, eggs, and Parmesan; beat. Stir in spinach. Saute onions and mushrooms in butter, add tarragon, nutmeg and salt. Add to spinach mix. Pour into pie shell, and bake on lowest shelf in 400°F. oven until crust is well browned and custard is set. Let rest 10 minutes before serving.

Serves 6

SPAGHETTI SQUASH WITH BUTTER-HERB SAUCE
(a main dish with chicken and vegetables)

Joyce Rosencrans

1 large spaghetti squash
½ cup butter or margarine
1 teaspoon salt
Grinding of black pepper
¼ teaspoon dried thyme leaves, crushed
2 cups finely chopped carrots (garden carrots are best for this)
1½ cups sliced celery
½ cup chopped onion
1 tablespoon or so chopped parsley stems
(add ruffly tops later)
2 cups diced, cooked, chicken
Grated Parmesan cheese

Use: Large skillet or Dutch oven

To prepare spaghetti squash, place in large pot and nearly cover with water. Bring to boiling, cover and cook 25 to 30 minutes. When done, the thin, hard shell should "give" when pressed with protected fingers. Drain off water and cool squash with cold tap water. Slice in half lengthwise and scoop out seed portion. Loosen strands at sides with fork tines and scoop out into large bowl. Set aside. (This may be done ahead of time.)

In large pot or skillet, melt the butter and blend with salt, pepper and thyme. Add the chopped vegetables. Cook over medium heat about five minutes, stirring occasionally. Vegetables should still be crisp. Add parsley stems and then cover the pan; cook until vegetables are crisp-tender. Add the strands of spaghetti squash and chicken to butter mixture and toss gently; heat through. Toss again with some chopped parsley and serve with plenty of grated Parmesan cheese.

Serves 6 to 9

STUFFED BUTTERNUT SQUASH

Bill Matthews

2 small butternut squash
Water
1 pound sausage (Matthews prefers to buy it unseasoned and season it with sage and garlic himself)
1½ tablespoons flour
½ cup chicken broth
1 cup uncooked egg noodles, preferably homemade
3 tablespoons dark brown sugar
¾ teaspoon Dijon mustard

Continued

84

Use: Baking dish and saucepans

Cut squash in half lengthwise, scoop out seeds, and place cut side down in baking dish with water to one-quarter inch depth. Bake for 30 minutes, 350°F.

While squash bakes, saute sausage, reserve fat. Mix flour with sausage and add broth. Bring to a boil.

Cook noodles in water and add to sausage sauce.

Mix brown sugar and mustard and spread half of the paste on the cut side of the squash. Fill the squash with the stuffing and drizzle with sugar-mustard, thinned with broth, if necessary. Bake 15 minutes in 375°F oven.

Serves 4

SUMMER SQUASH IN DILL AND SOUR CREAM

*From the book
"Across Canada with Herbs"*

2 lbs. summer squash, peeled and cubed
2 tablespoons butter
2 tablespoons flour
¾ cup dill pickle juice, warmed
2 tablespoons chopped fresh dill
2 tablespoons sour cream
3 tablespoons fresh parsley
Salt and pepper to taste

Melt butter in saucepan, remove from heat, and stir in flour. Add dill pickle juice and heat, stirring until mixture thickens. Add squash, dill, sour cream, parsley, salt and pepper. Simmer 10 to 15 minutes, until squash is tender.

Serves 4 to 6

WINTER SQUASH, BAKED

1 winter squash, quartered with seeds and stringy pulp removed
1 tablespoon lemon juice
1 tablespoon brown sugar
¼ teaspoon cinnamon
¼ teaspoon nutmeg
1 tablespoon fresh lemon thyme leaves, no stems
1 tablespoon butter

Drizzle quartered squash with lemon juice. Sprinkle brown sugar, cinnamon, nutmeg, and thyme leaves over squash and dot with butter. Bake at 400°F approximately 30 to 40 minutes or until a knife goes through squash easily. May be baked ahead and reheated.

Serves 4

BROILED TOMATOES

½ cup bread crumbs, dry
Salt, pepper to taste
3 tablespoons of mixed herbs, chopped fine (basil, chervil, marjoram, and summer savory)
4 tomatoes, sliced ¼" thick
1 tablespoon grated Romano or Parmesan cheese
1½ tablespoons butter

Mix all ingredients except tomatoes, cheese, and butter. Cover each tomato slice with bread crumb mixture, then add grated cheese and dots of butter. Arrange on a buttered cookie sheet and broil about 10 minutes.

Serves 4

BAKED CHERRY TOMATOES

2 cups cherry tomatoes
Salt and pepper to taste
1 tablespoon brown sugar
1 teaspoon basil, oregano, or both
1½ tablespoons olive oil

Toss all ingredients together except the olive oil. Place in a baking dish. Pour olive oil over tomatoes, cover, and bake in a 350°F oven for about 5 minutes. Remove cover. If necessary, bake a few minutes more.

Serves 4

TOMATOES PROVENCAL

2 lb. tomatoes, cut into ½" thick slices
4 slices bacon, diced
1 clove garlic, minced
1 onion, sliced
¼ lb. fresh mushrooms, sliced
1 teaspoon salt and ground pepper to taste
1 to 2 tablespoons basil, chopped, fresh
1 to 2 teaspoons oregano, chopped, fresh
6 tablespoons grated Parmesan cheese
1 tablespoon butter

Saute bacon until crisp. Add garlic, onion and mushrooms to skillet and saute until golden. Stir in salt, pepper, basil and oregano. Spread half of tomato slices in a shallow baking dish. Sprinkle with salt and pepper. Top with mushroom and bacon mixture. Sprinkle with half of Parmesan cheese. Top with remaining tomato slices. Sprinkle with salt and pepper and remaining Parmesan cheese. Dot with butter.

Bake at 350°F 40 minutes, or until tomatoes are just tender.

Serves 5 to 6

TOMATO PUDDING

1¼ cups tomato puree
1 (16-oz.) can whole tomatoes
2 or 3 fresh tomatoes, quartered
1 chopped onion
Salt and pepper to taste
½ teaspoon dried basil
4 tablespoons brown sugar, or less, if desired
1 cup (about 2 slices) bread, broken in pieces size of
thumbnail or larger
¼ stick butter
Pepperidge Farm Herb seasoned stuffing mix (crumb topping)

Use: 1½ quart casserole

Mix together tomato puree, broken whole tomatoes, fresh tomato quarters, chopped onion, salt, pepper, basil, sugar, and bread. Cut butter in pieces and sprinkle over top along with herb stuffing. Bake at 350°F until bubbling.

Serves 8 to 10

BAKED VEGETABLES

Broth
⅓ cup olive oil
3 cloves garlic, pressed
2 teaspoons salt
½ bay leaf
½ teaspoon summer savory
¼ teaspoon tarragon
1 cup beef bouillon

Vegetables such as:
½ cup peas, (if not fresh: frozen, uncooked)
½ cup celery
½ cup zucchini
1 yellow squash
¼ onion
½ head cauliflower
½ green pepper
1 cup broccoli
1 cup carrots
½ pt.-carton cherry tomatoes
½ lb. fresh asparagus, or
green beans, etc.

Vegetables* may be arranged, refrigerated, covered with plastic wrap, if you wish to prepare ahead. Bring to room temperature, pour over them, the broth, which has been heated almost to boiling. Cover (shallow casserole) with foil and bake 45-50 minutes in a 350°F oven.

*Cook all vegetables, except squashes and cherry tomatoes, for 30 minutes, adding those for a bare 15-20 minutes so they will be crisper. This is both beautiful and delicious with its "composed" arrangements of vegetables.

Serves 6 to 8

VEGETABLES IN SAVORY SAUCE

Use any of the following combinations of vegetables:

½ lb. fresh mini carrots or 1 (14½ oz.) can Belgian carrots (drained)
1 to 2 cups baby lima beans, preferably fresh but can use frozen
1 to 2 cups fresh whole green beans
1 to 2 cups tiny potato balls, made from whole potato
with a melon scooper

Cook the fresh or frozen vegetables until just tender. Drain and refresh them in cold water to retain color. Melt 1 tablespoon butter in sauce pan or casserole, add vegetables and keep warm while making sauce.

Sauce:
2 tablespoons butter (unsalted)
1½ cups well seasoned chicken stock
1 egg yolk
1½ teaspoons fresh minced summer savory (½ teaspoon, dried)
1½ teaspoons fresh minced marjoram (½ teaspoon, dried)
1 tablespoon chopped parsley
2 tablespoons flour
2 to 3 tablespoons heavy cream or Half and Half
Salt and pepper to taste

Melt butter, stir in flour and cook until straw-colored. Take off burner, whisk in chicken stock and cream, then bring to a boil, stirring. Reduce heat to a simmer. Taste for seasoning. Simmer a few minutes until thickened, remove from burner and quickly whisk in the egg yolk, put back on burner, add the herbs, salt and pepper and heat a few minutes, always keeping it under boiling point. Pour over hot vegetables.

Serves 4 to 6

STUFFED ZUCCHINI

This recipe may be used for a very large, overgrown zucchini or for several smaller ones. They must be large enough to scoop out and fill.

3 zucchinis, at least 6" long, or 1 large one
2 yellow squash, sliced ⅛" thick
12 to 15 fresh mushrooms, sliced
1 box frozen creamed spinach, defrosted, or your own favorite recipe
(about 2 cups)
¾ cup Pepperidge Farm herb stuffing (ground fine)
1 teaspoon marjoram
1 teaspoon oregano
Salt and pepper to taste
1 medium onion, chopped

Continued

1 garlic clove, chopped fine
1 tablespoon butter
1 tablespoon grated Parmesan cheese (optional)

Scoop out zucchini leaving ¼" shell. Cut scooped-out zucchini in small pieces. You can use a melon ball scooper for this, if you prefer. Parboil. DO NOT overcook; keep crisp. Cut squash slices in half and parboil the same way. Saute sliced mushrooms, chopped onion, marjoram, and garlic in butter about 2 minutes or until onions are transparent. Mix zucchini, mushroom, onion mixture (with juice), herb stuffing and spinach together. Add oregano, salt and pepper and blend well. Fill zucchini shells with above mixture, decorate with ½ slices of yellow squash, standing upright across the center. (Optional: sprinkle Parmesan cheese over top).

Bake in 350°F oven until bubbling.

Serves 8 to 10

ZUCCHINI UNDERCOVER

(Cheese and vegetables burrito-style)

Joyce Rosencrans

½ cup finely chopped onion
1 clove garlic, minced
3 medium zucchinis, chopped
1 (4 oz.) can chopped green chilies
1 teaspoon dried basil leaves, crushed
½ teaspoon dried oregano, crushed
¼ teaspoon ground cumin
¼ teaspoon salt
Small amount of cooking oil
1 cup grated Monterey Jack cheese
¾ cup toasted wheat germ
6-8 flour tortillas (large, refrigerated type)
Dairy sour cream
Fresh minced parsley

Use: Large skillet or griddle

Saute onion, garlic, zucchini, chilies, basil, oregano, cumin, and salt in a tablespoon of oil over medium heat five minutes. Stir in cheese and wheat germ, stirring until cheese melts and is blended with vegetables.

Have tortillas at room temperature and spoon vegetable mixture onto center of each, dividing evenly. Roll as for crepes, long and cigar-shaped. Fry bundles in small amount of oil until golden, turning once. Watch carefully and moderate heat; flour tortillas brown quickly and will burn. Top with sour cream and minced parsley. May be prepared ahead, browned, then chilled. Reheat in oven at 350°F or Microwave according to instructions.

Serves 4
(two bundles per person)

ZUCCHINI WITH BASIL

Golden Lamb

2 lbs. zucchini, washed, cut in 2-inch sticks
¼ onion, peeled and diced finely
2 tablespoons butter
Basil, fresh (leaves only) minced
Salt and pepper to taste
1 slice lemon

Saute onions in butter in large heavy skillet, add zucchini, stir. Add basil, salt, and pepper to taste. Don't overcook. Add few drops of fresh lemon juice.

Serves 4 to 6

ZUCCHINI WITH SUMMER HERBS

1½ lbs. zucchini
4 tablespoons olive oil
Salt and freshly ground pepper
2 tablespoons butter
2 teaspoons chopped garlic
1 tablespoon chopped parsley, fresh
1 tablespoon chopped chives, fresh
1 tablespoon chopped dill, fresh
1 teaspoon chopped tarragon, fresh
1 tablespoon chopped basil, fresh

Rinse the zucchini and pat dry. Trim off the ends, but do not peel. Cut the zucchini into thin slices, ⅛ inch thick. There should be about 6 cups. Heat the oil in a skillet and when it is quite hot, add the zucchini. Cook over relatively high heat, shaking the skillet, and tossing and stirring gently with a spatula to turn the slices. Add salt and pepper to taste. Cook about 5 to 7 minutes. Drain in a sieve. Do not wipe out the skillet.

Add the butter to the skillet. When melted and hot, return the zucchini to the skillet. Add the garlic and herbs. Add salt and pepper to taste. Toss and serve hot.

Serves 6

Beef,
Ham,
Lamb,
Pork,
Veal

BAKED HASH AU GRATIN

Shakertown

3 cups coarsely ground cooked beef or corned beef
1 teaspoon Worcestershire sauce
2 cups coarsely chopped cooked potatoes
¾ cup leftover gravy or
¾ cup beef bouillon stock
1 large onion, ground
1 green pepper, ground
¼ teaspoon thyme
1 teaspoon salt
1 teaspoon sherry
¼ teaspoon pepper

Topping:
2 tomatoes, sliced
½ cup grated cheese
¼ cup bread crumbs
2 teaspoons butter

Mix all ingredients for hash. Pour into an oiled 2-quart casserole. Press tomato slices into top of mixture, sprinkle with cheese and crumbs, and dot with butter. Bake in 375°F oven, uncovered, for 35 minutes, or until browned.

Serves 6 to 8

BEEF EN GELEE

You may use leftover roast beef, pot roast, brisket, or beef tenderloin.
You may also start from scratch. This recipe is based on a 4 pound piece of brisket. Cook the brisket according to your favorite recipe.
Let it cool in the sauce. This may be prepared 2 days before serving.
On the second day, take meat out of sauce (reserve sauce for another dish).
Slice as many pieces as you wish and according to the size of platter you have. Platter should be at least 1½" in depth. There should be at least 2 layers of sliced meat, unless you are doing tenderloin of beef or roast beef; a single layer will suffice then.

Continued

4 lbs. cooked brisket or other beef, sliced
Choice of vegetables:
1 box frozen peas, cooked
1 jar Belgian carrots
1 green pepper, sliced in rings
1 box frozen green beans, cooked
2 cans jellied beef consomme
1 teaspoon thyme
1 teaspoon basil
1 teaspoon Worcestershire sauce
Salt, pepper to taste
1 envelope gelatin (unflavored)
½ cup water or white wine

Arrange slices of meat in serving dish. Garnish with peas or other vegetables, green pepper slices, carrots, even snow peas may be used.

Heat 2 cans of consomme, but do not boil. Add thyme, basil, Worcestershire, salt, and pepper to consomme.

Soften gelatin in ½ cup cold water or white wine. Add to consomme, stir until gelatin is dissolved. Pour over meat slices and vegetables. Rearrange vegetables, for example: put carrots in middle of green pepper slices, if you are using this combination (peas will rearrange themselves).

Cool and then refrigerate.

Before serving, garnish with fresh sprigs of opal basil and regular basil and thyme, or watercress, if fresh herbs are not available.

Serve with horseradish sauce: 1 cup sour cream combined with horseradish, to taste.

Serves 8 to 10

BEEF STEW BORDELAISE

1½ lbs. beef chuck cut into 1" cubes
1 tablespoon shortening
1 clove garlic
1 medium onion, chopped
½ teaspoon salt
⅓ teaspoon pepper

1 can condensed tomato soup
¾ cup dry red wine
⅓ cup water
¼ teaspoon basil, dried
¼ teaspoon thyme, dried
½ cup tomato catsup

Lightly brown beef in shortening. Add garlic and onion. Saute until transparent. Sprinkle with salt and pepper. Stir in tomato soup, wine, water, basil, thyme, and catsup.

Continued

Arrange the following vegetables on top:

3 medium carrots, scraped
1½ cups sliced celery
4 medium potatoes, pared and cubed
1 cup cooked green beans
Additional water or bouillon, if needed

Cover and simmer 1½ hours. Add green beans during last few minutes to heat. Add more water or beef bouillon, if necessary.

Serves 6

BEEF WITH A VINAIGRETTE DRESSING

Charles Bolton

4 to 6 cups boiled or roasted beef, cut into ½" cubes (leftover roast or brisket)
2 ribs celery, thinly sliced
2 medium onions, thinly sliced and separated into rings
2 medium tomatoes, peeled, seeded and chopped
3 tablespoons capers, drained
2 tablespoons chopped fresh chives
2 cloves garlic, minced (optional)
2 tablespoons red wine vinegar
2 tablespoons prepared mustard (Dijon or other fine mustard)
¾ cup olive oil, peanut, or corn oil, chilled at least 3 hours

Mix beef, celery, onions, tomatoes, capers, chives, and garlic in large bowl.

In a chilled mixing bowl, whisk together the mustard and vinegar. Add the chilled oil slowly, in a constant stream, while beating rapidly. The dressing will look like a thin mayonnaise. Season the dressing with salt and pepper to taste; pour over salad and toss. Serve cold. This is a complete meal when served on a bed of lettuce, with a loaf of crusty French bread, butter, and wine.

Serves 4 to 6

HERBAL HINT
Add your favorite herb blend to buttered crackers. Heat in oven until slightly brown.

BEEF SHORT RIBS ALADDIN, BRAISED

Chef Gregory

2½ to 3 lbs. short ribs, trimmed of fat, or equivalent amount of chuck
roast, cut into comparable pieces
Flour for dredging
3 eggs and 3 tablespoons milk or water, beaten together
Sesame seeds for coating
1 stick butter
1 medium onion, diced
2 to 3 cloves garlic, minced
1 drop Tabasco
1 teaspoon Maggi
1 teaspoon white pepper
1 teaspoon coriander
½ teaspoon cumin
1 tablespoon chili powder
2 hot chili peppers (canned) plus 1 tablespoon of juice
1 cup tomato sauce
2 cups beef, chicken stock, or consomme
½ cup slivered almonds
1 cup pitted black olives, drained
½ cup chopped parsley

Dredge ribs in flour lightly. Dip into egg wash. Coat with sesame seeds.

Saute onion in butter until lightly browned. Brown ribs in butter, onion mixture on all sides. Add garlic and simmer a few minutes.

Remove from stove and add Tabasco, Maggi, pepper, coriander, cumin, chili powder, chili peppers and juice, tomato sauce, and stock. Shake pan and mix.

Put back on stove and bring up to boiling point. Bake in 350°F oven 2 hours, turning ribs every half hour. The last half hour, add almonds, olives, and parsley.

Serves 6 to 8

BEEF SHORT RIBS, HERBED

3 lbs. short ribs, cut in pieces
3 tablespoons flour
Salt and pepper to taste
3 tablespoons bacon drippings from 3 slices of bacon, reserve bacon;
and crumble
½ cup chopped onion
½ cup chopped celery
1 can beef consomme

¼ cup red wine
½ teaspoon rosemary, dried
½ teaspoon thyme, dried
3 sprigs parsley, chopped

Continued

Preheat over to 300°F.

Heat bacon drippings in a heavy-lidded casserole. Saute celery and onions in drippings until onion is transparent. Remove vegetables. Dredge ribs in salt and pepper, seasoned flour and brown in drippings. Remove from burner, add all other ingredients, including bacon. Cover and bake about 2½ hours, turning meat about 2 or 3 times. Cook until meat is tender. This may be done a day ahead and refrigerated. Remove excess fat before reheating.

Serves 3 to 4

BEEF STEW, HERBED

Melanie Barnard

2 tablespoons butter plus 2 tablespoons olive or vegetable oil
½ lb. small whole fresh mushrooms
½ cup chopped onions
1 clove garlic, crushed
1½ teaspoons salt
8 to 12 baby carrots
½ lb. small whole onions
1 teaspoon fresh dill or ¼ teaspoon dried dillweed
2 teaspoons fresh basil, minced or teaspoon dried basil
1 teaspoon fresh thyme or ¼ teaspoon dried thyme
¼ teaspoon powdered savory
1 bay leaf, crushed
2 lbs. lean beef chuck, cut in 1½ inch cubes
4 Italian plum tomatoes, quatered or 1 lb. can plum tomatoes, undrained
1½ cups good beef stock
1½ cups Burgundy wine
2 teaspoons potato starch
"Buerre manie" made by combining 3 tablespoons flour with 2 tablespoons butter

In a large stockpot, brown beef on all sides over medium heat in butter and oil. Do not crowd pan. When all is browned, lightly brown onions, carrots and mushrooms. Set aside. Lightly saute chopped onion and garlic adding more butter if necessary. Stir in potato starch till smooth. Return beef to pan. Add herbs, tomatoes, stock, and burgundy wine. Cover and bring to a boil. Lower heat to simmer and cover pan with a sheet of waxed paper, then cover with lid. Simmer about 1½ hours until meat is tender. Drain off accumulated liquid from top of waxed paper. Add onions and carrots and simmer about 30 minutes until tender. Add mushrooms and simmer 5 to 10 minutes. If desired, thicken, by swirling in bits of "buerre manie" till smooth and desired thickness. Correct seasoning. Serve with steamed rice or buttered noodles.

Serves 8

BRISKET OF BEEF

(Jewish style, with or without chicken)

1 well-trimmed flat brisket
1 to 3 cloves garlic, slivered
Kosher salt
Freshly ground black pepper
¼ teaspoon ground ginger
1 or 2 teaspoons paprika
2 tablespoons chicken fat, rendered with onion
1 large onion, diced
1 carrot, sliced
3 to 4 sprigs fresh thyme
3 to 4 sprigs fresh marjoram
3 to 4 sprigs fresh parsley
1 bay leaf
Chicken stock or water, enough to cover ½" depth of pan
Carrots and red potatoes, optional

Make slits in brisket with small pointed knife and insert slivers of garlic in them.

Season brisket liberally with salt, pepper, ginger, and paprika on both sides. Let stand ½ to 1 hour to absorb seasoning.

Saute onion and carrot in chicken fat in heavy roaster until onion is golden brown. Remove onion and carrot. Sear brisket on both sides in roaster, until well-browned. Return onion and carrot to roaster, scattering around meat.

Add herbs. Cover roaster tightly and roast in 325° F oven. After a short while, add a little stock or water, baste brisket and cover. Baste often, adding liquid a little at a time, if needed.

If you wish to cook carrots and potatoes in roaster with brisket, either add them about ½ hour before meat is tender or remove meat when tender and add vegetables to the roaster, until they are tender. Turn them several times and baste while cooking.

Let meat cool down. Slice thinly across the grain.

Either reheat the sliced meat and optional vegetables in the gravy, or puree the gravy in a food processor, and reheat with sliced meat and vegetables.

A disjointed roasting chicken that has been seasoned with salt, pepper, paprika, ground ginger, and garlic powder may be roasted along with the brisket the last hour of cooking or after the brisket has been removed from the pot.

Serve disjointed chicken pieces with beef.

Serves 8 to 10

CALVES LIVER AND SWEET BASIL

6 slices calves liver, about ¼" thick
Salt and pepper to taste
1½ tablespoons flour
6 tablespoons butter
½ cup white wine
1 tablespoon fresh basil, finely chopped
2 additional tablespoons butter

Season liver slices with salt and pepper and dredge with flour. Saute gently in hot butter in a skillet for about 3 minutes on each side, depending on how you like liver cooked. Remove liver to warm platter. Add wine to skillet, and stir in all the brown bits from bottom and sides of pan. Add basil and additional butter. Swirl pan until butter is melted. Pour over liver and serve.

Serves 4

HOMEMADE SAUSAGE

Mona Poynter (Mrs. Donald)

5 lbs. inexpensive fatty hamburger meat
5 rounded teaspoons Morton's Tender Quick Cure Salt
2½ teaspoons mustard seeds
2½ teaspoons coarse ground pepper
2½ teaspoons garlic salt
1 teaspoon Hickory Smoke Salt

1st day — Mix all ingredients together by kneading well in a bowl. Cover and refrigerate.
2nd day — Mix — knead — refrigerate
3rd day — Mix — knead — refrigerate
4th day — Form rolls about the size of Polish sausage, cut in 4" pieces or longer. Place rolls on rack of broiler pan.
Bake at 240° F for 8 hours. Turn every two hours. This sausage roll can be frozen and used as needed.

MARINATED BLUE CHEESE FLANK STEAK

Cris Carsman

Marinade:
½ cup salad oil
¼ cup lemon juice
1 tablespoon grated onion
2 tablespoons parsley
1 teaspoon marjoram
1 teaspoon thyme

1 teaspoon salt
¼ teaspoon garlic powder
½ teaspoon Tabasco
1½ lbs. flank steak, scored
¼ cup butter or margarine
2 tablespoons chopped chives

2 tablespoons blue cheese

Continued

Combine marinade ingredients and mix well. Pour over the steak in a shallow glass dish. Cover and refrigerate for two hours. Turn the steak over. Cover and refrigerate an additional two hours. Meanwhile, cream the butter, chives, and cheese together and set aside. Remove the steak from marinade and grill or broil, using the marinade to baste. Remove to carving board and spread with butter mixture. Slice on the diagonal.

Serves 4 to 5

MEATBALLS WITH DILL AND CARAWAY

Melanie Barnard

1 lb. ground round steak
1½ lbs. each ground pork and veal
1 cup dry bread crumbs
1 garlic clove
2 shallots
1 large onion, quartered
1 small green pepper, quartered
2 tablespoons fresh dillweed
2 tablespoons fresh parsley
1 tablespoon beef stock base or bouillon powder
½ cup milk
1 tablespoon caraway seeds
¼ teaspoon fresh ground nutmeg
2 eggs
Salt and freshly ground pepper to taste
½ cup unsalted butter
2 tablespoons olive or vegetable oil
1½ cup heavy cream
1 cup sour cream
Fresh dill for garnish

In a large bowl, combine the meats and bread crumbs. In a blender or processor, mince the garlic and shallots, then add the onion, green pepper, dill, parsley, beef base, and milk. Puree. Add to meat, along with caraway seeds, nutmeg, eggs, and salt and pepper. Combine well. Shape into about 4 dozen balls. Melt the oil and butter in a large skillet. Brown the meatballs on all sides without crowding pan. Place the meatballs, as they are browned, in a large saucepan. Pour cream over browned meatballs and keep them simmering till all balls are added. Add the sour cream and cook very slowly, not boiling, about 1 hour. If sauce is too thick, thin with beef broth. Garnish with dill.

Serves 8

MEAT LOAF

(Meat balls or Country pate)

Alice Galvin

Preheat oven to 350°.

2 lbs. lean beef	**½ teaspoon nutmeg**
½ lb. pork shoulder	**½ teaspoon ground black pepper**
½ lb. veal	**½ teaspoon basil**
½ lb. mild sausage	**½ teaspoon oregano**
½ cup chopped onions	**¼ teaspoon sage**
½ cup cream	**¼ teaspoon thyme**
½ cup fresh bread crumbs	**½ cup chopped parsley**
½ lb. chopped mushrooms	**2 eggs beaten with ½ cup cream**
1 clove chopped garlic	**Small amount of oil**
1 tablespoon salt	**Small amount of flour**

Chop meats in food processor.
Combine meats and onion and blend well with spoon or hands.
Heat cream and pour over bread crumbs
Add cream and bread crumbs. Mix well.
Add mushrooms, seasoning, and herbs. Mix well.
Add eggs and cream. Blend well.
Shape into 2 large or 4 small loaves.
Coat them slightly with cooking oil. Shake a small amount of flour over loaves, lightly coating them.
Bake in 350°F oven 1½ hours.

Additional notes:
Using lean meats insures that the loaves will not shrink a great deal.
This recipe may be used for meat balls or a delicious country pate. (Chop meats very fine for the pate.)
The recipe freezes very well and is easily doubled.

Serves 10 to 12

SERUNDENG
(Indonesian Beef)

Dora Ang

½ lb. beef tenderloin, sliced ⅛" thick	**2½ teaspoons sugar**
1 teaspoon salt	**2 teaspoons ground coriander**
2 tablespoons oil, preferably	**½ teaspoon ground cumin**
peanut or sesame	**Dash of turmeric powder**
¼ lb. grated coconut	**1 sprig lemon thyme (optional) or**
2 cloves garlic, chopped very fine	**Leaf from lemon tree, broken**
1 small onion	**into pieces**

Continued

Season beef slices with ½ teaspoon salt. Saute until half done in hot oil in wok. Remove from oil; keep warm.

Add all other ingredients to wok, stir-fry on low heat about 8 minutes. Add beef and stir until coconut is crisp and golden brown. Let cool and serve.

Serves 4 to 6

TERIYAKI STEAK STRIPS
(Barbecued Flank Steak)

Mona Poynter (Mrs. Donald)

2 lbs. flank steak
1 cup undiluted beef consomme or ¼ cup consomme and red or white wine
⅓ cup soy sauce
1½ teaspoons seasoned salt
¼ cup chopped green onions with tops
1 clove garlic, minced or mashed
2 tablespoons brown sugar or honey

Have your meatman remove the membrane, but don't have the meat scored in a mechanical tenderizer.

Cut meat into 1-inch wide strips, diagonally, from top to bottom. Marinate in refrigerator overnight in a marinade made by combining consomme, soy sauce, salt, green onions, garlic, and brown sugar or honey.

Drain meat and save marinade. Using a broiler, grill very quickly (2 to 3 minutes on each side) while brushing with marinade. Turn only once.

Serves 5 to 6

"Rosemary for Remembrance"

Shakespeare

Remember:
Use triple the amount of fresh herbs to dried herbs!

COTTAGE HAM AND GREEN BEANS

2 lbs. Kentucky Wonder green beans (string beans may be used)
1½ to 2 lbs. cottage ham
2 onions, quartered
Salt and pepper to taste
Approximately 1 pint of water, enough to fill pot, about 2" with
ingredients in it
2 teaspoons summer savory, fresh if available
1 teaspoon thyme, dried
6 small red potatoes, washed, not peeled
6 or 8 small white onions (optional)

Place all ingredients, except potatoes and whole onions, in heavy cooking pot. Bring to a boil, turn down heat, and simmer for about 2 hours, turning ham occasionally, until beans and ham are fork tender. The potatoes and whole onions should be added half way through cooking time. If they cook rapidly, remove and reheat later with beans. This dish may be prepared a day ahead, refrigerated, and excess fat removed before reheating and serving.

To serve, place cottage ham slices on a deep platter and surround with vegetables.

Small buttered carrots, cooked separately, will add color to the dish and blend nicely with the onions, beans, and potatoes.

Serves 4 to 6

CAUCASIAN SHASHLIK
(Lamb)

3 to 4 lbs. cubed lamb (with or without bone; leg is best)

Marinade:
Juice of 4 lemons
Olive oil, equal to about ½ volume of lemon juice
1 bunch parsley, finely chopped
3 to 4 cloves garlic, pressed or crushed
1 onion, thinly sliced
5 to 6 peppercorns
Salt and pepper
Mint, coriander leaves, oregano (optional)

Marinate lamb for a day or two, turning occasionally. Remove meat from marinade and skewer loosely, to grill over coals, turning to brown on all sides. Do not overcook; the meat will be too dry.

To broil in oven, the meat need not be skewered, and a rack is not necessary. If most of the marinade has been drained before cooking, you may cook for a brief time, if you prefer pink, or longer if you prefer your lamb well done. Browned scallions and green peppers are good accompaniments.

Serves 8 to 10

CROWN ROAST OF LAMB

Have your butcher prepare a crown roast of lamb. Young spring lamb is the best for this dish. Preheat oven to 400°F.

Put aluminum "mittens" on bone ends of chops to keep them from burning. Season lamb with salt, pepper, 1 slivered garlic clove, each sliver wrapped in a mint leaf. Insert these between chops. You may wish to use about 1 teaspoon finely chopped rosemary for seasoning too.

Place meat in roasting pan, turn oven down to 325°F and roast about 18 minutes per pound or, if you want it well done, an internal temperature of 175°F. Young lamb is very succulent when it is served medium rare, the French way (internal temperature of 140°F).

The following are suggested fillings for the unfilled center of the roast:

Lightly sauteed mushrooms and cooked fresh peas
Small buttered onions
Creamed carrots and peas
Small browned new potatoes

You may also wish to fill the crown with forcemeat stuffing. This is a regular bread stuffing plus one cup of very finely ground lamb. Mix your favorite poultry stuffing and add the lamb. You will need about 2 cups total. If you use forcemeat, fill the crown roast before roasting and bake at least 15 minutes longer.

When lamb is ready to be served, put paper frills on each chop and garnish center filling with parsley or mint.

Variation: A crown roast of pork.
This will require more cooking time. Allow 30 to 45 minutes to the pound. Do not use forcemeat stuffing. After roasting, fill pork roast with suggestions for lamb or with a sausage stuffing cooked separately and then put in center of roast before serving.

For sausage stuffing, brown and drain ½ cup sausage meat. Make your favorite dressing, adding 1 tart apple, cut up and browned sausage. Garnish with fresh sage leaves.

Serves 6 to 8

LAMB CASSEROLE

2 lbs. lamb shoulder, cut for stew *1 cup chicken stock*
½ stick butter or margarine *2 tablespoons fresh dill, chopped*
1 lb. green beans, cut in 1" pieces *2 teaspoons paprika*
2 large onions, sliced *Salt and pepper to taste*
Chopped parsley for garnish

Brown meat in butter in casserole. Add rest of ingredients, season with salt and pepper. Cover and bake in 350°F oven until meat is tender, about 1½ hours. Garnish with chopped parsley or mint.

Serves 6 to 8

LAMB CHOPS WITH HERB STUFFING

8 loin or rib lamb chops 1 to 1¼" thick
2 tablespoons butter

Herb stuffing:
¾ cup fresh bread crumbs
1 tablespoon parsley
2 or 3 teaspoons fresh thyme, minced
1 to 1½ teaspoons fresh rosemary
1 teaspoon fresh summer savory, if available
4 tablespoons butter
2 shallots, finely chopped
1 clove garlic, minced
Salt and pepper to taste

Sauce:
1 shallot, finely chopped
4 to 5 mushrooms, finely chopped
1½ tablespoons flour
2 cups well-seasoned chicken or veal stock or combination of both

Stuffing:

Combine bread crumbs and herbs. Cook shallots in 2 tablespoons butter until transparent, adding garlic at end of sauteeing time. Add two more tablespoons of butter to skillet, melt and mix shallots and garlic with bread crumbs and herbs. Add salt and pepper to taste.

If using rib chops, trim ends to expose 1 inch of bone. Cut a pocket in each chop and fill with stuffing mixture.

Heat 2 tablespoons of butter in skillet and saute chops on each side, 2 to 3 minutes or until nicely browned. Transfer to shallow baking dish. Cook in 300°F oven for about 10 minutes, or longer, if you prefer well done.

Sauce:

Saute chopped shallots in same skillet until transparent, stir in mushrooms and cook until mixture is dry. Add flour, stir well; add stock, bring to a boil, and simmer 5 minutes. Taste for seasoning; add salt and freshly ground pepper if needed.

Arrange chops on platter, spoon some sauce down the middle. Serve remaining sauce in sauceboat. Use paper frills on rib chops as an added plus.

Serves 8

LE CARRE D'AGNEAU AROMATES
(Rack of lamb with aromatic seasoning)

Chef George Pulver — Gourmet Room, Cincinnati, Ohio

Preheat oven 425°F.

1 rack of lamb
Salt and pepper to taste
1 teaspoon thyme
½ teaspoon rosemary, crushed
½ teaspoon sage, crushed
½ teaspoon mint leaves, chopped
1 teaspoon celery seed
2 tablespoons Swiss aromate
2 cloves garlic, mashed
1 tablespoon Dijon mustard
2 tablespoons fine bread crumbs
2 tablespoons melted butter

Season rack of lamb with salt and pepper. Roast 35 minutes in 425°F oven for medium rare. Remove from oven, pour off excess fat.

Mix all the herbs together and spread them over the lamb. Spoon mustard over herbs. Sprinkle bread crumbs over mustard. Pour butter over all, place under broiler for 10 minutes. Serve with fresh vegetables and mint garnish.

Serves 2

ROAST LEG OF LAMB MATTHEWS

Bill Matthews

One leg of lamb (allow three quarters of a pound per person)

Slivers of lemon rind	**½ cup orange juice concentrate**
Whole rosemary sprig	**½ cup brown sugar**
Pepper	**3 tablespoons soy sauce**
Garlic cloves, quartered lengthwise	**½ cup Dijon mustard**
½ cup honey	

Use: Baking pan

Pierce lamb all over at one-inch intervals by inserting paring knife blade one inch deep. Into each cut, insert one bit of lemon rind, one-fourth clove garlic and three "needles" of rosemary. Wrap tightly in plastic and set in a cool place outside the refrigerator for four to six hours.

Mix all remaining ingredients and rub onto lamb after curing period. Place uncovered in refrigerator for at least 24 hours before baking. Put lamb in preheated 500°F oven and immediately turn down to 375°F. Roast according to weight, or to desired doneness.

Yield: Depends on the size leg of lamb

SHOULDER OF LAMB OR BUTTERFLIED
LEG OF LAMB, STUFFED WITH
CHICKEN LIVERS AND HERBS

3½ lbs. lamb shoulder or butterflied leg of lamb (bone removed)
Salt and pepper to taste
1½ lbs. chicken livers, chopped coarsely
2 tablespoons butter
1 tablespoon grated onion
2 cups Pepperidge Farm Herb Stuffing
¾ cup chopped celery
2 tablespoons chives
1 tablespoon thyme
1 tablespoon marjoram
Several sprigs fresh mint
1 garlic clove, sliced thin
2 tablespoons white wine or sherry
⅓ cup chicken stock

Have bone removed from lamb to form pocket for stuffing. Salt and pepper roast, inside and out, cut about 6 to 8 small diagonal slashes in roast. Wrap garlic slivers in mint leaves and insert in roast. Brown chicken livers in butter and add rest of ingredients. Salt and pepper to taste.

Stuff lamb with dressing and skewer edges together just before roasting.

Preheat oven to 325°F.

Place roast in an uncovered roasting pan for approximately 2½ hours or use your thermometer for internal temperature you prefer, 170° F for medium and 180° F for well done.

If you wish sauce, remove fat from roasting pan, add about 1 tablespoon of water, bring to a boil and stir well. Add salt and pepper, if needed.

Serves 6 to 8

HERB PORK CHOPS

No quantities are given here. Use as many chops as you wish. This is a method recipe.

Sprinkle garlic powder (optional), salt and pepper, paprika, poultry seasoning and fine bread crumbs or Pepperidge Farm Herb Stuffing over both sides of chops. Bake uncovered in a 350° F oven until browned on both sides.

Add chicken stock to cover bottom of pan to ⅛" depth. Cover and bake until tender, about 40 minutes. You may substitute poultry seasoning with your own fresh, sage, thyme, marjoram, shallots, etc.

PORK CHOPS STUFFED WITH SPINACH AND HERBS

From the Civic Garden Center's "Herb Cookery"

4 double pork chops, at least 3" thick, cut with pocket
½ lb. fresh spinach or 2 boxes frozen, defrosted and drained
1 clove garlic, minced
1 tablespoon olive oil
½ cup chopped parsley
½ teaspoon thyme
1 tablespoon summer savory, fresh
Pinch of basil
½ cup dry bread crumbs
Salt and pepper to taste
⅓ cup chicken stock
2 tablespoons white wine

Wash spinach, salt, and cook until wilted. Drain and chop. Mince garlic and fry in oil for 5 minutes. Add parsley and herbs. Stir well and add crumbs and spinach, salt and pepper. Let cool. Then stuff into pork pockets. Bake at 325°F for 1 hour and 15 minutes, basting every 15 minutes with chicken stock and wine.

Serves 4

PORK ROAST

1 boned and rolled pork loin, well trimmed of fat
1 to 3 cloves garlic
1 teaspoon dried thyme or
5 to 6 sprigs fresh thyme
Salt, freshly ground black pepper
1 cup chicken, beef, or veal stock (approximately)

Cut garlic into slivers and insert into slits made with a small, sharp knife all over roast. Tuck sprigs of thyme into slits or sprinkle roast with dried thyme. Salt and pepper to taste.

Roast at 325°F until internal temperature registers 180°F. After roast has cooked for about an hour, add stock. Baste several times, adding more if needed. Let stand 15 to 20 minutes before slicing. Serve with sauce made from pan drippings.

Yield: According to size of roast

ROAST PORK L'ORANGE

5 lb. pork loin roast
Salt and pepper to taste
1 teaspoon thyme, dried
1 teaspoon grated orange rind and 3 pieces orange peel
½ teaspoon dry mustard
½ teaspoon ginger or ¼ teaspoon ginger root, chopped fine
½ cup orange juice
½ cup honey

Preheat oven to 325°F

Combine above seasonings, except orange juice and honey and rub over pork. Place in roasting pan and bake uncovered for 2½ hours or 30 minutes per pound.

Meantime, combine orange juice and honey. After roast has been in oven for about ½ hour, baste with orange juice/honey combination several times throughout remainder of cooking time.

Serve glazed roast on meat platter, surrounded by Mandarin oranges and Belgian carrots, garnished with watercress.

Serves 4 to 6

ALSATIAN VEAL STEW

Chef Gregory

2 lbs. veal shoulder, cut into 1" cubes, or if you prefer, lamb shoulder
½ lb. bacon, diced, sauteed till half done and well drained
1 medium onion, chopped
1 medium leek, chopped
2 medium carrots, peeled and diced
2 stalks celery, diced
2 to 3 cloves garlic, minced
1 teaspoon Maggi
1 drop Tabasco
1 tablespoon rosemary
1 teaspoon thyme
1 bay leaf
1 cup peeled, chopped tomatoes
½ cup dry sherry
2 cups beef or chicken stock
2 cups canned flageolets (rinsed) (small French kidney beans)
1 cup frozen pearl onions
Chopped parsley for garnish
Dash Madeira or brandy

Continued

Blanch veal (or lamb) by putting into a pot of cold water, bringing to a boil, and draining immediately.

Saute onion and leeks in bacon fat. Add remaining ingredients to pan except the flageolets and pearl onions, parsley and Madeira. Bring to boiling point, reduce heat, and simmer 20 to 30 minutes for veal and 30 to 40 minutes for lamb. About 15 to 20 minutes before done, add flageolets and onions. When ready to serve, sprinkle with chopped parsley, and add a dash of Madeira or brandy. May be served with rice or noodles.

Serves 6 to 8

ESCALOPES DE VEAU

"21" Restaurant

8 tablespoons sweet butter
2 medium onions, chopped
1 dozen medium-sized mushrooms, chopped
2 bay leaves
Pinch rosemary
1 cup raw long-grain rice
3 cups water
Salt and freshly ground black pepper to taste
2 egg yolks
2 cups unsweetened whipped heavy cream
½ cup grated Parmesan cheese
8 pieces pounded veal scallops, about 3½" in diameter
½ cup all-purpose flour
½ cup Madeira or dry sherry
1 cup brown sauce

Preheat the oven to 350°F. In deep casserole, melt 4 tablespoons of butter and, over a low flame, saute the onions and mushrooms until softened but not brown, about 10 minutes. Add the bay leaves and rosemary and cook for another 15 minutes, keeping the flame very low. Stirring constantly, add the rice and cook for a moment until it is coated with butter. Slowly stir in the water and season with salt and pepper. When the mixture comes to a boil, cover the casserole and bake in the oven for about 25 minutes, or until the rice is tender. After the mixture has cooked, puree, stirring well. Carefully fold in the whipped cream and half of the cheese. Put the mixture into a pastry bag and set aside.

Lightly dip the pounded veal slices in flour, shaking to remove excess. In a large skillet, melt the remaining butter (4 tablespoons) and brown the veal slices on both sides over a medium flame, cooking about 10 minutes in all. Arrange the veal on an oven-proof serving dish and preheat the broiler.

Into the skillet in which the veal was cooked, pour the Madeira and stir well. Boil over a high flame for a few minutes until the juices are reduced by about half. Mixing thoroughly with a whisk, slowly add the brown sauce and simmer until warmed through. Set aside.

Continued

Squeeze the mixture in the pastry bag over the veal, making a crisscross pattern on each piece, and sprinkle the remaining cheese over the top. Place the dish under the broiler until the top is golden brown. The Madeira sauce may be poured onto the serving dish around the veal or served separately.

Serves 4 to 6

ROLLED VEAL SCALLOPS WITH
VEAL STUFFING, ITALIANO

6 veal scallops
2 cups veal shoulder, ground
1 tablespoon chives
1 tablespoon olive oil
1 tablespoon dry white wine
1 teaspoon ground rosemary
½ teaspoon ground basil
½ teaspoon ground sage
Salt and pepper to taste
1 cup, your favorite tomato sauce
Grated Parmesan or Romano cheese for topping

Mix well ground veal and all ingredients except tomato sauce. Fill each scallop with mixture. Roll them, put on greased baking pan suitable for broiling. Broil for about 6 minutes on each side or until they are slightly browned. Serve with tomato sauce, topped with grated Parmesan or Romano cheese. Put under broiler for a few minutes to melt cheese.

Serves 6

VEAL PAPRIKA

Barbara Rosenberg

2 lbs. veal stew meat, cut into 1" pieces
⅓ cup lemon juice
4 tablespoons butter
½ teaspoon salt
⅛ teaspoon pepper
3 tablespoons Wondra flour
⅔ cup dry white wine
3 strips bacon, chopped
½ cup celery, chopped
½ cup carrots, chopped
½ cup onion, chopped
12 ozs. mushrooms
½ cup tomato, chopped
1 bay leaf
½ teaspoon marjoram
¼ teaspoon thyme
1 tablespoon caraway seed
3 tablespoons sour cream
2 tablespoons capers
2 tablespoons chopped parsley

Place veal in plastic bag with lemon juice; stir to coat. Marinate for 2 hours, turning occasionally. Drain juice and discard. Pat meat dry on paper towel.

Sprinkle meat with salt, pepper and flour.

Continued

Saute in butter until lightly browned.

Deglaze pan with wine. Add water to make 2 cups.

Saute chopped bacon, celery, onion, tomato and chopped mushroom stems. (Reserve mushroom caps).

Place meat and vegetables and liquid in covered heavy pan. Add herbs and spices. Simmer 2 hours or until meat is tender. Discard bay leaf.

Remove meat from sauce. Simmer sauce to reduce. Add meat and mushroom caps; continue cooking 10 minutes.

Just prior to serving, stir in sour cream and capers; heat just to boiling point. (Don't boil or cream will curdle.) Sprinkle with parsley.

Serve with spaetzle, noodles or rice.

Serves 6

VEAL SHANKS

2 veal shanks, sawed in 3 pieces
Salt and pepper to taste
¼ cup flour
1 tablespoon butter
1 tablespoon olive oil
1 onion, medium, chopped fine
1 or more garlic cloves to taste, chopped fine
1 large carrot, chopped
1 celery rib
¾ cup chicken stock
¾ cup dry white wine
1 tablespoon tomato paste
1 (16-oz.) can tomatoes
1 bay leaf, crumbled
1 teaspoon rosemary
1 teaspoon oregano
1 teaspoon grated lemon
1 tablespoon chopped parsley, for garnish

Salt and pepper shank pieces and dredge with flour. Heat oil and butter in skillet or heavy casserole you will use for baking. Brown shanks on all sides. Remove to warm platter, add to casserole all other ingredients except parsley. Cook gently until onion is transparent. Take off burner, return veal shanks to casserole. Be sure to scrape bottom of pan well to mix into sauce. Cover. Bake in a 350°F oven about 1½ hours or until meat on shanks is tender. Garnish with parsley.

Serves 3 to 4

VEAL SUPREME

1 lb. veal cutlet
3 tablespoons flour
3 tablespoons butter or drippings
½ cup onion, finely chopped
½ cup celery, diced
1 cup mushrooms, sliced
10½ oz. can chicken consomme
1 cup tomato juice
1 bay leaf
¼ teaspoon thyme
2 teaspoons salt
¼ teaspoon pepper
½ cup water chestnuts,
  thinly sliced (optional)

Cut veal in 1-inch cubes. Roll each cube in flour. Heat butter or drippings in heavy skillet; add veal and cook over low heat until browned. Add onions, celery and mushrooms; continue cooking until soft and lightly browned. Add consomme, tomato juice, and seasonings. Cover and simmer slowly about 1 hour or until meat is tender. Add water chestnuts; heat thoroughly.

Serve with wild rice (optional).

Serves 6

HERBAL HINT

Garnish Italian veal dishes with Italian Parsley.

Poultry

BAKED CHICKEN WITH HERBS

Chef Gregory

2 tablespoons cooking oil
1 (3½ to 4 lb.) frying or roasting chicken
1 small onion
1 clove garlic, peeled
1 teaspoon thyme
½ cup dry white wine
1 teaspoon Maggi
2 tablespoons butter
2 tablespoons parsley, chopped

Put oil in bottom of clay pot. Put onion, garlic, and thyme in cavity of chicken. Place chicken in clay pot, add wine, Maggi, and parsley to pot. Dot butter over chicken and cover tightly. Bake in a 400° F. oven for 1 to 1½ hours, or until tender. Before serving sprinkle with additional parsley. Can also be cooked in a heavy roasting pan.

Serves 4 to 6

CHICKEN AND CRAB IN
HERBED MADEIRA SAUCE

2 cups king crab in chunks
2 whole chicken breasts, skinned, boned, and cooked until just tender
1 stick butter
1 small onion, chopped
1 rib celery, diced
2 to 3 shallots, minced
1 clove garlic, minced
½ cup flour
2 to 3 sprigs thyme
1 sprig rosemary
1 bay leaf
2 tablespoons chopped parsley
1 tablespoon tomato paste
3 to 4 cups rich brown beef or chicken stock
1 tablespoon orange liqueur or orange juice
1 tablespoon sugar
¼ cup Madeira wine

Slice breasts.

Melt butter. Add onion, celery, and shallots. Saute until transparent. Add garlic and saute another half minute. Blend in flour, stirring until light brown.

Continued

Take off burner, whisk in 3 cups of stock; return to burner, bring to a boil, reduce heat to a simmer. Add more stock gradually, if sauce is too thick. Add thyme, rosemary, and bay leaf wrapped in a small cheesecloth bag. Add parsley. Simmer for an hour.

Remove cheesecloth bag and either strain or puree in a food processor. In another saucepan, heat sugar and orange juice or liqueur together until liquid is a light brown. Add Madeira, simmer a few minutes, making sure sugar is dissolved. Add this syrup to the strained or pureed stock mixture; add chicken and crabmeat. Simmer 5 to 10 minutes.

Correct seasoning, adding salt and a little freshly ground pepper, if needed.

Serve over rice and sprinkle with chopped parsley.

Serves 6 to 8

CHICKEN AND SAUERKRAUT

2 small fryers, quartered
1 lb. sauerkraut
1 medium onion, sliced
1 teaspoon caraway seeds
½ cup white wine
Salt and pepper to taste
2 tablespoons flour (optional)
1 cup light cream

Wash and dry chicken, salt and pepper. Place undrained sauerkraut in bottom of roasting pan. Scatter onion slices and caraway seeds over sauerkraut. Place chicken, skin side down, over this. Add wine. Bake in 350° F oven, covered, for about 1½ hours — turn half way through baking time and baste several times during baking. When chicken is tender, remove from pan. Place on dish to be served, surrounded by sauerkraut. Keep warm. Heat pan juices, add cream, salt and pepper to taste. If you wish, thicken sauce with flour. A must to accompany this dish, mashed potatoes.

Serves 8

CHICKEN BASQUE STYLE

3 frying chickens, quartered
Combination of butter and bacon fat to cover bottom of skillet to
about 1" depth
Salt and pepper
¾ lb. mushrooms, quartered
1 small eggplant, peeled and sliced in fingers
4 to 6 small tomatoes, peeled and quartered
2 green peppers, sliced
8 or 10 small white onions, cooked about 10 minutes in 1
tablespoon butter
2 cloves garlic, chopped (or more, according to taste)
¼ teaspoon dried thyme
2 bay leaves, broken
1 teaspoon dried basil
1 or 2 truffles, sliced (optional)
¾ cup dry white wine

Brown chicken in butter and bacon fat. Salt and pepper and place drained pieces in a deep casserole.

Saute rest of ingredients, except wine, in butter and bacon fat for a few minutes. Arrange them around the chicken. Pour wine in skillet. Heat slightly, scraping up all brown bits to pour over chicken. Add more salt and pepper if desired.

Cover casserole and cook in a 325° F oven (preheated) for about 45 minutes.

Serves 10 to 12

CHICKEN OR BEEF CURRY

(Gulai Ayam Daging) Indonesian

Dora Ang

2 tablespoons vegetable oil
2 buds garlic, sliced thin
2 onions, sliced thin
1 whole chicken, skinned, boned, and cut in small pieces or 1½ lbs.
beef, cut for stew
4 carrots, cut in 1" pieces
2 teaspoons salt
3 to 4 cups coconut milk
3 teaspoons paprika
¼ to ½ teaspoon cayenne pepper or chili pepper
1-2" piece ginger root, sliced thin
1-2" piece cinnamon stick, broken

Continued

1 to 2 lemon leaves (optional) or Indonesian Jeruk-purut leaves
3 cloves or ⅛ teaspoon powdered clove
⅛ teaspoon cardamom powder
2 teaspoons ground coriander
¼ teaspoon cumin powder
½ teaspoon turmeric powder

Heat oil in frying pan or wok. Cook onion and garlic until golden brown. Add all ingredients, including chicken or beef. Let simmer for about 30 minutes or until chicken or beef is tender. May be served hot or cold.

Serves 6 to 8

CHICKEN FRICASSEE

2 to 3½ lb. frying chicken, cut into serving pieces
½ cup flour
½ stick butter
1 large onion, finely chopped
1 garlic clove, chopped
1 teaspoon thyme
3 tablespoons tarragon, fresh
Salt and pepper to taste
1 cup chicken broth
2 bay leaves, broken
1 cup dry white wine
1 cup heavy cream
2 egg yolks, beaten
Juice of ½ lemon
Chopped parsley for garnish

Preheat oven to 350° F. Toss chicken pieces in flour. Melt butter in heavy skillet. Add chicken, onion, garlic, thyme, tarragon, salt, and pepper. Cook for under 10 minutes; do not brown chicken. Add chicken broth, bay leaves, and wine. Stir well. Bring to a boil. Place in a heavy casserole and cover. Put in 350°F oven for approximately 1 hour or until chicken is tender. Remove casserole from oven, place on top of stove. Add cream; heat. Do not boil. Stir in the egg yolks. Keep sauce warm, again do not boil. Add lemon juice — taste for seasoning, adding more salt and pepper if needed. If you wish, you may remove meat from bones to serve, garnished with chopped parsley.

Serves 6 to 8

CHICKEN, GREEN OLIVES AND FENNEL

Chef Gregory

3 fennel roots (Finocchio)
Juice and rind of 1 lemon
1 stick butter or ½ cup olive oil or combination
1 medium onion, chopped
2 cloves garlic, minced
2 frying chickens, cut up, wing tips removed, breasts boned, if desired
Flour
1 teaspoon Maggi
1 drop Tabasco
1 teaspoon dried thyme
2 to 3 tablespoons fennel seeds
1 cup pitted green olives
Dry white wine
Pinch ground black pepper
Juice of 1 lemon
Little chopped parsley
Little grated ricotta cheese
Dash of paprika
Bouquet of watercress for garnish

Cut each fennel root in quarters, cover with cold water, which has been salted, add juice and rind of a lemon, bring to the boiling point, simmer 30 to 40 minutes or until tender. Drain.

In a frying pan or stewing pot, melt butter and/or oil. Saute onion until transparent and add minced garlic.

Lightly dust the chicken with flour.

Quickly saute the chicken pieces in onion mixture over high heat, starting with the dark pieces, until chicken is just opaque. Remove chicken; add Maggi, Tabasco, thyme, fennel seeds, and olives to saucepan. Stir and replace chicken in pan; add enough white wine to come almost to the top of the chicken. Add pepper. Bring to a boil; reduce heat, and simmer about 25 minutes until chicken is tender.

Arrange drained fennel in bottom of casserole. Arrange chicken pieces over fennel. Stir up sauce and pour over chicken. Squeeze juice of a lemon over chicken and sprinkle with a little chopped parsley. (May be done ahead of time to this point.)

Bake in a 350° F. oven 20 to 25 minutes. Sprinkle a little grated ricotta cheese over top and then a dash of paprika. Put in oven for a few minutes before serving.

Place a bouquet of watercress in center of platter.

Serves 6 to 8

CHICKEN IN RED WINE SAUCE

1 chicken, cut into serving pieces
Salt and pepper to taste
3 tablespoons flour
2 tablespoons butter
1½ cups dry red wine
2 chicken bouillon cubes in 1 cup water or 1 cup chicken stock
¼ pound mushrooms, sliced
¼ cup onions, chopped
1 teaspoon finely chopped garlic
1 bay leaf
1 sprig parsley
2 sprigs fresh thyme or fresh lemon thyme
1 tablespoon flour or cornstarch for thickening

Sprinkle chicken pieces with salt and pepper, roll in flour.

Heat butter in skillet.

Brown chicken on all sides. Cover and cook until nearly done. Add wine and bouillon cubes, mushrooms, onions, garlic, bay leaf, parsley, and thyme. Cover and cook 15 minutes longer. Using a slotted spoon, transfer chicken and mushrooms to heated platter.

Remove bay leaf, parsley, and thyme sprigs from skillet; discard. Slightly thicken skillet juice with flour. Pour over chicken.

You may cook ahead, cool, remove excess fat, and then thicken as above.

Serves 4 to 6

HERBAL HINT

When barbecuing chicken, dried twigs of thyme or rosemary, added to the coals, give a delightful flavor and aroma.

CHICKEN LIVER GOUGERE

Pate a Choux Pastry:
1 cup water
½ teaspoon salt
6 tablespoons unsalted butter, cut into 6 equal pieces
1 cup flour, sifted
4 large eggs
1 egg beaten with 2 tablespoons milk, for glaze

Place water, salt, and butter in a heavy saucepan. Bring to boil (butter should be melted at this point). Add flour all at once, off heat, stirring mixture with a wooden spoon until flour is incorporated. Put back on heat and stir for about a minute. Mixture will have formed a ball. Remove from heat and beat in 4 eggs, 1 at a time, until each is completely absorbed. Continue beating until mixture is very smooth and shiny.

Line 4 lightly buttered individual oven-proof souffle dishes (3½ x 2 inches deep) or a 9-inch pie plate with pastry. Brush with egg and milk glaze.

Filling:
4 tablespoons unsalted butter
8 ounces chicken livers
2 tablespoons shallots, finely chopped
1 cup fresh mushrooms, sliced
1 tablespoon flour
½ cup chicken stock
1 medium tomato, seeded, cut into wedges or crescents
2 tablespoons finely chopped parsley (1 for topping)
1 teaspoon minced fresh summer savory or minced fresh marjoram
Salt and freshly ground pepper

Heat butter until hot in small skillet. Saute livers about 3 minutes, until nicely browned. Do not overcook. Remove livers with slotted spoon. Add chopped shallots to skillet and saute until transparent. Stir in mushrooms and saute a few minutes. Stir in flour.

Add stock, tomato, and herbs. Simmer about 5 minutes. Add livers, and heat through. Taste for salt and pepper. Fill pastry lined souffle dishes with mixture.

Bake in a preheated 400° F. oven about 20 minutes for individual, 30 to 40 minutes for large gougere. Sprinkle with 1 tablespoon chopped parsley.

Serves 4

CHICKEN MOUSSE

1 whole chicken cut up or chicken parts, enough for 2 cups of ground chicken.

Water to cover chicken
1 tablespoon salt
2 onions, studded with 6 cloves
Bouquet garni:
2 cut-up celery stalks with leaves
4 sprigs parsley
1 small bay leaf
1 sprig thyme or pinch of, dried

Cook chicken slowly until tender.

Bone enough chicken to yield 2 cups. Put through finest blade of food chopper or use food processor.

For Mousse:
1½ tablespoons unflavored gelatin
1 cup hot chicken stock
1½ cups milk
3 egg yolks, well beaten
Salt and pepper to taste
1 cup whipping cream, whipped until stiff

In a double boiler:
Dissolve gelatin in chicken stock. Add milk blended with well beaten egg yolks. Cook until sauce is thick and smooth, stirring with wire whisk; cool and add 2 cups ground chicken. Stir and slowly fold in whipped cream. Pour into an oiled mold. Chill until firm. May be made a day ahead. Unmold on a platter of lettuce or watercress.

Serve with curry mayonnaise.

Serves 6 to 8

"Rosemary for Remembrance"

Shakespeare

Remember:
Use triple the amount of fresh herbs to dried herbs!

CHICKEN TARRAGON

Maisonette

4 - 8 oz. boneless chicken breasts
Salt and pepper
2 ounces sweet butter
2 fresh shallots, chopped
1 glass dry white wine
1 pint heavy cream
2 tablespoons tarragon, chopped
1 tablespoon fresh parsley, chopped

Season the chicken breasts with salt and pepper. Saute the breasts in butter until golden brown on both sides. Cook in oven for 10 minutes at 400° F. Remove the chicken breasts; keep warm.

Remove the butter from the skillet. Add the chopped shallots; do not brown. Swirl in the white wine. Bring to a boil until reduced by one-half.

Add the cream, one tablespoon of the tarragon, and reduce the sauce until it thickens slightly. Correct seasoning. Add the rest of the tarragon and the parsley. Pour on the chicken breasts and serve hot. The dish may be accompanied by rice or noodles in butter.

Serves 4

CHICKEN WINGS WITH WATER CHESTNUTS (Chinese)

Dora Ang

10 chicken wings

Marinade for chicken wings:
¼ cup sweet soy sauce
¼ teaspoon salt
¼ teaspoon 5-spice powder
½ tablespoon wine
1 cup water
1 clove garlic, mashed
2 thin slices fresh ginger root
8 water chestnuts, cut in halves

For garnish:
Parsley
Radishes

Cut chicken wings in 2 pieces. Marinate chicken wings for 10 minutes. Place chicken wings and 1 cup water in a wok. Bring to a boil. Add garlic and ginger root slices. Boil, covered, for 15 minutes, then let simmer for 30 minutes, turning the chicken wings several times. Add the water chestnut halves and let simmer for another 10 minutes.

Place the chicken wings in a baking dish. Let the remaining sauce thicken on low heat until reduced to ½ cup.

Baste the chicken wings with sauce.

Broil for a few minutes.

Serve hot or cold. Garnish with chopped parsley or chopped radishes.

Serves 8 to 10

CHICKEN WITH GREEN GRAPES

¼ cup flour
1¼ teaspoons celery salt
⅛ teaspoon pepper
3 chicken breasts, boned, skinned, split in half
1 (10½ oz.) can cream of chicken soup, undiluted
¼ teaspoon rosemary, crushed
⅛ teaspoon tarragon leaves, crushed
Flour and dry white wine or water for thickening sauce
½ lb. seedless green grapes
1½ cups hot buttered rice, optional

Heat oven to 350° F. Combine flour, celery salt, and pepper in paper bag; shake each chicken breast in flour mixture to coat well. Brown chicken on top of stove. Combine soup and other ingredients, except grapes, flour and wine; pour over chicken; and bring to boil. Cover; bake in oven 40 to 45 minutes or until chicken is tender. Remove chicken; thicken sauce with flour and wine or water mixture, if desired. Stir in grapes and let stand 5 minutes. Arrange chicken on bed of rice; glaze with sauce.

Serves 6

CHICKEN WITH HERBS

4 tablespoons butter, approximately
3 lbs. chicken, disjointed
1 teaspoon salt
½ teaspoon freshly ground pepper
Dash of paprika
½ clove garlic, minced
1 teaspoon grated lemon peel
¼ bay leaf
½ teaspoon thyme, sage, or tarragon
2 teaspoons fresh marjoram, chopped
½ lb. mushrooms, washed, sliced, if large
3 to 4 teaspoons white wine

Melt ½ of the butter in shallow baking pan. Coat chicken pieces in butter and arrange in a single layer in pan. Dot with remaining butter. Season with salt, pepper, paprika, garlic, lemon peel and herbs. Arrange mushrooms in and around chicken pieces. Cover with foil and bake in 350° F. oven for 15 minutes. Turn and bake 15 more minutes. Remove foil. Add wine to cover bottom of pan. Increase oven temperature to 400° F. Bake 15 more minutes or until chicken is brown. Turn once.

Serves 6

COQ AU VIN WITH HERB PASTRY TOPPING

Topping:

Use your favorite pastry dough, enough to cover a 9" or 10" casserole. Blend 1 to 2 teaspoons of dried thyme in the dough. Chill.

2 lbs. chicken, fryer or roaster, disjointed
(You may select your favorite pieces but do use a few wings as they
add to the flavor.)
4 slices bacon, diced
½ stick butter
3 tablespoons flour, blended with
Salt and pepper to taste
2 teaspoons each fresh tarragon and thyme
½ cup onion, chopped
1 to 2 cloves garlic, chopped
2 cups mushrooms, sliced
2 bay leaves, broken
1 tablespoon parsley, chopped
1 tablespoon chervil
Salt and freshly ground pepper to taste
2 tablespoons brandy
1 cup chicken stock
1 cup dry red wine
1 dozen small white onions
1 dozen small carrots (may use canned Belgian)

Preheat oven to 325° F. Saute bacon in large skillet. Remove when crisp and brown. Add butter, onion, and garlic to bacon drippings, saute until transparent, remove from skillet. Dredge chicken pieces with herbed seasoned flour and saute until brown. Add more oil or butter if necessary.

Place chicken in casserole, add all ingredients except pastry crust and carrots, if canned. Bake until tender, turning occasionally and basting with juices. It will take about 1½ to 2 hours. If using canned carrots, add before last reheating.

Remove from oven, cool and degrease, if you wish. Roll out herb pastry, put on top of casserole as you would a pot pie, prick with fork and bake at 350° F., until pastry is lightly browned. Have casserole at room temperature before reheating and baking.

Serves 6 to 8

HERB STUFFING FOR TURKEY

¾ cup combination butter and rendered chicken fat
8 cups 2-to-3 day-old white bread or white and cornbread combination, cubed
1½ cups onions, diced
1 cup celery stalks and leaves, diced
⅓ pound bulk pork sausage
⅓ cup finely diced mushrooms
2 tablespoons chopped parsley
1 to 2 fresh sage leaves, minced
Several sprigs marjoram and thyme, minced
¼ teaspoon freshly ground pepper
1 to 2 teaspoons poultry seasoning, or to taste
Salt to taste
Strained chicken stock to moisten, about 1 cup

Melt chicken fat and butter in large skillet and saute onion and celery until vegetables are transparent and just beginning to brown.

Brown pork sausage and mushrooms in separate skillet until pork is cooked through.

Add all to bread cubes and toss lightly. Add parsley, sage, marjoram, thyme, and pepper. Then add poultry seasoning and salt gradually, testing until seasoning is correct. Add stock gradually, tossing to moisten bread cubes lightly.

Either stuff a 10-to-12 pound turkey,* or bake separately for 1 hour in greased, covered casserole, mixing in some of the turkey drippings while baking.

Also may be used in capon or chicken, in smaller quantity, according to size of bird.

* Do not make stuffing until ready to roast turkey. Poultry should never be stuffed until just before roasting.

HERBAL HINT
Purple flower heads of chives make an attractive rose-colored vinegar.

126

PATIO COUNTRY CHICKEN

Fern H. Storer

Microwave gives an assist to your conventional range in this version of oven-fried chicken with a bit of gravy - not too much but enough to add old-time flavor.

2 large chicken breasts, halved
Seasoned flour, see directions
¼ cup, half stick, butter or margarine

Gravy:
2 tablespoons butter or margarine
2 tablespoons seasoned flour, from coating chicken
1 cup milk, or Half and Half
¼ teaspoon garlic powder
¼ teaspoon powdered rosemary
2 tablespoons finely chopped parsley
¼ cup thin-sliced green onions or chives
½ cup finely diced celery
½ cup briefly cooked sliced fresh mushrooms, or canned, drained, optional
Salt and pepper

Use: Shallow baking dish to hold chicken pieces side by side; quart glass measure for gravy; conventional range oven at 350° F; microwave, high.

Melt butter in baking dish while preheating conventional range oven. Meanwhile rinse chicken pieces; blot off excess moisture. Mix together ½ cup flour, 2 teaspoons salt, ¼ teaspoon pepper and 1 teaspoon paprika; coat chicken pieces, reserving rest for gravy.

Set baking dish with melted butter out of oven; turn chicken pieces in the butter to coat; place all skin side down. Bake, uncovered in conventional range for 30 to 35 minutes.

Meanwhile prepare gravy in MICROWAVE OVEN. In a quart glass measure, melt butter, high, in microwave; stir in 2 tablespoons of the seasoned flour; when smooth, stir in milk; microwave-cook, high, until boiling and thickened, stirring several times (a medium-size wire whisk is best for this, but remember to remove it from the cooking container after each whisking). Cooking time will be about 5 minutes. Set sauce out and add all remaining ingredients; salt and pepper if needed.

When chicken has baked 30 to 35 minutes, set dish out and turn pieces skin side up. Spoon gravy on half of each piece to have the contrast of the golden chicken with the creamy gravy. Bake in conventional range oven only 20 minutes longer or until fork tender. Over-baking dries and toughens chicken. Take to table in baking dish.

Serves 4

ROAST CHICKEN WITH PARSLEY

Virginia Larson

2½ lbs. chicken (may use pheasant, cornish hen, or guinea hen)
5 tablespoons parsley
2 medium mushrooms
2 shallots or scallions
1 tablespoon chives
1 tablespoon tarragon
1 tablespoon ricotta cheese
Salt and pepper
1 teaspoon safflower oil
¾ cup chicken stock and additional for baking
1 clove garlic, minced
1 tablespoon parsley, minced
Salt and pepper

Chop parsley, mushrooms, and shallots or scallions very fine in food processor, using steel blade. Add chives, tarragon, and ricotta cheese; blend into a paste.

Remove excess fat from tail of bird. Salt and pepper inside of bird. Using fingers, gently release skin from flesh, starting with neck end to the tops of legs. Spread the parsley mixture under the skin and press skin back in place. Truss and paint skin lightly with oil.

Roast at 425° F for 20 minutes and then 40 minutes at 350° F. Use chicken broth to baste; do not use fat juices at bottom of pan. Remove bird when done. Let rest. Keep warm. Remove fat from pan juices. Add ¾ cup chicken stock, garlic and parsley to pan juices. Stir and scrape bottom of pan. Strain sauce through fine mesh strainer into small saucepan, season with salt and pepper and keep warm.

To serve: Quarter chicken, place in heated oval dish. Add juices from carving board to sauce and pour over bird.

Serves 6 to 8

ROAST TARRAGON-STUFFED CHICKEN

Linda Miller

1 whole frying chicken
3 to 4 large sprigs fresh tarragon
½ stick butter

Juice of 1 lemon
2 teaspoons Dijon mustard
Salt to taste

Stuff chicken with tarragon. Put in roasting pan and cut up butter over chicken. Roast at 350° F. for 1¼ hours, basting frequently with butter and juice from chicken. After chicken is cooked, put drippings from roasting pan into a small heavy saucepan. Put on low heat. Add lemon juice and mustard; whisk together. Salt the chicken, carve, and serve pieces with the sauce. Other herbs may be substituted, such as rosemary, sage, or lemon thyme.

Serves 4 to 5

SHRIMP AND CHICKEN WITH 10 VEGETABLES
(CHAP — CHYE, CHINESE)

Dora Ang

¾ lb. chicken breasts, skinned and boned
¾ lb. shrimp
½ lb. kee kian (the combination of vegetables listed below)
3 cloves garlic, chopped
1 yellow onion, sliced thin
3 green onions, cut in ½-inch lengths
2 carrots, sliced thin
½ cup bamboo-shoots, sliced
⅓ cup water chestnuts, sliced
2 cups Chinese cabbage, cut into 1-inch lengths
¼ cup lily flowers, soaked (optional)
¼ cup wood ears, soaked (optional)
4 pieces Chinese mushrooms, soaked and sliced
1 green pepper, sliced in strips
1 cup celery, cut into ½-inch lengths
2 tomatoes, cut in wedges

½ cup peanut oil

Marinate chicken in
1 tablespoon soy sauce
½ teaspoon cornstarch

Marinate shrimp in
1 teaspoon salt
½ teaspoon cornstarch

Seasoning Sauce:
¼ cup tomato catsup
1 tablespoon sweet soy sauce
1 teaspoon pepper
1 teaspoon salt
2 tablespoons sesame seeds, roasted
½ tablespoon sesame oil

Soak lily flowers, wood ears, and Chinese mushrooms in separate bowls for 15 minutes. Skin and bone chicken breast. Slice thin into 1-inch squares. Marinate chicken meat and shrimp for 20 minutes. Cut and slice the vegetables.

Heat ½ cup peanut oil in wok and stir-fry chicken and shrimp for a few minutes. Remove to platter.

Stir-fry the yellow onion until transparent. Add garlic, green onion and carrot. Stir-fry for another few minutes. Add the other vegetables and seasoning sauce. Stir in chicken and shrimp mixture. Add ½ tablespoon sesame oil and roasted sesame seeds. Stir-fry whole mixture for one minute. Serve hot.

Serves 8 to 10

THYME CHICKEN

Joan Stadler

2 lbs. chicken, cut in pieces
1 cup flour
2 teaspoons salt
¼ teaspoon pepper
2 teaspoons paprika
¾ stick melted butter

Sauce: (prepare early in the day)
1 clove garlic, mashed with 1 teaspoon salt
¼ cup oil
½ cup lemon juice
2 tablespoons finely chopped onion
½ teaspoon pepper
½ teaspoon dried thyme

Mix sauce ingredients together. Do not refrigerate. Stir occasionally.

Preheat oven to 400° F.

Shake chicken pieces in flour, salt, pepper and paprika in paper bag. Coat with melted butter.

Put skin side down in broiler pan. Bake about 45 minutes or until light brown. Turn with spatula: pour sauce over and bake another 30 minutes.

This recipe is excellent for quail or pheasant, but wild fowl must be steamed under foil for 30 to 40 minutes additional.

Serves 6 to 8

"Rosemary for Remembrance"

Shakespeare

Remember:
Use triple the amount of fresh herbs to dried herbs!

Fish and Shellfish

ALASKA KING CRAB LEGS

Bing Moy, China Gourmet

*12 ounces king crab legs, cut in ½" pieces, also excellent with blue
crab
3 ounces pork, ground fine
½ to 1 teaspoon black beans (according to taste, they are salty)
1 teaspoon garlic, chopped fine
1 teaspoon thin soy sauce
½ teaspoon sugar
1 tablespoon dry white wine, or slightly more
1 teaspoon cornstarch
1 egg
2 tablespoons peanut oil
2 tablespoons water (approximately)
1 green onion, chopped fine*

Pour oil in wok and heat until smoking. Add crab leg pieces and cover.
Cook about 1 minute. Place pork on top of crab legs, then add garlic and
black beans over pork. Cover and cook 2 more minutes. Add wine
around crab legs and approximately 2 tablespoons water. Blend soy
sauce, sugar and cornstarch and add to wine mixture. Take wok off heat.
Add whole egg and mix it quickly in the sauce and crab legs.

Serve at once, pouring sauce over crab legs and garnish with chopped
green onion.

Serves 3

BAKED MARINATED FISH

*½ cup corn oil
3 tablespoons grated lemon rind
⅓ cup lemon juice
2 cloves garlic, minced
2 teaspoons salt
2 teaspoons dried oregano leaves
2 teaspoons dried basil leaves
1 teaspoon dried thyme leaves
¼ teaspoon pepper
½ cup chopped onion
1 3-lb. whole dressed fish*

Stir together corn oil, lemon rind, lemon juice, garlic, salt, oregano, basil,
thyme, pepper, and onion. Pour half of marinade into bottom of large
baking dish. Lay fish in marinade. Spoon some marinade into fish cavity
and pour remaining over fish. Cover and refrigerate at least 4 hours,
turning and basting frequently. Collect marinade and pour into cavity.
Bake in 350° F oven, basting occasionally, for 30 minutes or until fish
flakes easily with a fork.

Serves 6

CHARCOAL BROILED FISH WITH FENNEL BUTTER

*2 to 2½ lb. whole fish, cleaned, with head left on and bone in
(white fish or red snapper, preferably)
Salt and pepper
2 sticks butter
2 to 3 tablespoons fennel, fresh
½ cup brandy*

Wash and dry fish. Season inside with salt and pepper. Mix fennel with softened butter, use ¼ of this mixture inside fish. Sew fish together, unless you have a fish grill form. Dot outside with fennel butter, save rest for marinade and serving at table.

Wrap fish in heavy-duty aluminum foil. Bake in 350° F oven about 30 minutes, depending on size. Fish should not be over cooked at this point.

If you are lucky enough to have some dried fennel branches, put these on coals before you put fish on the grill.

Have charcoal ready with coals red, grill not too close to coals. Place fish in buttered or oiled fish grill or finish cooking open on the foil. Baste occasionally with fennel butter and turn once.

15 to 20 minutes should be adequate. Test with fork to be sure fish flakes. Meanwhile, heat brandy in fireproof cup on grill. Remove fish from grill and place on heat-proof platter. Ignite brandy and pour over fish.

When fish is served, pass remainder of chilled fennel butter with it.

Serves 6 to 8

CIOPPINO

(Italian Fish Stew)

*½ cup chopped green pepper
¼ cup chopped onion
¼ cup chopped celery
1 tablespoon cooking oil (preferably olive)
1 (16-oz.) can tomatoes (preferably Italian)
1 (8-oz.) can tomato sauce
½ cup dry red wine
3 tablespoons minced parsley
Salt and pepper to taste
¼ teaspoon dried oregano, crushed, or ¾ teaspoon fresh, chopped
¼ teaspoon dried basil, crushed, or ¾ teaspoon fresh, chopped
1 clove minced garlic
1 lb. fish — sole, perch, or any good white fish
1 (7½-oz.) can minced clams
1 (4½-oz.) can shrimp, drained, or preferably 1 cup fresh peeled shrimp
1 cup scallops (optional)*

Continued

In a large saucepan, cook green pepper, onion, celery, and garlic in oil until tender, but not brown. Add undrained tomatoes, tomato sauce, wine, parsley, salt, pepper, oregano, basil, and garlic.

Bring to a boil and then reduce heat, simmer for 20 minutes.

Cut fish in bite-size pieces, leave shrimp and scallops whole, if not too large. Add these and drained clams to sauce and simmer gently, covered, for 5 to 8 minutes. Do not overcook. Sauce may be made ahead. Serve in individual bowls with a toasted slice of garlic Italian bread on top.

Serves 4 to 6

COLD SALMON

"21" Restaurant

1 (10 lb) salmon

Poaching liquid:

2 quarts dry white wine
1 quart white vinegar
1 gallon water
6 bay leaves
2 pinches thyme leaves
2 lbs. fish bones
3 medium onions, peeled and chopped
6 stalks celery, chopped
Salt and white pepper to taste

Garnish:
Truffles
Olives
Pimientos
Blanched strips of zucchini skin
Tiny shrimp
Sliced lemon
Parsley
2 tablespoons unflavored gelatin

Clean and scale the fish, leaving head and tail intact. Place the fish on a rack and lower into a large poacher. Combine the poaching-liquid ingredients and pour around the fish until it is covered with liquid. Simmer for about 25 minutes, uncovered. Remove the pan from the heat and let the salmon cool in the liquid for about 4 hours. Remove the salmon, peel off and discard the skin, and place the fish on a platter or wooden board. Reserve the poaching liquid. Decorate the fish with the remaining ingredients (except the gelatin), and arranged according to your own design. Chill in the refrigerator for 1 hour.

Add the gelatin to 1 quart of the strained poaching liquid, stirring well until it is dissolved; cool the aspic until it begins to jell. Spoon a layer over the decorated salmon and return the fish to the refrigerator. Chill for

Continued

½ hour, then repeat the process three times, chilling between each addition of aspic. (If the aspic becomes too thick to handle, warm it over boiling water until it liquefies) When ready to serve, cut the aspic around the salmon to separate it from the platter and transfer the fish carefully to a slab of white marble or a serving dish. Decorate with more sliced lemon and parsley. Serve with pressed cucumbers and sauce verte.

Serves 6 to 8

CREOLE JAMBALAYA

Marilyn Harris

2 tablespoons oil
1 large onion, sliced
½ lb. country ham, cut into pieces
3 cloves garlic, minced
2 tablespoons flour
1¾ cups tomato juice
3 cups tomatoes
½ cup chopped green pepper
½ cup chopped celery
½ chopped parsley
Large bay leaf
1 teaspoon thyme
Pinch sugar
Generous dash Tabasco
Salt and pepper to taste
1½ cups raw rice
1 lb. raw shrimp
½ pt. raw oysters

Melt shortening in heavy pot, saute onion. Add ham and garlic. Stir together for 2 minutes and add flour. Cook 2 minutes more, add tomato juice and tomatoes. Add all other ingredients down to shrimp. Be sure that the rice is covered with liquid. Bring to a boil, cover, and turn to simmer. Cook, stirring occasionally, for 20 minutes. Add shrimp and oysters and cook 10 to 15 minutes more — rice should be very tender and liquid absorbed. Let rest for 15 minutes, pot lid ajar, before serving. Top with more chopped parsley before serving.

Serves 8 to 10

DILL MARINADE FOR SHRIMP

Chef Scott Berman
Longwharf Restaurant — Sag Harbor, L.I., N.Y.

3 cloves crushed garlic
3 tablespoons soy sauce
3 tablespoons lemon juice
3 tablespoons lime juice
1 teaspoon dill vinegar
1 tablespoon dry mustard
2 tablespoons fresh dill, chopped
3 teaspoons oil

Blend everything except the oil. Add oil slowly, beating constantly. Marinate shelled, steamed shrimp at least 2 hours in this mixture.

Yield: Enough to marinate about 1 lb. of shrimp

FILET OF SOLE WITH
CUCUMBERS AND CRAB

Chef Gregory

2 lbs. lemon sole
1 cup dry white wine
Juice of 1 lemon
2 medium cucumbers, peeled and seeded
2 medium leeks, with some of the green part removed
½ stick butter (unsalted)
1 teaspoon garlic salt
1 teaspoon Maggi
1 drop Tabasco
1 tablespoon powdered chicken base
2 to 3 tablespoons fresh dill, finely chopped, or 1 tablespoon dried dill
1 tablespoon Dijon Mustard (or Mr. Mustard)
2 tablespoons arrowroot or flour
½ cup light cream
2 to 3 egg yolks
1 cup lump crab meat
2 tablespoons chopped parsley for garnish

Place sole in shallow casserole and pour 1 cup white wine over fish. Sprinkle with juice of 1 lemon. Poach in 350° F oven 3 to 5 minutes, if fresh and 10 to 15 minutes if frozen, or poach on top of range. Should be cooked just enough to become opaque, to be firm but wiggly. Drain and reserve poaching liquid.

Thinly slice the peeled and seeded cucumbers. Cover them with cold salted water, bring to the boiling point, and drain well; refresh under cold water; drain.

Continued

Sauce:

Split leeks, thinly slice them, and wash well with lukewarm water. Braise leeks in butter, cooking slowly till they are transparent. While braising, add garlic salt, Maggi, Tabasco, chicken base, dill weed, and mustard. When leeks are transparent, add arrowroot or flour and stir in well. Add the reserved poaching liquid from the fish; there should be about 1½ cups. Bring to boiling point, whisking till liquid thickens. When it comes up to the boiling point, add light cream. Simmer 4 to 5 minutes. Remove from fire, let stand a minute, and whisk in egg yolks. Taste for seasoning. Add any additional poaching liquid from fish so latter is dry. (If doing this recipe ahead of time, grate 2 to 3 tablespoons bread crumbs over the fish.) Spread crab meat over fish. Place cucumbers over crab. Sprinkle 2 tablespoons chopped parsley over cucumbers. Mask with the sauce. (May do ahead to here, let cool down, wrap in plastic wrap, and refrigerate. Remove from refrigerator, and let come to room temperature, which will take 1½ to 2 hours.)

Bake in a 350° F oven about 20 minutes, just enough to heat through. Sprinkle with chopped parsley.

Serves 6 to 8

MACKEREL WITH FENNEL SAUCE

Gertrude Foster
From the book, "Herbs for Every Garden"

1 mackerel
½ cup water
Salt to taste
1 teaspoon vinegar
5 sprigs fennel
Parsley for garnish
Lemon wedges to garnish

Fennel Sauce:
½ cup cream
1½ cups chicken stock
3 tablespoons potato flour
2 tablespoons chopped fennel leaves

Combine cream and chicken stock, thicken with flour, and add chopped fennel leaves.

Place cleaned mackerel in a shallow frying pan with water, salt, vinegar, and fennel. Bring to a boil quickly and boil hard for a few seconds. Turn down heat and simmer for fifteen minutes. Drain fish on cloth or paper toweling and scrape off the skin carefully. Serve with a garnish of parsley and lemon slices on a heated platter. Pass fennel sauce with fish.

Editor's Note: Other fish may be substituted: white fish, salmon, halibut.

Serves 2 to 3

RESTIGOUCHE SALMON

From the book, "Across Canada with Herbs"

4 (8 to 10 oz) salmon steaks
¼ cup vegetable oil
2 teaspoons finely grated lemon peel
3 tablespoons lemon juice
2 tablespoons chopped scallions (white part only)
½ teaspoon dried marjoram
½ teaspoon salt
¼ teaspoon freshly ground pepper
1 tablespoon soft butter
4 tablespoons melted butter
2 lemons, quartered

Lay salmon steaks in shallow baking dish in a single layer. In bowl, mix oil, lemon juice, lemon peel, scallions, marjoram, salt and pepper. Beat marinade with whisk, then coat salmon steaks on both sides. Marinate at room temperature about 40 minutes, turning once or twice. Spread softened butter on broiling pan. Arrange steaks on pan and broil 4" from heat, about 6 to 7 minutes per side, basting every 3 minutes with melted butter. Transfer to serving platter; arrange lemon wedges around fish. Garnish with fresh dill or fennel, if available.

Serves 4

SALMON MOUSSE WITH DILL SAUCE

An oiled fish mold will make this dish more attractive than a ring mold, but either may be used.

2½ cups fresh poached salmon, skinned and bones removed or canned salmon. If using canned, remove skin and small bones.
½ cup cold water to soften gelatin
1½ envelopes unflavored gelatin
¾ cup mayonnaise
Juice of ½ lemon
1 tablespoon onion, grated
1 tablespoon fresh dill or fennel, chopped fine
Dash of Tabasco
Dash of Worcestershire sauce
¼ teaspoon paprika
Salt and white pepper to taste
½ cup whipped cream
Garnish: 1 tablespoon capers, pimiento, thinly sliced cucumbers, thinly sliced lemons, thinly sliced olives (black or stuffed), fresh fennel, or dill.

Continued

Soften gelatin in cold water. Blend briefly in food processor all ingredients, except gelatin and whipped cream. Remove mixture from food processor; blend in gelatin, and then slowly fold whipped cream into mixture. Place in oiled fish mold. Chill until set. This may be done the day before serving.

Unmold on chilled platter and decorate using strips of pimiento for mouth and tail fin, black olives sliced thin, or capers for eyes, sliced cucumbers for scales. Sliced lemons and dill or fennel can be used for added garnish around fish.

Serve with dill cucumber sauce.

Serves 6 to 8

SCALLOPS REMOULADE

1½ teaspoons prepared mustard
1½ teaspoons chopped capers
1½ teaspoons parsley flakes
1 teaspoon chives, minced
1 small clove garlic, minced
1 cup sour cream
1 pkg. (12 oz.) frozen scallops, thawed, or 3/4 lb. fresh
2 tablespoons butter

In a bowl, blend mustard, capers, parsley, chives and garlic into sour cream. Cover and chill several hours or overnight. Makes 1 cup.

In skillet, saute scallops in butter 6 minutes or until lightly browned. Serve remoulade sauce in separate bowl.

Serves: 3

SEAFOOD IN HERB BUTTER

½ cup butter
1 medium onion, chopped
1 clove garlic, crushed
1 teaspoon paprika
2 to 3 teaspoons chives, chopped
1 teaspoon chopped fresh basil
1 teaspoon chopped fresh marjoram
1 teaspoon chopped fresh oregano
½ teaspoon Worcestershire sauce
3 drops Tabasco
1 tablespoon minced parsley
2 cups Cooked shrimp, lump crab, or poached scallops
[or combination]

Saute onion in butter until transparent. Add garlic and paprika and cook another half minute. Add other ingredients, except parsley. Simmer few minutes until flavors are blended. Stir in parsley. Serve in heated ramekins or serve from chafing dish.

Serves 4 to 6

SHRIMP CURRY

2 medium onions, diced
3 to 4 stalks of celery, diced
1 stick butter
4 (10 oz.) cans cream mushroom soup
1½ cups milk
4 lbs. peeled raw shrimp
1 tablespoon curry, or more to taste

Condiments, about a cup of each:
Major Grey chutney
Crushed salted peanuts
Grated hard-cooked egg yolk
Grated hard-cooked egg white
Toasted coconut flakes
Crumbled crisp cooked bacon or bacon bits
Currants softened in warm water

Saute onions and celery in butter until onions are slightly transparent. Mix soup and milk well, add celery, onions, and curry. When sauce is smooth, bring to a boil, add raw shrimp, boiling them for about 3 minutes until they are pink. Remove from heat but keep warm or reheat at a low temperature, just before serving. Serve with the above condiments.

Serves 16

SHRIMP AND GREEN BEANS
IN COCONUT MILK

Sambel Goreng Bunces (Indonesian)

Dora Ang

4 tablespoons vegetable oil
1 onion sliced
3 buds garlic, chopped
8 oz. shrimp (whole, medium size) peeled
1 lb. green beans, cut diagonally in 1" pieces
1 teaspoon salt
2 teaspoons sugar
¼ - ½ teaspoon shrimp paste (trasi) dissolved in water
1 teaspoon paprika
1-1" piece Laos root or ⅛ teaspoon Laos powder
(galangal powder)
1½ to 2 cups coconut milk

In 2 tablespoons oil, stir-fry the onion and garlic for a short time until transparent.

Continued

Fry the shrimp in 2 tablespoons oil for 2 minutes. Add the green beans and other ingredients. Finally, add the coconut milk.

Let simmer for 10 minutes more until beans are tender.

Serve hot or cold.

Serves 6 to 8

SHRIMP DE JONGHE

Stanley Demos
From the book, "Stanley Suggests"

6 shrimp, cooked
1 clove garlic
⅓ teaspoon tarragon
⅓ teaspoon parsley, chopped
⅓ teaspoon chervil
⅓ teaspoon shallots
⅓ teaspoon onion
½ stick butter
1 cup bread crumbs
⅓ teaspoon nutmeg
⅓ teaspoon mace
⅓ teaspoon thyme
½ cup sherry wine
Salt and pepper to taste
¼ cup buttered bread crumbs (optional)

Mix all ingredients except shrimp together. Place shrimp in individual dish suitable for oven. Cover with mixture and bake 20 minutes at 325° F. Top with buttered bread crumbs, if you wish, before baking.

Serves 1

Here's flowers for you;
Hot *lavender, mints, savory, marjoram;*
The *marigold,* that goes to bed wi' the sun,
and with him rises weeping; these are flowers
Of middle summer, and, I think, they are given
To men of middle age. Y'are very welcome.

Shakespeare

The Winter's Tale

Eggs and Cheese

DANISH DEVILED EGGS

6 hard-cooked eggs
1 cup pickled beets, finely chopped
2 tablespoons mayonnaise or more, if needed to blend yolks and
beets
Salt and pepper to taste
Caraway seeds for garnish
Basil, chopped for garnish

Cut eggs in half lengthwise. Remove yolks and mash. Add chopped beets
and mayonnaise; blend well. Season with salt and pepper. Fill whites with
mixture and sprinkle caraway seeds and chopped fresh basil over all.

FRENCH TOAST

Shakertown

Use this fresh or frozen — freeze if you have a small family or wish to do
ahead for house guests.

4 eggs
1 cup milk
2 tablespoons sugar
1 teaspoon vanilla
½ teaspoon ground coriander
8 slices day-old French bread cut ¾-inch thick
Melted butter or margarine
Powdered sugar, honey or syrup

Beat together the eggs, milk, sugar, vanilla, and coriander. Place bread
slices on a rimmed baking sheet, pour egg mixture over bread and let
stand a few minutes. Turn slices over and let stand until all egg mixture is
absorbed. Freeze, uncovered, until firm; transfer to a plastic bag and
return to freezer.

To serve, place desired number of frozen slices on a greased baking sheet
and cover with foil. Brush each with melted butter or margarine. Bake in
a 500°F oven (or portable toaster-oven) for 8 minutes. Turn slices over,
brush with melted butter, and bake 10 minutes longer or until nicely
browned on both sides. Serve with powdered sugar, honey, or syrup as
desired.

Serves 4 to 6

HERBED-STUFFED EGGS

6 hard-cooked eggs
¼ cup yogurt
¼ cup sesame seeds, ground
1 tablespoon chopped parsley
¼ teaspoon marjoram
Seasoned salt to taste
Toasted sesame seeds for garnish

Remove yolks, reserve whites, and mash yolks in bowl. Stir in all ingredients except toasted sesame seeds; blend well. Refill whites and garnish with toasted sesame seeds.

Serves 5

OMELETTE aux FINES HERBES

From the Book
"Herbs for Every Garden"
Gertrude Foster

1 teaspoon fresh chervil
½ teaspoon fresh chives
½ teaspoon fresh marjoram
2 eggs
1 tablespoon butter
2 tablespoons cream
Pinch of salt
Dusting of pepper

Mince the herbs with a knife on a chopping block. Break eggs into a small bowl and add cream. Beat slightly to blend. Place butter in a heavy flat frying pan (or omelette pan). Place over heat and roll the melting butter around the pan. Pour eggs into the pan just before the butter begins to smoke. Cook over a quick fire until bubbles around the edges show the eggs are getting set. Lift the edges with a fork and let the uncooked liquid run against the heated pan. When most of the egg mixture is beginning to firm, sprinkle with salt, pepper, and fines herbes.

When you fold in the herbs, lift the edges of the omelette and fold one side over the other. Turn once, it you wish to brown more. Then slide on a heated plate. It is better to make one omelette at a time than to try to make a larger quantity.

Editor's note: Other combinations of herbs may be used:
chives, chervil, parsley, tarragon
chives, basil, oregano
chives, chervil, basil, marjoram, tarragon

Serves 1

FLUFFY HAM OMELET

Joyce Rosencrans

5 eggs, separated
½ cup sour cream
¼ teaspoon salt
1 cup finely chopped ham (fully cooked)
About one tablespoon freshly snipped chives
2 tablespoons butter or margarine
2 tablespoons additional sour cream, about
Additional snipped chives
Thin crescents of avocado, optional

Use: 10-inch skillet with heavy bottom and heat-proof handle (or protect with foil)

In large mixing bowl, beat egg whites first, until stiff, at high speed of electric mixer. Then beat egg yolks (without washing beaters) in smaller bowl until yolks are light colored. Beat in sour cream and salt into the yolks. Pour over egg whites in larger bowl and fold together with snipped chives and ham. Blend well, being careful not to let too much air escape from the egg whites.

Melt butter in skillet over low heat; pour in omelet mixture and level the top. Cook over low heat until lightly browned on the bottom, about five minutes. Time this step, because you can't peek.

Have oven preheating to 325°F. Transfer skillet to oven after initial five minutes; finish by baking the omelet until set, about 12 minutes. Loosen around edges and invert onto warm, buttered serving plate. Spread top thinly with sour cream, sprinkle with chives, and arrange a circle of avocado cresents on top. Cut wedges by inserting tines of 2 forks back to back and separating.

Good for brunch with tomato juice cocktails, English muffins.

Serves 6

PICKLED EGGS

2 tablespoons mild mustard
2 cups white or cider vinegar
1 teaspoon dill
½ cup water
1 cup granulated sugar
1 teaspoon salt

1 teaspoon celery salt
1 teaspoon mustard seed
6 whole cloves
2 sliced medium onions
12 hard-cooked eggs

Blend mustard with a little vinegar in a saucepan, add remaining ingredients, except onions and eggs. Heat just to boiling; simmer 10 minutes. Cool. Pour over onions and eggs. Cover. Refrigerate overnight.

Serves 10 to 12

POACHED EGGS CARUSO

Chef Gregory

½ cup cider or white vinegar
1 tablespoon salt
1 to 2 eggs per person (at room temperature)
2 pounds fresh spinach
1 small onion, chopped
½ stick butter (unsalted)
1 teaspoon garlic salt
1 teaspoon Maggi
1 drop Tabasco
Little freshly ground black pepper
1 teaspoon freshly grated nutmeg
¼ cup flour
½ cup heavy cream
3 tablespoons freshly grated Parmesan cheese
¼ pound baked ham or prosciutto
⅛ pound Italian hard salami
1 cup grated mozzarella cheese
Chopped parsley for garnish

Tomato Sauce:
2 cups tomato puree
2 tablespoons olive oil
1 drop Tabasco
1 teaspoon garlic salt
1 teaspoon Maggi
2 teaspoons basil, fresh
1 teaspoon sugar
Little ground black pepper

Place 2" of water in a copper, enamel, or stainless steel shallow pan. Add vinegar and salt. Bring up to boiling point, reduce heat till under the simmer. Break eggs into pan and cook a few minutes till set. (Eggs may be cooked ahead of time and kept in cold tap water in refrigerator and reheated in warm, not hot, water in any recipe in which eggs are not baked.)

Wilt spinach by placing in a large pot with about 1 cup of water and heating till spinach wilts down. Saute onion in butter till transparent. Add garlic salt, Maggi, Tabasco, ground black pepper, and nutmeg. Stir in flour, then cream. Stir over heat till combined. Sauce will be thick. Add spinach, which has been well drained, and simmer about five minutes. Place spinach mixture in bottom of a shallow casserole or in individual ramekins. Hollow out nests in spinach. Sprinkle lightly with about two tablespoons Parmesan. Lift eggs out of water, dry with a paper towel, and place in nests. Sprinkle a light dusting of Parmesan over eggs.

Continued

For tomato sauce, put puree in saucepan and add remaining ingredients. Heat about five minutes, stirring occasionally.

Slice ham and salami in julienne strips. Place over eggs. Sprinkle half of mozzarella over ham and salami. Sprinkle a little chopped parsley over top. Spoon tomato sauce over; add remainder of mozzarella and a sprinkling of parsley over it. (May be done ahead to this point.)

Reheat in a 350°F oven about 25 minutes.

POACHED EGGS IN ASPIC

2 to 3 quarts water
⅓ cup vinegar
6 to 8 large eggs

Fill a shallow saucepan or deep skillet ¾ full of water. Add vinegar. Bring to a boil, reduce heat immediately. Break the eggs one at a time into the water, holding as close to the water as possible (or first break into a saucer and slip into water), or use a French egg poacher. Cook each egg until the whites are firm, 4 to 5 minutes. Remove eggs and place in bowl of cold water to stop the cooking process. When ready to proceed, lift out onto a towel to dry. Trim edges with scissors to remove ragged edges.

Aspic:
2 tablespoons gelatin
⅓ cup cold water
4 cups clear chicken broth, clarified, or canned chicken broth, room temperature
Tabasco, dash
Salt to taste
Tarragon leaves (leaves trimmed from scallion stems may be substituted)

Soak gelatin in cold water. Add broth, stir, and heat till dissolved. Add Tabasco and salt if needed. Chill, but keep liquid. Spoon a thin layer of aspic into individual egg molds or custard cups. Chill till set. Dip tarragon leaves in aspic and place on layer of set aspic in a decorative pattern, such as a V. Chill. Place an egg on top of tarragon. Carefully fill each mold with chilled, but still liquid aspic. Chill.

To unmold, dip the outside of the mold quickly into a bowl of warm water and turn out on a serving dish or serve individually. Garnish with watercress and chopped aspic and, or cherry tomatoes.

Serves 6 to 8

SAMBEL — GORENG — TELOR

(Indonesian Eggs)

Dora Ang

6 hard-cooked eggs
1 medium size onion, chopped
2 buds garlic, sliced
2 tablespoons cooking oil
Dash turmeric
Dash cayenne pepper or chili powder
Ginger root, sliced
1 bay leaf
½ teaspoon salt
½ cup coconut milk

Peel the eggs. Stir-fry the chopped onion and garlic in 2 tablespoons oil until golden. Add remaining ingredients, except eggs and coconut milk. Finally, add the eggs and coconut milk. Simmer over slow heat until sauce has thickened.

To serve: Cut eggs in halves and pour the sauce over the eggs.

Serves 4 to 5

SCRAMBLED EGGS

Shakertown

18 eggs
1½ cups heavy cream
Salt and freshly ground pepper
1 tablespoon chopped parsley
1 tablespoon chopped chives
1 teaspoon chopped fresh tarragon or
1 teaspoon dried leaf tarragon
1 cup butter or margarine

Beat eggs lightly in half the cream and season with salt, pepper, and herbs. Heat 1 to 2 cups water to boiling and pour into water pan or bain-marie of chafing dish. Light Sterno or alcohol burner under chafing dish. Melt half the butter in large heavy skillet over low heat. Pour in eggs and stir with wooden spoon for a few minutes, until eggs are warmed and beginning to cook. Turn into warm, buttered top pan or blazer of chafing dish. Set over hot water. Cook, stirring occasionally with wooden spoon in long even strokes, until eggs are lightly cooked but still soft and moist. Cut rest of butter into small pieces. Stir balance of cream and butter into eggs. Keep warm over hot, not boiling water.

Serves 12

SUNNY EGGS

6 hard-cooked eggs, peeled and sliced lengthwise
3 tablespoons mayonnaise
1 tablespoon cider vinegar
¼ teaspoon salt
½ teaspoon dry mustard
Pepper
3 tablespoons sunflower seed meal
1 tablespoon minced chives or grated onion
¼ cup alfalfa sprouts
Sunflower seeds

Remove yolks and mash in bowl. Add mayonnaise, vinegar, salt, mustard, pepper, sunflower seed meal, onion or chives; mix well.

Spoon yolk mixture back into whites. Garnish with sprouts and several sunflower kernels stuck into each egg half.

CANADIAN CHEDDAR SOUFFLE

From the book, "Across Canada with Herbs"

2½ tablespoons butter
3 tablespoons flour
1 teaspoon basil
1 teaspoon prepared mustard
Salt and pepper to taste
1 cup warm milk
4 egg yolks
6 egg whites
1 cup grated Canadian Cheddar cheese
1 tablespoon fine bread crumbs

Butter and prepare souffle dish with collar. Heat oven to 375°F. In saucepan, melt butter, blend in flour, basil, mustard, salt, pepper to taste. Gradually stir in milk and cook over medium heat, stirring until thick. Remove from heat and beat in egg yolks one at a time. Then fold in egg whites that have been beaten stiff, but not dry. When mixed, fold in grated cheese and turn into souffle dish. Sprinkle bread crumbs over top. Bake 35 to 40 minutes until souffle is puffed and brown. Serve at once.

Serves 4 or 5

ONION CHEESE PIE

Pastry for 9" pie pan　　　**2 tablespoons butter**
1 cup finely sliced onion　　**¾ cup grated Cheddar cheese**

Saute onion slices in butter until transparent. Place onions in pie pan lined with pastry crust. Preheat oven to 350° F, cover with cheese. Blend the following ingredients and pour over onions and cheese:

3 eggs, slightly beaten
1½ tablespoons flour
½ cup milk
2 teaspoons prepared mustard
2 tablespoons chopped parsley
1 can (10¾ oz.) mushroom soup
1 teaspoon marjoram, dried

Bake in 350°F. oven for about 45 minutes or until custard sets.
Excellent for luncheon dish with salad or serve as an hors d'oeuvre.

Serves 4 or 5

TOMATO-SALAMI QUICHE

Joyce Rosencrans

One 10-inch prepared pastry shell, unbaked
1 cup (4 oz.) shredded Cheddar cheese
2 cups diced tomatoes, seeded and well drained (about three medium tomatoes)
¼ pound thinly sliced hard salami, cut into small pieces.
4 eggs
1 cup milk (or Half and Half, if preferred)
1 tablespoon instant minced onion
2 tablespoons freshly minced parsley
1 teaspoon dried oregano, crushed
½ teaspoon garlic salt
Freshly ground black pepper

Use: 10-inch pie plate or quiche pan with highstanding rim.

Line pan with pastry and have oven preheating to 450°F. Prick bottom of pie shell with fork. Bake for eight minutes. Remove from oven. Do not reduce oven temperature.

While pie shell is baking, prepare shredded cheese, tomatoes, and salami. Be sure tomatoes are well drained. In prebaked pie shell, sprinkle half the cheese, salami, and tomatoes. Repeat layers. In medium mixing bowl, beat the eggs to blend. Add milk, minced onion, parsley, oregano, garlic salt, and pepper. Beat well and pour evenly over quiche ingredients. Spread parsley with tines of fork, if it tends to clump. Bake quiche at 450°F for 10 minutes; reduce temperature to 325°F; bake 30 to 35 minutes more. Let stand five minutes before cutting.

Serves 8

ARMADO — Peace! —

The armipotent Mars, of lances the almighty,
    Gave Hector a gift, the heir of Ilion;
A man so breathed, that certain he would fight; yea
    From morn till night, out of his pavilion.
I am that flower, —

DUMAINE — That *mint.*

SHAKESPEARE

Love's Labour's Lost

Butters, Vinegars, Blends
Mayonnaise, Sauces,
Dressings

Butters

HERB BUTTER I

½ pound butter or margarine
1 finely chopped scallion with part of green top
¼ teaspoon thyme
¼ teaspoon basil
¼ teaspoon marjoram

Mix herbs into softened butter or margarine. Allow flavors to blend at least several hours. Excellent on heated French bread, broiled meats, vegetables and baked potatoes.

HERB BUTTER II

1 stick butter
1 clove garlic, minced (optional)
Few drops lemon juice
1 to 4 tablespoons finely minced fresh herbs (depending upon your taste and the pungency of the herbs used)

Cream butter. Blend in garlic, lemon juice and herbs. Let mellow, covered in refrigerator overnight to bring out flavor. Refrigerate up to one month or freeze.

Herb butters are delicious on breads, vegetables, grilled meats and fish, on seafood, with eggs, on poultry and game, in stuffing and gravy, in soups and stews, and in sauces. Some herbs and herb combinations that make good butters are:
basil, oregano, or a combination of the two.
chives, parsley, and dill.
fennel, tarragon, chives, parsley and chervil.
savory, thyme and marjoram.
a combination of the previous two or three.
tarragon, rosemary, salad burnet, chives, and parsley, sorrel, and sage.
Try your own combination!

HERB BUTTER III

Shakertown

1 stick butter or margarine
Pinch of thyme
Pinch of ground anise seed
Pinch of parsley

Blend well and let stand covered, for 24 hours at least. May use either fresh or dried herbs.

HERB BUTTER IV

Shakertown

Bring 1 stick (¼ pound) of butter to room temperature, then with a wooden spoon work in 2 or 3 teaspoons of any fresh green herb and a dash of lemon juice. When mixed, mold in table-type (pretty) container. Cover with plastic and refrigerate overnight.

Recommended blends ;

Basil butter — tomato dishes, eggs, roast Cornish hen, bean soup

Chive butter — almost anything hot

Dill butter — use on boiled, mashed or baked potatoes, scrambled eggs, seafood, potatoes

Parsley butter — vegetables, fish, potatoes, and in Hollandaise sauce

HERB BUTTER V

Daisy Sticksel

Make a year's supply of herb butter in July or early August. If stored in the deep freeze, the herbs in the butter will retain their green color and flavor for at least 3 months or longer.

The following herbs can be used: tarragon, dill, parsley, chives, thyme, chervil, sweet marjoram, summer savory, and cress. As few as three herbs may be used, but eight or nine make a delicious blend.

Cream the butter (unsalted butter is preferred)
Cut the chives in small bits with scissors
Chop the leaves (no stems) in a wooden bowl with a hand chopper.
Do not use a food chopper.
For 1 pound of butter use 2 tablespoons chopped herbs.
For 10 pounds use 1½ cups chopped herbs.

Store in deep freeze for winter use.

HERB BUTTER VI

¾ *cup butter*
¼ *teaspoon salt*
Dash cayenne pepper
½ *teaspoon dried summer savory*
¾ *teaspoon dried thyme*

Spread on toast, or spread on Syrian bread and bake until slightly browned and crisp. Good with salad, soup, or as an hors d'oeuvre.

HERB BUTTER FOR STEAK OR VEGETABLES

Chef Scott Berman
Longwharf Restaurant — Sag Harbor, L.I., N.Y.

½ *cup butter*
1 tablespoon chopped parsley
2 teaspoons chopped chives
¼ *teaspoon dry mustard*
¼ *teaspoon thyme*

Beat butter until fluffy. Blend all herbs into it. Serve over steak or vegetables.

LEMON HERB BUTTER

1 lb. butter
¼ *cup mixed herbs (your choice)*
1½ teaspoons grated lemon peel
2 tablespoons lemon juice
Freshly ground black pepper to taste

Beat butter until light and fluffy. Add other ingredients. Store in jar refrigerated, until needed.

Good on vegetables, fish, steak, pork, English muffins.

Melt for lobster, shrimp, and artichokes.

Yield: 2 cups

Vinegars

HERB VINEGAR

Add several sprigs of any one fresh herb, or a compatible combination of two or three, to a bottle of red or white wine vinegar or cider vinegar. Let stand, tightly capped, for several weeks in a dark cupboard, until the flavor has developed. Add more herbs if a stronger flavor is desired.

If giving as a gift, remove herbs and add a fresh green sprig.

To speed up the process, heat the vinegar to just below the boiling point and pour over crushed herbs. Tightly cap and stand in a sunny spot. Strain before serving.

Herbs that make good vinegars are:
sweet or opal basil (if using opal, use white wine vinegar to achieve a beautiful ruby red color)
oregano
a combination of the two
dill, chives (preferably garlic chives), and salad burnet
tarragon, thyme and marjoram
a combination of the latter two
rosemary, sage and mint

VINAIGRE AROMATISE

½ oz. dried mint
½ oz. dried parsley
1 clove garlic, mashed or 2 teaspoons juice of onion
2 whole cloves
1 teaspoon freshly ground pepper
Dash of grated nutmeg
Salt to taste
2 teaspoons sugar
1 teaspoon good brandy
1 quart cider vinegar

Add all ingredients to vinegar and let it stand covered for 3 weeks. Strain and bottle.

"Rosemary for Remembrance"
        Shakespeare

Remember:
Use triple the amount of fresh herbs to dried herbs!

Blends

Fines Herbes Blends

For ground beef mixture: 1 tablespoon each summer savory, basil, marjoram, thyme, parsley, lovage or celery leaves.

For vegetables: 1 tablespoon each summer savory, majoram, basil, chervil.

For pork dishes: 1 tablespoon each sage, basil, summer savory.

For lamb and veal dishes: 1 tablespoon each marjoram, summer savory, rosemary.

For egg and chicken dishes: 1 tablespoon each summer savory, tarragon, chervil, basil, chives.

For poultry stuffing: 1 tablespoon each summer savory, marjoram, basil, thyme, parsley, celery or lovage leaves; 1 teaspoon ground dried lemon peel; 1 teaspoon sage may be added.

For vegetable cocktails: (for 1 pint liquid) ½ teaspoon each marjoram, basil, tarragon, thyme, summer savory; 1 tablespoon chopped chives.

For fish: (2 cups liquid) ¼ teaspoon each marjoram, thyme, basil, sage, crushed seeds of fennel.

For soups and stews: (2 quarts liquid) 1 teaspoon each parsley or chervil, thyme or summer savory, basil, marjoram, celery or lovage leaves; ½ teaspoon each sage, rosemary, dried ground lemon peel.

Flavor granulated sugar, with any of the sweet herbs, use in iced drinks, icings, cookies, or with fruit. Herbs excellent for this purpose are, rose geranium leaves, mints, or lemon verbena. Add a few leaves to a pint of sugar and screw lid on tightly. Use powdered sugar, flavored with rose geranium leaves to make a thin white icing for cakes.

ITALIAN HERB MIXTURE

Shakertown

3 tablespoons leaf oregano	3 tablespoons leaf basil
3 tablespoons leaf marjoram	3 tablespoons rosemary,
1 tablespoons leaf thyme	crumbled
3 tablespoons leaf savory	1 tablespoon sage

For: meatballs, salad dressings, tomato sauce, eggplant dishes, sauteed chicken and veal.

Combine all ingredients. Keep in tightly closed containers.

Makes 2 gifts of ½ cup each.

CHINESE 5 SPICE

2 tablespoons fennel seed
2 tablespoons cinnamon
2 tablespoons peppercorns
6 whole star anise
2 tablespoons cloves

Put in blender or spice grinder. Use in salad dressings, sauces, etc.

QUATRE EPICES (4 SPICES)

Shakertown

¾ cup ground white pepper
4 teaspoons ground cloves
4 teaspoons ground ginger
2 teaspoons ground nutmeg

For: pates, meat loaves, ground beef casseroles, soups, and pepper cookies.

Combine all ingredients. Keep in tightly closed containers.

Makes 2 gifts of ½ cup each.

HERB FLOUR

Keep a glass pint jar filled with herbed flour to use in dusting chicken or chops, for pastry, biscuits, pizza crust, and dumplings, or to stir into sauces and gravies.

2 cups flour
1 to 2 teaspoons minced dried herbs (thyme, marjoram, and sage or savory are a good combination)
½ teaspoon salt
Freshly ground pepper

HERB SALT

Coarse salt

In slow oven* put variety of herb leaves on glass pie plate: rosemary, thyme, basil, sage, tarragon, parsley, dill. When leaves are dry, crumble and mix with salt. Suit your own taste as to variety of herbs and proportions used.

*Or microwave, according to directions

Mayonnaise

DILL MAYONNAISE

1 cup sour cream
½ cup mayonnaise
1 tablespoon lemon juice
½ teaspoon Lowry's salt
2 teaspoons dill weed

Mix and store in refrigerator a few hours before serving.

Serve with cold salmon or shrimp. Garnish with fresh dill.

GREEN GODDESS DRESSING

4 anchovy fillets, finely cut
2 tablespoons chopped onion
1 teaspoon chopped parsley
1 teaspoon chopped tarragon
2 teaspoons chopped chives
1 teaspoon tarragon vinegar
1½ cups mayonnaise
1 clove garlic

Combine anchovies, onion, parsley, tarragon, chives, and tarragon vinegar. Add mayonnaise; gently mix until blended. Serve over romaine, escarole, and chicory, and add endive if you wish, tossed lightly together in a wooden salad bowl rubbed with a cut clove of garlic.

Yield: 1¾ cups

HERBAL HINT

Cucumber flavored salad burnet, delicious blended with cream cheese.

HERB MAYONNAISE

Shakertown

So many combinations of herbs are possible that one must choose one's own preferences. Below are some favorites, but sometimes you can vary them, depending on what food they will be used with, plus availability in the garden.

1 cup firm mayonnaise (blender is easy and about as good as the old fashioned way)
2 tablespoons each parsley, chives, tarragon (minced) or
2 tablespoons each parsley, dill, chives or
2 tablespoons each parsley, basil, chives
1 teaspoon lemon juice (optional)
¼ lb. spinach (optional)

Mix herbs thoroughly with mayonnaise — add 1 teaspoon lemon juice if desired. If green color is desired, blanch ¼ pound spinach for 2 minutes, mince and add. Will keep well in refrigerator 2 to 3 weeks.

HERB MAYONNAISE HEATED SAUCE

Civic Garden Center "Herb Cookery"

½ cup mayonnaise
6 tablespoons rich milk or Half and Half
2 tablespoons minced parsley
2 tablespoons minced green pepper
2 tablespoons minced scallions
1 tablespoon minced pimiento
2 hard cooked eggs, chopped
2 tablespoons watercress, minced

Blend mayonnaise and milk in top of double boiler, over boiling water. Heat until lukewarm. Gently stir in all the herbs except watercress. Add chopped eggs. Heat thoroughly for 5 minutes Add cress, and pimientos, stir gently. Serve immediately over hot vegetables, such as asparagus, broccoli, celery, Belgian endive, carrots, peas, or string beans.

HERB TARTAR SAUCE

1 cup mayonnaise
⅓ cup sour cream
⅓ cup finely chopped pickles (pressed between paper towel to remove moisture)
2 teaspoons finely chopped capers
2 tablespoons stuffed green olives, chopped
1 tablespoon prepared mustard
2 tablespoons minced parsley
¼ teaspoon dried chervil
¼ teaspoon dried chives
¼ teaspoon tarragon

Blend mayonnaise and sour cream. Add remaining ingredients. Stir to blend.

Yield: 1½ cups

MUSTARD MAYONNAISE

⅓ cup dry mustard
⅔ cup brown sugar
3 ounces tarragon vinegar, heated
½ cup mayonnaise

Mix all together while vinegar is hot. Excellent with ham or Canadian bacon.

Yield: 1½ cups

PARSLEY MAYONNAISE DRESSING

1 cup parsley, ground
1 small onion and 1 clove garlic, ground
¼ pound blue cheese, finely broken
1 pint mayonnaise
Juice of 1 lemon
1 teaspoon Worcestershire sauce
⅛ teaspoon each salt and pepper

Mix cheese, parsley, onion and garlic. Add mayonnaise, lemon juice, Worcestershire sauce, salt and pepper. Mix well.

Yield: Approximately 1 pint

SAUCE VERTE I

"21" Restaurant

1 cup fresh spinach
½ cup watercress
1 tablespoon chives
½ cup chopped leeks
½ cup parsley
2 cups mayonnaise

Boil the spinach, watercress, chives, leeks, and parsley together for 7 minutes in salted water. Drain well and cool. When the greens are cold, pass them through a grinder. Blend the puree with the mayonnaise and serve with salmon.

Yield: Approximately 2½ cups

SAUCE VERTE II

2 cups homemade mayonnaise.
1 bunch parsley, heads only, very finely minced
2 bunches watercress, stems removed, very finely minced
4 tablespoons sieved yolks of hard-cooked eggs
2 tablespoons Gulden's mustard
2 tablespoons Grey's Poupon mustard or Dijon
Juice of 1 lemon
Dash of white vinegar

Combine the ingredients and stir well until well blended. Cover and refrigerate until ready to serve. Excellent with cold salmon or salmon mousse.

Yield: 2½ cups

"Rosemary for Remembrance"

Shakespeare

Remember:
Use triple the amount of fresh herbs to dried herbs!

Sauces and Dressings

BASIL SAUCE FROM GENOA

Inelda Tajo

In Italy, especially in Genoa (where this recipe comes from) it is used as often as a tomato sauce to dress pasta, potatoes gnocchi, or to add to an already made vegetable soup.

¾ cup olive oil
3 cloves garlic
1 teaspoon salt
2 cups fresh basil leaves
¾ cup grated Parmesan cheese
2 tablespoons Romano cheese (optional)
2 tablespoons pine nuts
4 tablespoons butter, softened

In a blender put the first three ingredients and mix for about a minute at high speed, then add the basil (never use dried leaves) and mix it until it is reduced to small bits; pour into a bowl, add the Parmesan cheese, the Romano cheese (if you like its strong taste), the pine nuts and the butter. Mix well with a wooden spoon. The sauce is now ready to use.

This quantity will serve 8 portions of pasta. Three-fourths of a cup will be enough for 8 servings of vegetable soup.

Basil sauce may be frozen, but do not add either the cheese or the butter. I often use those plastic ice cube trays and when the "pesto" is frozen I put the "pesto cubes" in small zipped plastic bags.

Serves 8

BASTING SAUCE AND MARINADE
WITH JUNIPER BERRIES

Marny Dilts

(Use to flavor and tenderize beef and wild game)

½ cup red wine vinegar
3 cups Burgundy wine
12 black peppercorns
1 large onion, sliced
1 clove garlic, crushed
½ teaspoon celery salt
5 juniper berries
1½ teaspoons salt
⅛ teaspoon nutmeg
4 whole cloves
¼ teaspoon thyme
1 bay leaf, crushed

Blend all in large bowl. Store overnight in covered jar at room temperature. Store in refrigerator. Pour marinade over meat, let stand overnight. Use liquid for basting while cooking.

BEARNAISE SAUCE I

Chester's Road House

1 tablespoon fresh shallots, chopped
2 oz. fresh tarragon stalks, chopped
10 peppercorns — crushed
1 pinch of salt
4 tablespoons of white vinegar
5 egg yolks
6 oz. melted butter
1 teaspoon fresh tarragon leaves, chopped
1 teaspoon fresh parsley, chopped
1 teaspoon fresh chervil, chopped

Bring to a boil shallots, tarragon, peppercorns, salt, and vinegar, reduce to two thirds. Take off the fire. Let cool. Add 5 egg yolks, put the saucepan on a low fire, beat with whisk until it has the consistency of heavy cream.

Add gradually 6 oz. of melted butter. Whisk the sauce briskly to ensure the cooking of the yolks which, alone, by gradual cooking, effect the thickening of the sauce.

When the sauce is finished, rub through a fine sieve, add fresh chopped parsley, chervil, and tarragon leaves.

The sauce should not be served very hot. It will curdle if overheated.

Yield: 1½ cups

BEARNAISE SAUCE II
(Using food processor)

Melanie Barnard

¼ cup tarragon vinegar
¼ cup dry white wine
1 tablespoon minced shallots
1½ teaspoons fresh tarragon, minced, or ½ teaspoon dried tarragon
Salt and pepper to taste
⅓ cup butter
3 egg yolks

Boil the vinegar, wine, shallots, and seasonings slowly until reduced to about 2 tablespoons. Add butter and heat till bubbly, but do not brown. In the work bowl with the steel blade, process the yolks about 15 seconds till light. With motor running, dribble the hot butter mixture through the feed tube. Serve warm or at room temperature, with steak or poultry.

Yield: 1 - 1½ cups

BROWN SAUCE

"21" Restaurant

5 cups strong beef stock
4 tablespoons unsalted butter
4 tablespoons all-purpose flour
1 clove garlic, peeled
1 bay leaf
½ teaspoon dried chopped thyme
1 small onion, chopped
¼ teaspoon Worcestershire sauce
Madeira wine to taste
Salt and freshly ground black pepper to taste

Preheat the oven to 350°F. Bring the stock to a boil. In a small heavy-bottomed saucepan, melt the butter and add the flour, blending thoroughly with a whisk. Allow to cook for a few minutes until the mixture is slightly browned. Pour the stock into a casserole dish and stir in the "roux" (butter-flour mixture). Simmer over a low flame until the stock is slightly thickened. Add the garlic, bay leaf, thyme, onion, and Worcestershire sauce and place the casserole in the oven, "roasting" for about 1½ hours. Strain the sauce into a bowl or pan, add the wine, and season to taste with salt and pepper.

Yield: 1 quart

CHILI SAUCE

12 large tomatoes, chopped
3 large onions, chopped
1 cup sugar
1 tablespoon salt
½ cup vinegar

3 green peppers, chopped
1 red pepper, chopped
1 stick cinnamon
¼ cup, approximately,
mixed pickling spices wrapped
in cheesecloth bag

Cook until thick, 1 to 2 hours.

DILL CUCUMBER SAUCE

1 (8 oz.) carton sour cream
Salt and white pepper to taste
1 teaspoon onion, grated
½ cup very thinly sliced cucumbers, peeled or unpeeled, as you like,
pat dry to remove excess moisture.
1 tablespoon fresh dill, chopped
⅛ teaspoon fresh horseradish
Fresh dill for garnish

Continued

Mix all ingredients together. Chill for several hours before serving. Garnish with sprigs of fresh dill. Excellent with fish, mousse, or cold salmon.

FINES HERBES SAUCE FOR COLD FISH

Pigall's

6 egg yolks
2 tablespoons hot water
1 cup oil
¼ cup wine vinegar
2 tablespoons Dijon mustard

2 tablespoons tarragon
2 tablespoons fresh chopped
parsley
1 tablespoon fresh chopped dill

Mix egg yolks and water and beat until fluffy; add oil slowly, mix, for two minutes. Add mustard, vinegar and remaining ingredients; mix for two more minutes. Refrigerate for 15 minutes before using.

Yields: Approximately 3 cups

FENNEL SAUCE

Jane Miller

For baked or boiled fish:

1 teaspoon fennel seeds, ground
1 cup white wine
1 cup mushrooms, sliced
¼ stick butter
1 egg, beaten
½ cup chopped parsley

Grind fennel into white wine. Cook, reducing wine by one half. In separate pan, saute sliced mushrooms in butter. Whisk wine and fennel into beaten egg. Add mushrooms and butter to mixture. Add parsley just before serving. Pour sauce over cooked fish.

FRENCH DRESSING

Shakertown

Make your own favorite dressing. (Commercial ones are not as good). Often an herb vinegar is used and additions are not necessary. However, chopped basil, tarragon, chives, parsley, or dill — or some combination is very nice and adds color and flavor to your salad.

Basic dressing:
3 tablespoons salad oil (preferably olive oil)
1 tablespoon herb vinegar
½ teaspoon dry mustard
½ teaspoon salt
¼ teaspoon freshly ground black pepper
Split clove garlic left in 24 to 48 hours if desired

This recipe may be made in much larger quantities and put in a tightly covered jar and kept in refrigerator indefinitely.

Often, in our kitchen, we add the minced herbs directly to the salad, mix with greens, and then add dressing at the last minute, after greens are well dried and very cold.

GREEN SAUCE

"The International Review of Food and Wine Magazine"
Editor-In-Chief, Michael Batterberry

Watercress stems
1½ cups olive oil
6 cups fresh herbs plucked from stems (Italian parsley and watercress mandatory, plus dill or whatever else you like that's available)
1 heaping tablespoon minced white of leek
4 little scallions in 1 inch lengths
2½ tablespoons capers
6 inch squirt anchovy paste
½ cup lemon juice
2½ tablespoons fresh tarragon leaves or 1 tablespoon dried tarragon
1 teaspoon sugar
2 soft boiled eggs (3-4 minutes)
Salt and black pepper to taste

Place whatever fresh watercress stems you have, once leaves have been plucked, in blender or food processor with olive oil. Blend until liquefied (Italian parsley stems may also be treated in this way if they are not tough). Add all other ingredients except fresh herbs, eggs, salt, and pepper. Blend well. Add egg yolks and blend briefly. Add fresh herbs and egg whites and

Continued

blend only until a "chopped" consistency is achieved. Season to taste with salt and pepper, remembering brininess of anchovy paste and capers. A couple of cornichons or other tiny sour pickles may be blended along with the sauce base, but in the process the garden-fresh brilliance of the flavor may be somewhat dimmed.

GREEN HERBS AND GREEN PEPPERCORN SAUCE

London Chop House

1 cup yogurt
¾ cup homemade mayonnaise
3 teaspoons white wine, dry
⅛ teaspoon salt
1 ½ tablespoon green peppercorns, mashed with flat French knife
1 tablespoon minced chives
1 tablespoon minced capers
1 tablespoon minced parsley
2 tablespoons minced basil, 7 large leaves
3 teaspoons minced scallions, 5 medium

Whip together the yogurt, mayonnaise, white wine and salt. Add all herbs and spices. Rest the mixture at room temperature for 1 hour, then refrigerate until ready to serve. This piquant herb sauce is excellent with fish, especially a salmon mousse, cold sliced beef, or lamb.

Yield: 2 cups

HORSERADISH

1 horseradish root (about 1 pound)
1 cup white vinegar
½ teaspoon sugar
1 teaspoon salt
1 small turnip, peeled and cubed, optional*

Vigorously scrub the horseradish root (or peel), cutting away dark parts. (The whiter and cleaner the root, the whiter is the finished product.) Cut into cubes — you should have about 3 cups. It is important that you make it in a blender, covered, to protect your eyes from the hot fumes that rise from the fresh root. Add vinegar, sugar, salt and gradually add the horseradish cubes.

*(If you wish to make it milder, add the turnip.)

Blend until smooth. Can be refrigerated up to 3 months or frozen.

Yields: about 3 cups

LOVAGE SAUCE

Barbara Remington, Dutch Mill Herb Farm

2 tablespoons butter
1 tender stalk of lovage
2 tablespoons flour
Salt & pepper to taste
1 cup milk

Melt butter and add lovage which has been diced and cooked until tender. Stir in flour, cooking long enough for flour to become a deep golden color. Add salt and pepper. Stir milk in gradually. Cook, stirring until sauce is thick. Serve over fish or pot roast.

MINT SAUCE I

Mix together ½ cup (packed) fresh mint leaves cut fine with ½ cup white vinegar and ¼ cup water, 1 tablespoon sugar. Steep uncovered, at least 30 minutes to an hour. Strain. Mint sauce in its natural state is an amber color, so if you want it green add a dash of green food color. Bottle and label.

MINT SAUCE FOR LAMB OR BEEF II

Shakertown

2 tablespoons sugar
½ cup cider vinegar
4 tablespoons chopped mint leaves

Pour vinegar over sugar. When dissolved, add mint. Put in warm place for 1 hour or more before serving.

MINT CHILI SAUCE FOR LAMB
OR ROAST BEEF

Shakertown

½ cup chili sauce
½ cup mint jelly
1 tablespoon Worcestershire sauce
1 tablespoon horseradish mustard
1 pint drippings from roast

Mix together in saucepan, simmer about 10 minutes. Serve hot.

170

MOCK CHEESE SAUCE

1 tablespoon vinegar or cider vinegar
½ cup plain yogurt
1 cup cottage cheese
1 onion, thinly sliced
1 teaspoon sugar
½ teaspoon salt
⅛ teaspoon pepper
2 tablespoons chopped parsley
½ teaspoon dillweed

In electric blender container, combine all ingredients, except parsley and dill. Blend until smooth. Stir in parsley and dill. Pass in sauceboat to serve with hot potatoes.

Yield: about 1½ cups

MUSTARD

With variations

¼ cup white wine vinegar, preferably tarragon
¼ cup dry mustard
1 tablespoon sugar
½ teaspoon salt
⅓ cup dry white wine
3 egg yolks, beaten

Blend all ingredients except egg yolks and let stand for two hours.

Put mixture into top of a double boiler over hot, but not boiling water. Beat the egg yolks into this mixture, stirring constantly with a wire whisk. It should thicken slightly in a few minutes. Pour into a jar. Cool and cover tightly. This may be stored in the refrigerator for at least 3 weeks.

Variations:
Add ½ teaspoon fresh tarragon leaves, chopped

Use with chicken, lamb or steak.

Add ½ teaspoon mint leaves and 2 tablespoons tomato paste. Great for hamburger, baked ham and hot dogs.

SALSA VERDE PIQUANTE

Linda Miller

4 cloves garlic (small)
4 anchovies (rinsed)
1 hard cooked egg yolk
lemon juice (1 whole lemon or more)
1 large bunch parsley
Salt
Freshly ground black pepper
¼ cup olive oil (more if necessary)

Combine in blender or food processor. Sauce should be slightly coarse, and very tart.

Serve with cold meats.

SPAGHETTI SAUCE

1 to 2 quarts condensed turkey or meat stock, prepared with
2 bay leaves
2 ounces dried Italian mushrooms, cut up, soaked in water
to cover 1-2 hours
10 onions, diced
8 cloves garlic, minced
¼-½ cup imported olive oil
2 large cans imported pear-shaped tomatoes
6 6-oz. cans tomato paste
½ teaspoon rosemary, dried
1½ tablespoons oregano, dried
1 tablespoon basil, dried
1 to 2 teaspoons Tabasco
3 quarts water, approximately
Salt to taste

Prepare a strong stock, salted to taste, in advance. For this purpose, it is convenient to use a leftover turkey carcass, adding additional turkey parts if needed. Refrigerate overnight. Skim fat off the top the next day.

Heat stock in a large heavy pot. Add mushrooms and water, in which they have been soaked, to pot.

Saute onions in oil until transparent. Add garlic and saute a few minutes longer. Add to pot along with remaining ingredients. Simmer slowly, occasionally skimming off oil which rises to the top. Cool until thick. Correct seasoning.

VINAIGRETTE SAUCE WITH PIMIENTO

½ cup white wine vinegar
½ cup dry white wine
2 tablespoons vegetable oil
3 green onions, sliced
1 teaspoon salt
⅛ teaspoon pepper
⅛ teaspoon thyme
2 whole, canned pimientos, drained and chopped

In small saucepan, combine all ingredients except pimientos. Simmer three minutes. Stir in pimientos and heat. Pass in sauceboat. Serve with hot baked potatoes.

Yield: 1½ cups

YOGURT DRESSING (LOW CALORIE)

Civic Garden Center "Herb Cookery"

3 tablespoons Yogurt
3 or 4 drops lemon juice
1 teaspoon onion, garlic, or chives, according to your taste
1 teaspoon dill or any other favorite herb

Mix and chill, use on tossed salad.

CLEOPATRA — As sweet as *balm*, as soft as air, as gentle — 0
Anthony! — Nay, I will take thee, too. (Applying another asp to her
arm, Dies.)
What should I stay —

CHARMIAN — In this vile world? So, fare thee well.

Shakespeare

Antony and Cleopatra

Breads, Crepes, Grains, Pastas

CARAWAY RAISIN BREAD

5 cups sifted flour
1 cup sugar
1 tablespoon baking powder
1½ teaspoons salt
1 teaspoon baking soda
½ cup butter
2½ cups white seedless raisins, washed and drained
3 tablespoons caraway seeds
2½ cups buttermilk
1 egg, slightly beaten

Sift together flour, sugar, baking powder, salt, and baking soda. Cut in butter until mixture resembles cornmeal. Stir in raisins and caraway seeds. Add buttermilk and egg to dry mixture. Blend until moistened. Butter 11¾" cast iron skillet. Turn batter into skillet; bake in 350° F oven 1 hour or until firm.

Yield: 1-12" round loaf

CHIVE BISCUITS
Shakertown

2 cups sifted flour
2 teaspoons baking powder
½ teaspoon salt
4 teaspoons butter
½ cup finely chopped chives
¾ cup milk or enough to make a soft dough

Melt enough butter to cover 25 biscuits. Preheat oven to 450° F.
Sift flour, baking powder and salt. With 2 knives or pastry blender, cut in butter and add chives. Stir in milk with fork. Turn dough out on lightly floured board and knead briefly. Roll out to ½" thickness and cut into small rounds. Put biscuits on a buttered baking sheet, brush the tops with the melted butter. Bake in a very hot oven 450° F. for 12 to 15 minutes or until they are golden brown.

Yield: 25 biscuits

CRESCENT HERB SWIRL

1 (8 oz) can refrigerated crescent dinner rolls
2 tablespoons butter or margarine, softened
1 teaspoon parsley flakes
¼ teaspoon oregano

Continued

¼ teaspoon dillweed
⅛ to ¼ teaspoon garlic powder

Separate dough into 2 long rectangles. Slightly overlap long sides to form a 12-inch by 7-inch rectangle; firmly press perforations and edges to seal. Combine butter, parsley, oregano, dill, and garlic powder. Spread about 1½ tablespoons of the herb butter evenly over dough. Reserve remaining mixture. Starting at shorter side of dough, loosely roll up; seal long edge. Place in ungreased loaf pan, eight inch or nine inch size. Bake at 375° F for 20 to 25 minutes or until deep golden brown. Cool slightly. Brush with remaining herb butter. Serve warm. May be made up two hours ahead of baking and chilled.

Serves 6

CROUTONS, HERB SEASONED

To make your own:

One half of a 1 lb. loaf of bread will make about 3 cups of croutons. Day old French bread is the best, but other may be used. Slice bread and cut in ½" cubes. Spread on a rimmed baking sheet. Bake in a 300° F oven for about 10 minutes. Then coat croutons with one of the following herb butters, and bake at 275° F for about 30 minutes, turning occasionally until light brown and crispy. Store in covered jar. Croutons are excellent addition to salads, and soups, and make marvelous casserole toppings.

I — Garlic
¼ cup butter, melted
1 clove garlic, minced finely
2 tablespoons fresh parsley, minced

II — Onion and Herbs
¼ cup butter, melted with 1 teaspoon onion powder
½ teaspoon each basil, chervil, and oregano

III — Cheese and Herbs
¼ cup butter, melted
¼ teaspoon each basil, oregano, marjoram, thyme
Dash of Worcestershire sauce
Dash of Tabasco
1 tablespoon grated Parmesan cheese

HERBAL HINT

Add your favorite herb blend to buttered crackers.
Heat in oven until slightly brown.

DILL AND ONION BREAD CASSEROLE

1 pkg. active dry yeast in ¼ cup warm water
1 cup creamed cottage cheese, small curd
1 tablespoon butter
2 tablespoons sugar
1 tablespoon instant minced onion
2 tablespoons dill seed or ½ seed and ½ weed
1 teaspoon salt
¼ teaspoon soda
1 egg
2¼ to 2½ cups flour

Soften yeast in water. Heat cottage cheese to lukewarm. Add butter to melt.

In mixing bowl mix: cottage cheese, butter, yeast, sugar, onion, dill, salt, soda, and egg.

Add flour to form stiff dough, beating well after each addition.

Cover, let rise in warm place until double in bulk. (About 50 minutes.)

Stir down and put in well oiled 2 qt. casserole.

Let rise until light (30 to 40 minutes). Bake at 350° F for 40 to 50 minutes or until golden brown.

Brush with soft butter and sprinkle with salt.

Serves 6 to 8

FEATHER BREAD WITH HERBS

Jerry East - Shillito's

2 pkgs. active dry yeast
3 tablespoons 115° F. milk
3 tablespoons sugar
3 whole eggs
1 tablespoon chopped tarragon
1 tablespoon chopped marjoram
1 tablespoon chopped shallots or onion
½ cup soft butter (¼ lb.)
2 cups sifted all-purpose flour
½ teaspoon salt

Combine yeast and milk, let stand 3 minutes. Meanwhile beat together sugar, eggs, tarragon, marjoram, and shallots. Add butter, flour and salt. Add the yeast mixture to the batter. Beat well 3 minutes. Place in a greased bread pan or a 9-inch tube pan. Let rise in a warm place (90° F.) until double in bulk, about 2 to 2½ hours. Bake in a preheated 450° F. oven about 15 to 20 minutes. Should be amber brown and spring back to the touch very readily.

Yield: 1 loaf

HERB BREAD I

Shakertown

1 pkg. yeast
¼ cup warm water
¼ cup sugar
1½ cups milk, scalded, and cooled to lukewarm
½ cup shortening, melted
2 eggs, beaten
1 tablespoon salt
6 to 7 cups sifted flour
1 teaspoon dried sage leaves
¾ teaspoon dried thyme leaves
¾ teaspoon dried marjoram leaves

Dissolve the yeast in the warm water along with one tablespoon of the sugar. Add the milk, remaining sugar, shortening, eggs, salt, and two cups of the flour. Mix well. Cover and let rise in a warm place (80 to 85 degrees) until bubbly, about one hour.

Mix the herbs and crumble them. Add to the yeast mixture.

Stir in enough of the remaining flour to make a stiff dough. Knead on a floured board until satiny and elastic. Place in a bowl, cover, and let stand in a warm place (80 to 85 degrees) until double in bulk.

Punch down the dough and let it rest ten minutes.

Shape into two loaves and place in two greased 9x5x3 inch bread pans. Brush the tops with milk and let rise until double in bulk.

Bake in a preheated 375° F oven until done, about 50 minutes.

Yield: Two loaves

HERB BREAD II

1 cup lukewarm milk
2 tablespoons shortening
1 teaspoon salt
2 tablespoons sugar
1 cake yeast
1 egg beaten
3¾ cups flour
1 tablespoon sage
2 teaspoons caraway seeds
½ teaspoon nutmeg

While milk is hot, add shortening, salt, and sugar. Cool, add yeast and dissolve. Add egg, flour and seasonings. Knead, let rise to double in bulk. Mold into 2 small loaves. Put in greased pans, let rise until double. Bake in preheated 375° F oven for 40 minutes, or until done.

Yield: 2 loaves

HERB BREAD III

Mix 1 stick butter with combination of chives, thyme and parsley. Spread liberally on French bread. Heat 10 minutes at 400° F.

HERBED CHEESE BREAD

Melanie Barnard

½ cup milk, scalded
3 tablespoons sugar
2 teaspoons salt
3 tablespoons butter
2 pkgs. active dry yeast
1½ cups warm water (105-115°)
6 to 6½ cups all purpose flour
2 tablespoons melted butter
1 cup fresh chives, chopped
1 cup fresh parsley, chopped
½ cup fresh dill, minced
3 tablespoons chervil, minced
½ cup Edam cheese, shredded

Add sugar, salt, and 3 tablespoons butter to scalded milk and cool to tepid. Dissolve the yeast in the warm water in a mixer bowl. Stir in the milk mixture and 3 cups flour. Beat about 2 minutes at low speed. Stir in enough additional flour to make a stiff dough. On a lightly floured surface, knead till smooth and elastic, about 10 minutes. Place in a greased bowl, turning to grease top. Cover and let rise until doubled, 1½ hours. Punch down and let rest 10 minutes. Divide in half and roll each half to a 9x16 inch rectangle. Brush with half of melted butter. Combine herbs and cheese and sprinkle half over dough. Roll up tightly from the short side, pinching ends to seal. Repeat with other half of dough. Place in 2 greased 9 x 5 inch loaf pans. Cover and let rise in a warm place till doubled — about 1 hour. Bake 40-45 minutes at 375° F. until loaves sound hollow when tapped, or make 8 small loaves and place in greased 3 x 5 inch loaf pans. Bake about 20-25 minutes.

Yield: 2 large loaves
or 8 small loaves

"Rosemary for Remembrance"

Shakespeare

Remember:
Use triple the amount of fresh herbs to dried herbs!

HERB RYE BREAD
(1st Prize, Cincinnati Post Contest)
Jerry Natowitz

1¾ cups warm water (110°)
⅓ cup brown sugar
1 pkg. active dry yeast
¼ cup dried onion flakes
¼ cup dried parsley flakes
1 or 1½ teaspoons thyme, crushed
1 or 1½ teaspoons rosemary, crushed
¼ cup vegetable oil
1 egg
3 teaspoons salt
2 cups medium rye flour (not coarse pumpernickel rye)
3 to 3½ cups all purpose flour (hard wheat flour or bread flour is superior)
1 additional egg, beaten with 2 tablespoons milk
  (there will be excess for just 2 loaves)
2 tablespoons sesame seeds

Use 1 large baking sheet, ungreased or oiled lightly with spray product if desired.

Oven: 350° F.

Dissolve brown sugar in warm water in a large mixing bowl. Sprinkle on yeast and stir to mix. Let sit in warm, draft-free place for five minutes. Add onion and parsley flakes, crushed rosemary, thyme, oil, egg, salt and rye flour, and three cups white flour. Mix well, adding more white flour only if necessary, until dough barely sticks to sides of bowl. Turn out onto a floured surface and knead, adding additional flour only if necessary. Continue kneading and turning dough about five minutes, until dough is smooth and elastic. Expect dough to be somewhat sticky at this point, but add flour sparingly to the surface of the dough for kneading.

Place dough in clean, oiled bowl and turn to grease the top of the dough. Cover with damp towel and set in warm draft-free place until dough is almost doubled, about one hour.

Punch down, turn onto a floured surface and knead for 30 seconds. Divide dough into two equal portions and then divide each of these into three equal portions. Cover with bowl or cloth and let rest for five minutes.

Roll each piece of dough with your hands into a rope about 15 inches long. Braid three ropes to form a loaf and repeat with other three ropes. Place loaves, spaced as far apart as possible to allow for rising, on lightly oiled baking sheet. Cover lightly with damp towel or plastic wrap and let rise until nearly double, about 50 minutes.

Brush loaves with egg-milk mixture and sprinkle with sesame seeds. Bake in a preheated oven at 350° F for 30 to 40 minutes or until golden brown. Remove loaves from baking sheet and cool on a rack.

Yield: 2 braided loaves

HERB TOAST* I

*To accompany soups — it is particularly good with curried lima bean soup!

Put ½ cup (1 stick) butter, ¼ teaspoon each dried thyme, oregano, freshly ground black pepper, and minced garlic, ½ teaspoon each salt and minced shallots, and 1 teaspoon chopped parsley in a small skillet and melt over low heat; stir to mix. Trim crusts from 6 slices of day-old bread and cut into fingers. Dip both sides in the herb butter and place on baking sheet. Bake in a preheated 350° F oven until brown, turning them once — it takes about 20 minutes. Serve hot, warm or at room temperature.

Note: Use a pastry brush to brush the butter onto the bread, for less "soaking in" and better flavor.

HERB TOAST II

Pepperidge Farm thin sliced white bread
Remove crust — cut one slice into 3 portions

Melt butter and brush on both sides of bread. Preheat oven to 350° F. Sprinkle fines herbes on both sides of buttered bread. Place on cookie sheet and brown both sides.

Same with Lebanese bread. Split bread and heat in pieces.

HERBED ROLLS

¼ teaspoon nutmeg
⅛ teaspoon thyme
⅛ teaspoon sugar
⅛ teaspoon oregano

Add seasonings to flour mixture of your favorite hot roll or bread recipe and proceed as usual. Excellent addition to hot roll mix.

WHEAT GERM HERB BREAD

5½ to 6½ cups unsifted all purpose flour
2 pkgs Red Star Instant dry yeast
⅓ cup sugar
1 teaspoon salt
1 teaspoon thyme leaves, crushed
1 teaspoon marjoram leaves, crushed

1½ cups milk
½ cup water
½ cup butter or margarine
2 whole eggs
1 egg yolk
1⅓ cups wheat germ, regular or sugar and honey
1 egg white, beaten
1 tablespoon wheat germ

Oven: 350° F.

In large mixer bowl, combine 3 cups flour, yeast, sugar, salt and herbs; mix well. In saucepan, heat milk, water and butter until warm (120° to 130° F; butter does not need to melt); add to flour mixture. Add eggs and egg yolk. Blend at low speed until moistened; beat 3 minutes at medium speed. By hand, gradually stir in wheat germ and enough remaining flour to make a soft dough. Knead on floured surface until smooth and elastic, about 10 minutes. Place in greased bowl, turning to grease top. Cover; let rise in warm place until light and doubled, about 1 hour.

Punch down dough. Divide into 2 parts. Roll or pat each part on lightly floured surface to a 12 x 8 inch rectangle. Cut each rectangle into 2 equal strips. Pinch ends of each strip together to make a rope. Twist 2 ropes together; seal ends and tuck under loaf. Place in well greased 8½ x 4½ x 2⅝ inch loaf pans.* Cover; let rise 30 to 40 minutes. Lightly brush with egg white; sprinkle with 1 tablespoon wheat germ. Bake at 350° F for 35 to 45 minutes. Cover loosely with foil the last 5 to 10 minutes of baking. Remove from pans; cool.

*Two 9 x 5 x 3 inch loaf pans may be used.

Yield: 2 loaves

OATMEAL BREAD

Sister Linda — Shakertown

3 cups flour
1¼ cups quick oats
1½ tablespoons baking powder
2 teaspoons salt
1 egg
1½ cups milk
1 tablespoon melted margarine
1 teaspoon dill or marjoram
¼ cup honey

Oil 9 x 5 x 3 inch pan. Mix dry ingredients in a separate bowl. Stir in rest of ingredients until moist. Will not be smooth. Spread in pan. Bake at 350° F for 1 hour and 15 minutes. Turn out and butter top.

Yield: 1 loaf

ONION CHEESE SUPPER BREAD

½ cup onions, chopped
1 egg, beaten
½ cup milk
1½ cup biscuit mix (Bisquick)

1 cup sharp cheese, shredded
2 tablespoons snipped parsley
2 tablespoons butter, melted

Cook onions in small amount of hot fat until tender, but not brown. Combine egg and milk. Add to biscuit mix and stir until just moistened. Add onions to half the cheese and parsley. Spread dough in round greased cake pan. Sprinkle with remaining cheese and drizzle with butter. Bake in 400° F oven for 20 minutes or until pick comes out clean.

Serves 6 to 8

PARMESAN BREAD STICKS

Shakertown

10 slices firm white bread
2 sticks of butter, melted
1½ cups Parmesan cheese
Dill or other herb

Remove crusts from bread cut to make 4 fingers. Dip in melted butter. Roll in cheese. Sprinkle with desired herb. Bake at 250° F. for 1 hour. Store in tightly covered jar.

Yield 40 sticks

PULL-APART ONION ROLLS

½ cup margarine or butter
2 tablespoons instant minced onion
1 tablespoon instant beef bouillon
1 teaspoon parsley flakes
¼ teaspoon onion powder
2 cups biscuit mix (Bisquick)
½ cup cold water

Heat oven to 425° F. Mix margarine, onion, instant bouillon, parsley, and onion powder in saucepan. Heat until margarine is melted and bouillon is dissolved; cool slightly. Pour about half of the margarine mixture into round layer pan, 9 x 11½ inches; spread onions evenly in pan.

Mix baking mix and water until soft dough forms; beat vigorously 20 strokes. Drop dough by teaspoonfuls onto margarine mixture in pan; drizzle with remaining margarine mixture. Bake until golden brown, about 12 minutes. Invert pan on heatproof serving plate. Cover rolls with pan for a few minutes.

Yield: About 2 dozen

SAGE BREAD

1 pkg. dry yeast
¼ cup warm water
2 tablespoons shortening
2 tablespoons sugar
1 teaspoon salt
2 teaspoons caraway seeds
½ teaspoon nutmeg
1 teaspoon sage
2⅔ cups flour

In large bowl dissolve yeast in warm water.

Add all ingredients but flour. Mix well. Then add 2 cups flour,* mix until smooth. Cover, let rise until double. Stir down. Dough will be sticky.

Put into greased loaf pan (cover lightly). Bake at 375° F for 50 minutes until brown.

*Extra 2/3 cup of flour may be added if needed.

Yield: 1 loaf

TANSY BREAD

2 cups boiling water, potato water may be used
1 cup rolled oats
1 tablespoon butter
½ cup brown sugar
1 pkg. dry yeast
½ cup warm water
1 teaspoon salt
1 teaspoon nutmeg
1 teaspoon celery seed
2 tablespoons parsley flakes
1 pimiento, chopped fine
½ teaspoon ground sage
½ teaspoon ground marjoram
2 tablespoons dried tansy, crumbled
2 tablespoons grated cheese
4½ cups sifted flour
Butter, melted for 2 baking pans

Mix boiling water and rolled oats. Add butter and brown sugar; set aside 2 hours. Dissolve yeast in water, add to rolled oats. Add rest of ingredients; mix. Let stand until light; stir down. Butter two tins, 8¾" x 4¾" x 2¾"; allow to rise again. When doubled in size, brush with melted butter. Bake in 375° F oven for 20 minutes reduce heat to 350° F and bake until done.

Yield: 2 loaves

TOASTED GARLIC BREAD

¼ lb. butter or margarine, softened
1 4 oz. pkg. blue cheese
2 tablespoons sesame seeds
2 cloves garlic, pressed
½ teaspoon salt
1 loaf French bread

Mix together first five ingredients. Spread on slices of French bread. Broil until golden brown. Serve hot.

YOGURT-DILL BREAD

2 cups biscuit mix, Bisquick
1 carton (8 oz.) unflavored yogurt or dairy sour cream
2 tablespoons instant minced onion
1 tablespoon dill seed
Minced parsley, for garnish

Heat oven to 400° F. Grease 9 inch pie plate or square pan, 8 x 8 x 2 inches. Mix all ingredients, except parsley, until soft dough forms. Spread in plate; sprinkle with snipped parsley if desired. Bake until wooden pick inserted in center comes out clean, about 20 minutes. Cool 10 minutes; cut into wedges or squares.

Great flavor with fish.

Serves 8 to 9

SMOKED SALMON CREPES

8 warm crepes, made from your favorite recipe
1 tablespoon shallots or onion, chopped finely
1 tablespoon butter
1 tablespoon flour
1 cup light cream
¼ lb. smoked Nova Scotia salmon, diced
3 hard cooked eggs, diced
1 tablespoon capers
Salt and pepper to taste
1 tablespoon fresh dill weed, minced
1 tablespoon parsley, minced
1 to 2 tablespoons chives, minced
Dash lemon juice
2 tablespoons grated Parmesan cheese
1 tablespoon butter

Saute shallots in butter until they are transparent. Blend in flour, then cream and stir over medium heat till thickened. Mix with salmon, eggs, capers, salt and pepper, dill, parsley, chives, and lemon. Place about 2 tablespoons on each crepe and roll up. Place in a buttered shallow oven proof casserole. Sprinkle Parmesan cheese over, dot with butter and reheat in a preheated 400°F oven 15 minutes.

Serves 4

BAKED RICE

½ lb. butter or margarine
2 cups rice, uncooked, long grain
2 cups mushrooms, canned-drained (save liquid)
1 large onion, diced
2 heaping teaspoons oregano, dried
3 cans beef consomme
2 cans liquid juice of mushrooms and water

Simmer butter, uncooked rice, oregano and mushrooms 20 minutes in uncovered skillet, stirring occasionally. Place all ingredients in large casserole in 375° F oven. Bake 1½ hours covered. If mixture seems to be drying out after 1 hour add a little water or consomme to moisten.

Serves 12

GREEN NOODLES AND BASIL

16 oz. (1 lb.) spinach noodles *½ cup fresh basil leaves*
¼ lb. butter *1 cup Parmesan cheese*

Cook noodles until just done (al dente). Drain well in colander, and return to saucepan. Over low heat, add butter and stir noodles until coated. While stirring gently, add cheese and basil. Basil turns black but it does not change flavor.

Serves 8

187

HERB BARLEY CASSEROLE

3 cups water or consomme
2 teaspoons salt (use less, if using consomme)
1 tablespoon vegetable oil
1 cup pearl barley (quick kind)
½ cup minced onion
½ cup butter
2 (4 oz.) cans sliced button mushrooms, drained
⅛ teaspoon marjoram (dried)
⅛ teaspoon rosemary (dried)
1 cup cooked peas

Combine first three ingredients in 2-quart saucepan. Bring to boiling, add barley, and stir until mixture boils again. Reduce heat, cover, and simmer 20 to 30 minutes, stirring occasionally. Meanwhile, saute onion in butter until soft, but not brown. Add mushrooms and saute about 5 minutes.

Combine all ingredients.

Turn into buttered casserole and reheat before serving.

Serves 6 to 8

NOODLES WITH HERB SAUCE

Chef Gregory

Basic pasta dough:
1½ cups all purpose flour
2 large eggs
Pinch of salt

Blend in food processor. Add about 2 tablespoons cold water until a ball forms. Wrap dough in plastic wrap and let rest at least 1 hour.

Roll out dough, sprinkling lightly with flour. Let dry about 30 minutes, then cut in strips or if you have one, use a pasta machine. After cutting strips you may let them dry or cook them immediately in boiling salted water. Cook al dente:, or until just tender with a slight texture, but not soft. Drain immediately.

Sauce for noodles

1 stick butter
4 chopped green onions and tops
2 or 3 garlic cloves, according to taste
1 cup heavy cream
3 beaten egg yolks
1 dash Maggi seasoning
Salt and pepper to taste

188

2 teaspoons marjoram, fresh
2 teaspoons parsley
2 teaspoons chives, fresh
½ teaspoon thyme, dry
½ teaspoon basil, dry
2 tablespoons Romano or Parmesan cheese

Saute onions and garlic in butter until transparent. Add cream. Bring to a boil but do not boil. Add egg yolks, Maggi, salt and pepper. Add chopped herbs. When thoroughly heated, pour over noodles which have been drained, and heaped on a serving platter. Sprinkle with grated cheese.

Serves 8 to 10

PIZZA

Margy Robson

Baking pizza at home is rapidly becoming an American tradition. There are almost as many recipes for pizza as there are pizzerias. Once you've mastered the basics, let your family or friends determine the ingredients you use. Don't be bashful to add an extra layer of cheese, to embellish your pizza with your favorite vegetable, or even to add garlic or herbs to the dough.

Basic dough:

1 teaspoon salt
3½ cups flour
2 teaspoons sugar
1 pkg. active dry yeast
1 cup lukewarm water
2 tablespoons olive oil

Mix flour, sugar and salt together in a large bowl. Dissolve yeast in lukewarm water and add to flour mixture. Stir again, then add olive oil. Stir until the dough begins to form a ball in the bowl. Place the ball of dough on a lightly floured board and knead for 8-10 minutes and let rise in a warm, draft-free place until double in size. Punch down and knead again, allow to rise an additional 20 minutes Roll out dough to form a circle slightly larger than your pizza pan. Place in pan and form a rim about ¼" high around the edges with the excess dough.

Basic tomato sauce:

2 tablespoons olive oil
1 cup chopped onions
3 cups canned Italian plum tomatoes
1 small can tomato paste
¼ teaspoon garlic salt

Continued

¼ teaspoon freshly ground pepper
½ teaspoon salt
1½ teaspoons sugar
1 bay leaf
1 teaspoon oregano, or more to taste
1 teaspoon basil

Saute onions in olive oil until they become transparent. Add remaining ingredients and stir thoroughly (you may cut up the tomatoes if you like). Simmer uncovered for at least 1 hour. Remove bay leaf.

Basic ingredients for pizza
1 batch dough
1 lb. grated Mozzarella cheese
1 batch tomato sauce
½ lb. grated Parmesan or Romano cheese

Layer about 1/3 of the Mozzarella on the dough, then spread the tomato sauce evenly over the cheese. Top the sauce with embellishment of your choice. (Italian sausage, mushrooms, green peppers). Sprinkle on Romano/Parmesan. Bake in a preheated 450° F. oven for 25 minutes or until crust is golden brown.

Whatever you do, don't forget the vino and cold beer.

SISTER ROBERTA'S COLD RICE DISH

Shakertown

6 tablespoons oil
¼ cup parsley, chopped
½ cup onions, chopped
½ cup green pepper, chopped
3 cups cooked rice
3 tablespoons vinegar (white)
1 teaspoon salt (or to your taste)
1 teaspoon tarragon, minced
1 pkg. frozen peas, cooked crunchy

Saute parsley, onions, and green pepper in 1 tablespoon oil, until soft but not browned. Add rest of ingredients.

Toss all together and permit to stand overnight in the refrigerator. Other herbs are tasty such, as chive blossoms, curry powder, or basil. If a more hearty dish is desired, add cubed ham, cheese, and dill pickles.

Serves 4 to 5

Desserts, Candies, Jellies, Beverages, Teas

CARAWAY COOKIES, SOFT

1 cup butter
¾ cup sugar
1 egg
1 cup unsweetened apple juice
1 teaspoon vanilla
2 cups flour, sifted
2 teaspoons baking powder
1 teaspoon salt
1 tablespoon caraway or cumin seeds

Glaze:
Juice of half a lemon
Juice of half an orange
Powdered sugar

Preheat oven to 375° F.

Cream butter and sugar. Add egg to creamed mixture. Blend. Add apple juice. Blend. Add vanilla.

Sift flour, baking powder, and salt together. Add to creamed mixture and blend well. Add seeds last.

Drop onto greased cookie sheet and bake about 10 minutes until light brown. While still warm, glaze with a mixture of orange and lemon juice combined with enough powdered sugar to be of spreading consistency.

Yield: About 5 dozen

FROZEN MINT JULEP PIE

Fern H. Storer

There is no more consensus on the authentic Derby Pie than on the authentic Kentucky Mint Julep. You can safely bet, however, that both will be made with bourbon, Kentuckians' native libation. Derby Day hostesses cherish this pie because it is made and frozen a day ahead of serving.

CAUTION: Do not freeze longer — the filling will become rubbery and the crunchy crust, soggy. Cook the custard base of the filling in your microwave oven, - the easiest way, - or in a saucepan on conventional range, with more stirring and watching.

Crumb Crust:
½ stick butter or margarine
1⅓ cups crushed chocolate wafers, about half of a 9½-ounce package.
1 to 2 tablespoons sugar, depends on sweetness of wafers

Continued

Filling:
¼ cup sugar, additional
¼ envelope unflavored gelatin
⅛ teaspoon salt
1 cup milk or coffee cream or half and half
3 egg yolks
¼ cup bourbon
1 tablespoon green creme de menthe
3 egg whites
½ cup whipping cream
Tiny mint sprigs to garnish

Use: Nine-inch oven-glass pie plate; batter bowl, 2½ quart

Melt butter in pie plate in MICROWAVE OVEN, high, 45 seconds; mix in cookie crumbs and sugar with a fork; press evenly in pie plate to make a crust; chill in refrigerator or freezer.

In batter bowl mix ¼ cup sugar, gelatin and salt; whisk in milk with wire whip to mix well; let stand 5 minutes to soften gelatin. Meanwhile separate eggs, putting yolks in small bowl, whites in medium-size mixer bowl. Start cream chilling in bowl in which you will whip it.

Heat milk mixture in batter bowl, high, uncovered, whisking twice, until near boiling — about 5 minutes. Beat yolks with wire whisk, then rapidly whisk in about a ½ cup of hot milk mixture; when smoothly blended, whisk into rest of hot milk and cook, high, 30 seconds.

Set bowl out and immediately whisk vigorously to prevent curdling; let stand 5 minutes, whisking often. Add bourbon and creme de menthe. Set bowl in container of cold water with ice cubes to hasten cooling, stirring often. When beginning to thicken, work rapidly; if custard becomes too thick it is impossible to fold the whipped ingredients in smoothly.

Proceed in this order: beat egg whites to soft mounds, slowly add the additional ¼ cup sugar while beating at high speed to form stiff peaks; beat 2 minutes longer. Transfer beater to cream and whip stiff. Add both whipped ingredients to custard, folding gently, do not whip, with wire whisk or rubber spatula; turn into chilled crust swirling attractively.

Refrigerate until set, then freeze. When firm, cover pie with clear plastic wrap or foil. Take pie from freezer when just ready to serve — do not defrost. Garnish each serving with a pair of fresh mint leaves, or tiny tip sprigs.

To cook custard filling base on conventional range: Combine sugar, gelatin and salt in a one-quart heavy saucepan, whisking to mix; whisk in milk. Let stand 5 minutes to soften gelatin. Cook, stirring constantly, on range unit on medium-high heat until boiling, and gelatin is dissolved. Whisk some of hot milk into beaten egg yolks as directed above, then combine with rest of yolks; cook, stirring constantly, until custard is near boiling; proceed as directed above.

Serves 6 to 8

FRUIT COMPOTE

2 boxes frozen mixed fruit
1 (10 oz.) can pineapple chunks
2 bananas or any fresh fruit of your choice, sliced

Mix together:
1 teaspoon curry
½ cup brown sugar
2 teaspoons Mr. Mustard
¼ cup melted butter
1 teaspoon chopped candied ginger

Several sprigs mint, as garnish

Drain frozen fruit thoroughly after defrosting and combine with fresh fruit. Add above mixture. Bake at 325° F until heated through. Garnish with mint leaves.

This is an excellent dessert, but also a great accompaniment to Canadian bacon or ham.

Serves 4 to 6

LEMON BASIL DROP COOKIES

¼ cup butter
1 (8 oz.) pkg. cream cheese
1 egg yolk
1 teaspoon lemon juice
½ teaspoon grated lemon peel
1 box lemon cake mix
1¼ cups currants or 1 cup raisins
¼ cup shredded coconut
¼ cup chopped walnuts
1 tablespoon dried basil

Cream butter, cheese, egg yolk, and lemon juice until well blended and fluffy. Blend in cake mix, ⅓ at a time, mixing last portion by hand. Stir in remaining ingredients. Drop by level tablespoonfuls onto greased baking sheet. Bake in preheated 350° F. oven 15 to 18 minutes, or until lightly browned.

Yields 4 dozen

LEMON — CORIANDER BARS

Mrs. E. E. Lohmolder

½ cup butter
1 cup flour
¼ cup powdered sugar

Filling:
2 tablespoons lemon juice
Grated rind of 1 lemon
2 eggs, beaten
1 cup sugar
2 tablespoons flour
½ teaspoon baking powder
¾ teaspoon ground coriander seed

Combine butter, flour and sugar. Mix well. Pat into bottom of 8-inch square pan. Bake at 350° F. for 15 minutes.

Combine filling ingredients, place on baked crust. Bake at 350° F. for 25 minutes. Cool and cut into bars.

Yields: about 48

LEMON-MINT CHEESECAKE

Civic Garden Center "Herb Cookery"

1 (16 oz.) carton smooth cottage cheese
1 3⅝ oz package Lemon Instant Pudding
1 graham cracker crust for 9-inch pie pan, plus crumbs for topping
Dash of salt
Sprig lemon mint or any other mint

Mix cottage cheese and instant pudding until smooth. Add a tiny bit of salt to graham cracker crust and bake 10 minutes. Cool. Fill with cheese mixture, top with graham cracker crumbs or whipped cream. Before serving garnish with sprigs of fresh mint.

Serves 6

MINT MARINADE WITH ROSE GERANIUM

Civic Garden Center "Herb Cookery"

1 cup sugar
1 cup water or ½ water and ½ white wine
3 rose geranium leaves
2 mint sprigs

Bring sugar and water/wine to boil. Stir well to dissolve sugar. Add geranium leaves and mint. Cover. Allow herbs to marinate for 10 minutes. Remove and chill marinade for one day at least. This is excellent over fresh fruit, melon, or ice cream.

MINTED BAVARIAN

From the Book
"Across Canada with Herbs"

4 teaspoons unflavored gelatin
2 tablespoons cold water
1 cup milk
2 egg yolks

½ cup sugar
Pinch of salt
¾ cup creme de menthe
½ pint whipping cream, whipped
3 or 4 mint sprigs

Soften gelatin in cold water. Scald milk in top of double boiler, add mixture of slightly beaten egg yolks, sugar and salt. Stir until mixture thickens slightly, then fold in creme de menthe and whipped cream. Garnish with mint sprigs.

Serves 6 to 8

PEARS IN RED WINE

Chef Gregory

12 Large ripe pears, peeled, sprinkled with lemon juice. Cores should be loosened but not removed, and stems should be left on. Blossom ends of pears should be trimmed off so that pears will stand.

Sauce:
1 cup powdered or fine sugar or ⅓ cup honey
Juice of a small lemon
8 whole cloves
2-3 cinnamon sticks
35 black peppercorns
2 cups dry red wine
Mint sprigs, candied violets and strawberries for garnish

Continued

In a deep enamel or stainless steel pan, bring ingredients to the boiling point, stirring until sugar is dissolved. When dissolved, place pears with their stems up in the pan and cover. Poach 8 to 10 minutes over medium heat. Baste occasionally. Cook until just tender. Remove pears from syrup and let cool.

Strain sauce and reduce until it is a nice, bubbly syrup. If not thick enough, add 1 small tablespoon of arrowroot dissolved in a little water. Let syrup cool.

Spoon syrup over a large platter or on a bed of apricots or "into individual compotes." Stand pears on top in a ring and fill center with whipped cream. Garnish cream with mint and candied violets. Garnish outside of ring with whole fresh strawberries. Raspberry or strawberry puree may be spooned over all (optional).

Peaches, apples, strawberries, or sliced oranges may be substituted for pears. Stones may be left in peaches. Sauce should be poured over them while it is still warm. If using strawberries, cool sauce before pouring over fruit.

Serves 12

ROSE GERANIUM ROLLS

½ cup melted butter
1 cup sugar
½ cup orange honey
18 rose geranium leaves, finely minced
2 orange rinds, grated

Use basic dough recipe for rolls. After it rises, roll into a rectangle until it is about 2 inches thick. Brush with butter and spread on above ingredients. Roll crosswise. Cut in 1 inch slices and place in greased muffin tins. Let rise according to instructions. Bake 15-20 minutes at 375° F.

SEED CAKE

To your favorite pound cake recipe (or package mix for hurry-up cookies) add:

¼ teaspoon anise seeds
⅛ teaspoon caraway seeds
⅛ teaspoon cardamom granules (removed from cardamom seeds)
¼ teaspoon whole coriander
⅛ teaspoon lemon rind

Mix and bake as usual.

SEED COOKIES

2 cups sifted flour
1 teaspoon salt
1 teaspoon baking powder
1 cup whole wheat flour
⅓ cup sugar
1 cup shortening
6 to 7 tablespoons water

Topping:
1 teaspoon anise seeds
½ teaspoon caraway seeds
1 teaspoon coriander seeds
½ teaspoon shelled cardamom seeds
¼ cup sugar, approximately

Sift flour, baking powder, and salt together. Add whole wheat flour and mix. Cream shortening and sugar. Add dry ingredients and mix with pastry blender. Sprinkle water over mixture, tossing lightly until, mixture is moist enough to hold together. Roll out to ⅛" thickness. Cut into leaf shapes or circles. Place on greased baking sheet. Sprinkle with topping and press lightly to make it stay on top of cookie.

Topping:
Grind in a mortar, anise seeds, caraway seeds, coriander seeds, shelled cardamom seeds, until very fine. Add about ¼ cup sugar. Bake at 350° F for 15 to 18 minutes. Remove from sheet immediately. They improve with age and freeze well.

Yield: about 5 dozen

SHAKER HERB COOKIES

Shakertown

½ cup shortening, butter, or chicken fat

½ cup sugar	*2 tablespoons ground ginger*
½ cup molasses	*1 teaspoon ground cinnamon*
1 egg, unbeaten	*1 teaspoon powdered cloves*
2½ cups sifted flour	*6 tablespoons hot water*
¼ teaspoon salt	*2 tablespoons anise seeds*
½ teaspoon baking powder	*1 tablespoon coriander seeds*

Cream shortening, sugar, and molasses. Stir in egg. Sift dry ingredients together, except seeds. Soften anise and coriander seeds in hot water and crush. Add dry ingredients and hot water with crushed seeds alternately to creamed mixture. Drop on greased baking sheet about 2" apart. Bake in 350° F oven for about 10 minutes or until light brown.

Yield: about 4 dozen

SWEET CICELY COFFEE CAKE

2 cups sweet biscuit dough
1½ cups almond paste
1 (10½ oz.) can crushed pineapple
2 tablespoons flour
¾ cup sugar
4 sweet cicely leaves, chopped

Roll out biscuit dough until about ½ inch thick and oblong in shape. Spread almond paste and crushed pineapple in layers. Sprinkle with 2 tablespoons flour and ¾ cup of sugar. Top with sweet cicely leaves. Fold both sides over filling. Press seams to seal. Sprinkle top with sugar. Bake on lightly buttered and floured cookie sheet for 30 minutes at 350° F.

TANSY COOKIES

Shakertown

2½ cups flour
1 teaspoon baking powder
½ teaspoon salt
½ cup shortening
½ teaspoon baking soda

1 cup sugar
2 eggs
1 teaspoon vanilla
1½ teaspoons tansy, minced
1 tablespoon milk
Tansy for topping

Cream sugar and shortening, add eggs, then rest of ingredients. Beat until well blended. Roll out to ⅛-inch thickness on floured board. Cut with cookie cutter. Sprinkle cookies with more tansy and bake at 400° F for 10 minutes.

Yield: About 5 dozen

CANDIED BORAGE STARS

Shakertown

Pick flowers when they have fully opened. Brush with egg whites beaten just enough so that it can be applied easily (use a small brush). Dust with sifted granulated sugar and spread on waxed paper to dry in a cool place. Store in air-tight cans with waxed paper between layers. Mint leaves, rose petals, and violets may be candied the same way.

CANDIED MINT LEAVES OR VIOLETS

With fork, beat until frothy 1 egg white and 1 tablespoon orange juice. With small paint brush, paint violets or leaves with mixture. Then spoon superfine sugar over them, covering all sides. Use small dish in which you keep adding more dry unlumpy sugar. Lay violets or mint leaves on waxed paper and move often enough to keep from sticking to paper. Dry completely for a few days and then store in sealed can.

HERB INFUSION FOR JELLIES

4 tablespoons dried
or
8 tablespoons fresh herbs of your choice

Simmer with 1 cup of water 10 minutes. Strain through cloth-lined strainer.

HERB JELLY

Virginia Larson

1 cup fresh herb leaves (rosemary, tarragon, or mint)
1½ cups boiling water
5 cups sugar
1 cup cider vinegar
8 ounces pectin
A few drops green food coloring
Paraffin — melted

Cover fresh herb leaves with 1½ cups boiling water. Add sugar and cider vinegar. Boil for 10 minutes, stirring to dissolve sugar. Strain through a fine sieve or cheesecloth. Add 8 ounces pectin and a few drops green food coloring. Pour into sterile hot glasses. Seal with melted paraffin, while hot.

Yield: about 3 pints

HERB APPLE JELLY

Shakertown

Place the herb of your choice in the bottom of the glass and pour in the apple jelly. Some favorite choices are; angelica, apple mint, basil, costmary, lavender, lemon verbena, spearmint, rose geranium, or rose petals. Quince and apple makes an excellent combination — use equal parts.

ROSE GERANIUM JELLY

Daisy N. Sticksel

Use any basic recipe for apple or rhubarb jelly. Three minutes before the product is ready to pour into the glasses, drop the leaves of rose geranium into the boiling jelly. The fragrant scent of these leaves will be diffused into the jelly giving it a delightful new flavor.

Beverages

HERB TOMATO JUICE

1 peck unpeeled tomatoes
3 sweet peppers
1 handful each celery, parsley leaves, onions to taste
1 sprig each: basil, thyme, savory, marjoram, fresh or 1 teaspoon each, dried

Stew all but herbs until done. Put through strainer. Bring to boil and add one sprig each of fresh cut basil, thyme, savory and marjoram (or 1 teaspoon each dried). Add salt and pepper to taste. Slow boil 10 minutes and put in hot sterilized jars. Take out herb sprigs as you finish. Serve cold with lemon wedge.

MAY WINE (Maibowle)

Shakertown

5 bunches sweet woodruff (Waldmeister)   *1 bottle Moselle or Chablis*
¾ cups fine sugar   *4 Additional bottles of wine*
1 cup brandy

Place sweet woodruff in a half gallon, wide mouth, glass jar. Sprinkle sugar on top; let set one hour. Add brandy and one bottle of wine. Cover and let stand overnight in a cool place. Strain. Add 4 additional bottles of wine. Chill. Served in champagne glasses.

Variation: To make a punch, add only 3 bottles of wine. Blend in 2 bottles of champagne. Float slices of orange, pineapple and fresh strawberries on top.

MINT JULEP #1

A good julep takes time, care, 100 proof bourbon whiskey and mint.

Here's how to make them individually. The best are made in silver julep cups but glasses may be substituted.

1 teaspoon powdered sugar
2 teaspoons water
Several spearmint leaves
Finely chopped ice, pulverized
100 proof Kentucky bourbon
Fresh mint sprigs for garnish

Dissolve sugar in water in silver cup or glass. Muddle spearmint leaves into sugar, water mixture. Pack cup tightly to the top with pulverized ice. Fill with bourbon. Stick a sprig of mint on top. Add a straw or just let your guests bury their nose in that fragrant mint.

Caution:
They should be sipped and one should move about while sipping. They are so good you may find your guests partaking of more than one.

MINT JULEP II

Jump-Ahead of the DerbyJulep

hot simple syrup made of 1 part water to 1 part sugar.
spearmint leaves, preferably, or pappermint
Crushed ice
100 proof bourbon whiskey
Fresh mint for garnish

Muddle or crush the mint leaves, the amount depending upon the type and the fragrance. Add to the hot syrup and let syrup cool. Strain mint leaves out of syrup.

When ready to serve, fill silver julep cups or glasses tightly with crushed ice to the top. Pour one jigger of mint syrup mixture over the ice and about 2 jiggers of whiskey.

Garnish with a sprig of fresh mint. Add a short straw.

Hint: If cups are not packed tightly with pulverized ice, frost will not form on the outside of the julep cup.

MINT LEMONADE CONCENTRATE

2 cups sugar
2½ cups water
Juice of 2 oranges
Juice of 6 lemons
Grated peel of 1 orange
1 cup mint leaves, chopped

Boil sugar and water for 5 minutes, cool. Add juices and orange peel. Pour over mint leaves. Cover and let stand for at least 1 hour. Strain into jar and refrigerate.

To Serve: Use about ½ cup concentrate in a 6 to 8 ounce glass. Fill with crushed ice and water. Add vodka, gin, or rum, if desired.

PINEAPPLE COMFREY DRINK

Rosella Mathieu
"Complete Herb Guide"

8 ounces unsweetened pineapple juice
3 young, tender comfrey leaves

Whirl in blender till well blended

Hint: For a tasty and nourishing breakfast drink, try combining comfrey with apple, orange, tomato, or mixed fruit juice.

ROSEMARY FRUIT PUNCH

Shakertown

1 large can pineapple juice
2½ teaspoons dried rosemary leaves or 5 teaspoons fresh
½ cup sugar — optional
1½ cups lemon juice
2 cups water
Fresh lemon slices and rosemary leaves
1 large bottle pale dry gingerale

Bring to a boil 1 cup pineapple juice and rosemary. Remove from heat, simmer 5 minutes, strain, and cool. Add all other ingredients except the gingerale. Pour into a punch bowl over ice and add gingerale just before serving. Float fresh lemon slices and rosemary leaves in bowl.

HERBADE

Shakertown

½ cup lemon balm, cut fine
½ cup mint, cut fine
½ cup regular sugar syrup or honey
½ cup lemon juice
½ cup orange juice

Combine and let stand one hour. Add 4 quarts of gingerale.

ZEBROVKA

Version 1
Into a quart bottle of Vodka put about 6 blades of buffalo grass. Let steep for at least 2 weeks and, voila, you have a delicious "Russian" liqueur. Chill before serving "neat".

Version 2 (Aphrodisia)
1 Qt. Vodka, pinch of salt, 1 tsp. glycerine, ½ teaspoon lemon peel, 5 or 6 blades of "buffalo grass".

Combine all ingredients, store in a dark place for 2 weeks. Chill and drink or serve over lemon sherbet.

HERB TEAS

Prepare in the same way as other teas but steep a little longer. Make with either fresh or dried herbs, with or without the flowers. Or add a leaf or sprig or two to your other teas. A delicious addition for 1 cup of tea is a rose geranium leaf or several lemon verbena or mint leaves placed in the cup.

Do not serve cream or milk with herb teas. A drop or two of honey, however, enhances herb teas. Lemon may be added.

Among herbs that can be used for tea are lemon balm, lemon thyme, sage, lavender, marjoram, catnip, basil, horehound, hyssop, rosemary, burnet, comfrey, costmary, lovage, oregano, parsley, southernwood, and woodruff. Teas are also made from borage, calendula, chamomile and red clover blossoms as well as from rose petals and rose hips.

Sassafras tea is made from the bark of roots, ginger tea from the roots of wild ginger. Teas are also made from anise, caraway, dill, fennel and fenugreek seeds.

To make herb teas, use approximately 1 teaspoon of dried herbs or approximately 1 tablespoon of fresh herbs to 2 cups of water. Proportions vary according to personal tastes and strength of herb used.

HERB TEA

Shakertown

Brew a pot of hot Orange Pekoe tea, steep according to directions on box. Pour one cup hot tea into a cup containing a single rose geranium leaf or several mint leaves. Cream or milk are not served with herb teas. Add only a drop or two of honey or lemon if desired.

HERB TEA MIX

Shakertown

This tea may be served with fresh lemon or orange. Try it unsweetened to enjoy the true taste of herbs. If you want to sweeten, use honey or rock candy.

Combine equal parts of the following dried herbs: mint (spearmint, orange mint, or apple mint), chamomile, and rosemary. Use 1 teaspoon of the herb mixture to 1 cup of boiling water. Steep for 10 minutes and serve.

SAGE TEA

Shakertown

Steep 1 teaspoon dried sage in 1 cup of boiling water for 10 minutes and serve.

Sweeten tea with honey or maple syrup. Very good for the throat.

GROW YOUR OWN HERBS AND MAKE YOUR OWN TEA

Lee Cain

Have you ever thought about raising your own tea?

Does that commercial package of herb tea or no-tea represent the ultimate flavor for its kind of brew?

Is the mint tea from the market shelf the same brew that you remembered drinking at your grandmother's home?

Just because it is a commercial product does not mean that the producer knows the proper or accepted way to make tea. For instance, I recently purchased a package of sassafras tea. When I opened it, I found dried leaves. Perhaps I had been mistaken, maybe you can make sassafras tea out of sassafras leaves. I wasn't mistaken. The brew made from steeping the dried leaves was terrible. It bore no resemblance to the sassafras brew made by long-steeping the bark from sassafras roots.

Mint tea made from fresh mint leaves is different from the brew made from dried mint leaves. Peppermint is unlike spearmint and applemint tastes different from pineapple or orange mint.

The mint clan is variable both in flavor and growing habits so the teas made from mint can range from a pale green nippy brew to a dark green pungent beverage even though the tea is steeped in the same way each time.

Most kinds of mint are very easy to raise. In fact, some are downright invasive and should be planted in a container such as a bottomless pail or upright clay tile so the rampant habit can be controlled.

Pineapple and golden spearmint seem to be the exceptions to the rule. The pineapple with its lovely green and white varigation is apt to die out unless it is carefully tended and the golden spearmint succumbs if it must compete with other plants.

Balm is another tea favorite but, again, there are two distinct types.

Lemon balm is as delightful in the garden as in the tea pot. It is an easy to raise perennial which is refined in habit of growth as well as appearance.

One of the most aromatic herbs, it can be dried for potpourri, flavoring for stuffings and sandwich spreads, or used alone, or in combination with other herbs for a delicious tea.

The other balm is bee balm, or Oswego tea monarda. This is a much more rank growing plant and the flavor which it imparts is more heady than lemon balm.

One note of caution about using bee balm: Always immerse the flowers in water for a few minutes whether you are using them for drying or flower design. There is a small insect, the earwig, that hides out in the cozy corollas of the flowers.

Continued

Bee balm is an excellent perennial for those areas where poor drainage creates a boggy condition. There are several named varieties that range in color from white to bright red. This is a plant that is continually aflutter with bees and butterflies when it is in bloom.

There are several plants that are commonly referred to as chamomile but the daisy-flowered Anthemis nobilis seems to be the time-honored species that we used in the bathtub to soothe and relax, in the wine or liquor to relieve pain, or in the tea cup to produce a pale tea.

In the garden, the low-growing plant with its finely-cut "ferny" leaves is a super ground cover for that sunny spot. It tolerates being walked on and is a pretty cover for the garden path which is used only occasionally.

Herb teas are fun to make and to use. You can choose your favorite flavor or combine teas either in the cannister or in the pot.

Dried and stored separately, the leaves or flowers can be used in many ways but if you have a small herb garden or even an herb barrel, you can combine a few leaves of each type as they are available.

A delightful herb tea can be made by combining two fresh or four dried chamomile flowers, one fresh or two dried peppermint leaves, two fresh or dried (small) lemon balm leaves and one whole clove.

Pour one cup of very hot (not quite boiling) water over the mixture, cover the container and allow it to steep in a warm place for about 10 minutes.

Most herb teas as well as sassafras tea should be steeped longer than traditional tea. Ten minutes to a half hour usually allows flavors to develop. Never boil the brew.

Herb teas have character all of their own. You can mix and match to suit yourself. You can add fresh lemon to the brew, dried lemon or orange peel to the mix, cloves, cinnamon or nutmeg to the brew. They may be served piping hot or over ice cubes. They cost next to nothing and they will not keep you awake at night. I rest my case.

Lee Cain is garden writer for The Cincinnati Post. This article appeared in The Post in June, 1979. She has shared her gardening expertise with Cincinnatians for many years.

METHODS OF PRESERVING HERBS
Marge Haller

Generally it is best to use dried or frozen herbs within one year from date of preservation.

A. DRYING (sage, mint, oregano, savory, basil, lemon balm, thyme, marjoram, chives, parsley, rosemary):

Harvest in quantity just before flowers have opened. Wash and dry or hose off day before harvesting. Harvest before noon after dew has dried, but before sun is hot.

1. Hanging:

   Hang by stems upside down in small bunches in a dark, dry, airy room. May hang inside brown paper bag, with holes punched in sides, to keep herbs from getting dusty. Strip leaves from stems when dry and store in airtight container out of light.

2. Tray drying, oven drying, or microwave drying:

   Large herb leaves, such as sage, basil, and mint, will dry more quickly if picked from stems first.

   a. To tray dry, spread leaves out in a single layer on a screen mesh or cheesecloth-lined box. Turn leaves over every few days until dry.

   b. Dry in slow oven on cookie sheets with door ajar.

   c. Microwave* on high setting with herbs placed between paper towels. Dry a few sprigs at a time for 2 to 4 minutes, turning over in middle of each drying cycle. Repeat, if needed, until herbs are crisp.

      * Some microwave ovens require 1 cup of water placed in rear of oven while drying herbs. Check your microwave instruction book.

3. Drying herb seeds (coriander, cumin, caraway, dill, fennel):

   Cut stems with seed heads when seeds are ripe, before they begin to drop from the heads. Turn stems upside down in a paper bag and hang in a dry room for a few days. Then shake bag so that seeds fall to bottom. Spread out, remove chaff, and put seeds in an airtight jar, labeled with name and date.

B. FREEZING (basil, chervil, chives, dill, parsley, tarragon, fennel):

Herbs that freeze will retain their fresh flavor and are fine for cooking but cannot be used as garnishes because they will wilt when thawed. Harvest at same time as for drying.

1. Put sprigs of clean, dry herbs in a small plastic bag and close tightly with a twister. Label.

2. Put small bags inside a large plastic bag or other container.

   a. It is convenient to freeze amount of herbs to be used in an individual recipe in a small bag.

    b.   Compatible herbs, to be used in any one recipe, may be frozen in same bag. Example: tarragon, chervil, chives, parsley.

C.   SALT CURING (basil, burnet, dill, fennel, parsley):

These may be packed in salt. Wash and drain, remove leaves from stems. Place in alternate layers with table salt in a container, beginning and ending with salt. Fill container to top and cover with an airtight lid. Store in a cool, dark place. Rinse before using.

D.   PACKING IN VINEGAR:

Leafy herbs, such as tarragon, may be packed into jars and covered with vinegar.

Salad burnet, the cucumber-flavored fern-like leaf makes a stunning garnish on almost anything. Particularly good with cold salmon.

Put bay laurel leaves on the buffet table for after graduation celebration. The word baccalaureate is derived from the name of this herb, as is poet laureate.

Put slivers of garlic wrapped in mint leaves in lamb roast. Make gash and insert.

Try fennel or dill on a buttered English muffin and broil.

Season dumplings with your favorite herbs, e.g. for beef — thyme and marjoram, for chicken — tarragon or rosemary.

For a cool summer treat:

Add chopped celery, thyme or marjoram to jellied beef bouillon with a drop of sour cream on top, but for madrilene, use basil and for chicken consomme, use tarragon. Serve in individual bowls.

Slice cantaloupe, casaba, honey-dew or other melon in individual portions, leaving on the skin. With a toothpick, anchor a small cluster of seedless green grapes together with a sprig of mint and place at end of melon.

Cut a quarter off of an orange, scoop out the middle. This can be used for making your own sherbet or ice or eaten, as is.

Fill the orange cup with orange, lemon or lime sherbet. Freeze. Take out of freezer about 20 minutes before serving time. Garnish top with a sprig of mint or borage flowers, if you have them.

Orange shells can be rinsed, frozen and reused.

In a bowl, place attractively the fruit of your choice, melon, berries, etc. or in winter, canned fruit may be used.

Use clusters of green grapes, Catawbas or black, arranged around bowl. Garnish with mint leaves and sprigs of mint. Varigated mint is especially attractive on this dish. A dash of liqueur or white wine adds flavor.

Fines Herbes Blends

For ground beef mixture: 1 tablespoon each summer savory, basil, marjoram, thyme, parsley, lovage or celery leaves.

For vegetables: 1 tablespoon each summer savory, majoram, basil, chervil.

Continued

For pork dishes: 1 tablespoon each sage, basil, summer savory.

For lamb and veal dishes: 1 tablespoon each marjoram, summer savory, rosemary.

For egg and chicken dishes: 1 tablespoon each summer savory, tarragon, chervil, basil, chives.

For poultry stuffing: 1 tablespoon each summer savory, marjoram, basil, thyme, parsley, celery or lovage leaves; 1 teaspoon ground dried lemon peel; 1 teaspoon sage may be added.

For vegetable cocktails: (for 1 pint liquid) ½ teaspoon each marjoram, basil, tarragon, thyme, summer savory; 1 tablespoon chopped chives.

For fish: (2 cups liquid) ¼ teaspoon each marjoram, thyme, basil, sage, crushed seeds of fennel.

For soups and stews: (2 quarts liquid) 1 teaspoon each parsley or chervil, thyme or summer savory, basil, marjoram, celery or lovage leaves; ½ teaspoon each sage, rosemary, dried ground lemon peel.

MORE HERBAL HINTS AND GLAMOROUS GARNISHES

Try substituting fresh dill weed for basil in pesto sauce. This is especially good on shrimp.

Flavor granulated sugar with any of the sweet herbs and use in iced drinks, icings, cookies, or with fruit. Herbs excellent for this purpose are, rose geranium leaves, mints, or lemon verbena. Add a few leaves to a pint of sugar and screw lid on tightly. Use powdered sugar, flavored with rose geranium leaves to make a thin white icing for cakes.

Parsley is a versatile herb — always attractive for a garnish, full of vitamin C and a great breath purifier. Munch on a few leaves and garlic, cigarette odor, etc. will disappear.

To improve the flavor of dishes containing herbs and spices cooked in a microwave, add more than you would for conventional cooking. The short cooking times do not allow sufficient time to release the flavors of the herbs and spices so you can compensate by adding more.

Saute a little thyme in butter to brush on fresh corn on the cob.

Use fresh sage on pork chops (one leaf to each chop.)

Rosemary may be used with chicken, swiss steak or a little, cut up fine, in potato salad.

Try using chives, parsley or dill weed on baked potatoes with sour cream and a little lemon juice.

Mint can be used in green peas, pea soup and fruit cups.

Oregano is an essential in Italian dishes such as pizza and spaghetti.

Tarragon adds that extra zip to fish, fowl and wild game.

Pesto sauce is excellent over spaghetti squash.

Season scrambled eggs with herb salts.

Verbena is a pleasant and different garnish.

Three ways to add fresh herbs to salads:

a) Cut fresh leaves of such herbs as dill, salad burnet, parsley, fennel, basil, directly into the salad greens.

b) Make a paste of garlic, salt, pepper, mustard (Dijon or dry), and mince fresh herbs with a mortar and pestle. Beat in vinegar and oil.

c) Use herb vinegar

Chopped fresh basil, combined with chopped parsley and minced chives or shallots, makes a delicious topping for sliced home-grown tomatoes. Tomatoes are then dressed with a good vinaigrette or a good wine vinegar.

A simple sauce made with either fennel or dill is delicious on poached or broiled fish. Add to ½ cup butter, melted and slightly cooled, ¼ cup finely chopped fennel or dill leaves, 1 tablespoon lemon juice, salt and freshly ground black pepper to taste.

Add freshly chopped mint to hollandaise sauce to be served with lamb.

Branches of some herbs, such as rosemary, thyme, savory thrown on hot coals at end of barcecuing, will add marvelous flavor to the food.

Give roast chicken a delicious flavor by putting sprigs of herbs, such as tarragon, rosemary, basil, thyme, parsley, bay leaves or compatible combinations of these, into cavity of chicken before roasting. Alternative way is to make a thick herb butter and work it under the chicken skin.

Add a favorite herb to your crepe batter, e.g. dill for chicken, shrimp or scallops.

Tomatoes, slices — scatter blue borage flowers over.

Tomato baskets — fill with parsley or herb bouquet of edible herbs, such as parsley, common and lemon thyme, marjoram, salad burnet, oregano, borage, sage, rosemary.

Tomato towers — slice a large tomato in thirds, and, using broad end for base, layer crab, shrimp, tuna, or chicken salad between tomato slices. Put together with a long toothpick and place a yellow calendula or a spray of borage with flowers on top to hide pick.

Tomato cups — cut small tomatoes in half and scoop out. Fill with a fish, chicken, or marinated vegetable salad; decorate top with criss-cross strips of pimiento, tiny olives, and parsley, or salad burnet sprigs.

Large mushrooms or artichoke bottoms may be used in place of tomatoes.

Cucumber cups — score cucumbers, cut in slices about 1" thick, let drain on paper towels in refrigerator overnight. Spread a boursin cheese or a cream cheese mixed with chopped salad burnet, chives, and parsley, adding a little horseradish if desired, over top of cucumber, mounding in the center. Criss-cross thin strips of Nova Scotia salmon over cheese and garnish with a sprig of salad burnet or parsley. (May use pimiento instead of salmon.)

Lemons — make zig-zag cuts all around middle of lemon, twist apart, and dip points in parsley and paprika.

Fill hollowed-out lemon halves with cranberry sauce and garnish with a sprig of mint or borage flowers, lemon balm or lemon verbena.

Fruit platters — garnish with any of the following: mint leaves, lemon balm, lemon verbena, pineapple sage, scented geranium leaves, borage.

Desserts, such as ices, ice creams, cold souffles — pipe a rosette of whipped cream over top, and put a sprig of fresh mint or candied mint leaves and fresh or candied violets or borage or rose petals in whipped cream; add a fresh strawberry or a few fresh raspberries if desired.

Applesauce — garnish with a few apple-scented geranium leaves.

Tube cake — glaze with a chocolate or white icing. Fill center with fresh strawberries, marinated if desired in a little liqueur, and just before serving, press three or four sprigs of fraises des boises (tiny strawberries) leaves around sides of cakes and one on top, next to strawberries.

Green vegetables — garnish with opal basil.

Vegetable platters — garnish with green or opal basil and borage flowers.

Fish — cold fish platters masked with mayonnaise — garnish with sprigs of dill, fennel or tarragon, and cherry tomatoes or tomato wedges.

HERBAL HINTS AND GLAMOROUS GARNISHES

Cold cucumber soup — garnish with a few salad burnet leaves

Garnish a turkey platter with large bunches of sage leaves, common, tri-color, bi-color, or purple.

Poached eggs in aspic — garnish with tarragon leaves.

Radishes — push a skewer through the top of a radish and insert a sprig of parsley.

Salads — add nasturtium leaves and flowers, chive flowers, or violets or calendula flowers, for color, flavor, and vitamins.

Chicken chaud-froid (chicken glazed with a white aspic) — decorate top of each piece of glazed chicken with a variety of herbs combined with other foods to make flowers. Use blanched leeks, chives, or scallions for stems; tarragon, chervil, parsley, or salad burnet for leaves. Use tomato skins, pimiento, black olives, capers, hard-cooked eggs, etc. for flowers.

Garnish a roast chicken platter with sprigs of tarragon.

Garnish a crown roast of lamb with sprays of blooming rosemary.

Garnish a May wine bowl with sprigs of sweet woodruff, myrtle flowers and strawberries.

Use herbs in an ice ring for punch. (can be combined with fruit).

Before making herb tea always warm the pot and use boiling water.

Marinate lamb in oil, wine and rosemary.

Caraway is an herb, but the seeds are a spice.

Tarragon gets bitter and tough when boiled.

Try mint or tarragon, instead of parsley, over new potatoes.

Herbs have no calories.

Use marigold, calendula or nasturium petals for color.

Float a nasturtium leaf or flower on cold soup for added color and a different taste treat.

Sweet woodruff in cold cider.

Mint leaves in fruit salad.

Scatter potpourri on the floor and vacuum for a delightful fragrance.

Tuck potpourri sachets in your chairs and suitcases.

To prolong the life of dried herbs, keep in a cool dark place.

Winter and summer savory go especially well with green beans.

DECORATING WITH HERBS THROUGHOUT THE YEAR
Rosemarie Culver

An herb garden can be utilized indoors every month of the year. As any herbalist knows, growing and cooking with herbs are but two facets of the delights of herb gardening.

Decorating with herbs can be as simple as placing bottles of herb vinegars on a windowsill, or as complicated as creating an herbal Christmas tree.

The harvest can be enjoyed year round.

JANUARY — POMANDERS

A bowl of pomanders is a lovely sight as well as a pleasing fragrance in the house.

Pomanders are made of whole citrus fruits studded with cloves. Insert cloves in rows around the fruit. After covering the fruit, roll the pomander in a mixture of your favorite spices and orris root.

The finished pomanders may remain in the spice mixture in an open bowl until dry. After drying, they may be trimmed with sprigs of dried herbs and tied with a ribbon.

Try making some with kumquats and attach to a ribbon in groups of three. Cinnamon sticks or dried flowers may be added.

FEBRUARY — POTPOURRI CRAFTS

A potpourri is a blend of herbs, buds, and petals of flowers. Add essential oils and spices to reinforce the fragrance. Recipes are varied and may be found in many herb books, including this one.

There are many beautiful ways to use potpourri. A lovely bowl brimming to the top with your favorite mixture is a pleasing sight on a table. Scatter whole flowers over the top as a final touch. At Christmas time, place it in the center of an herb wreath. Old china pieces picked up at antique shops make lovely containers. Fill a basket or glass jar and trim it with a sprig of herbs and ribbon.

Herb, sachet pillows scattered around the house give a warm and aromatic touch. Colors and shapes may be changed according to the decor or the season.

For Valentine's Day, sew a heart-shaped pillow and enclose in it a small cotton muslin or linen bag of your favorite mixture. Make sure your fabric is tightly woven to prevent leakage. Save your Valentine's Day candy box and use it as a container for potpourri. When mailing valentines, enclose a bit in the envelope. Make a heart-shaped potholder and add a linen bag of spicy cinnamon mixture to the filler. It makes for a delightful kitchen smell.

Stuffed dolls and animals with potpourri in the filler make lovely gifts.

MARCH — PRESSED HERB PICTURE

Herbs can easily be pressed in an old telephone book between pieces of paper towel. The small flowers can be pressed whole. Separate the petals of larger ones. Lamb's ears, thyme, rosemary, violets, and lady's mantle are but a few that are suitable for pressing. Press plant material all spring and summer and put aside to use on a rainy day.

To make a picture, select a background of linen, velvet, or an attractive heavy paper, cut to fit your frame. Glue this to a heavy backing of cardboard. Arrange the pressed herbs on your fabric. Carefully glue the herbs onto your background. A milk-based glue should be used.

An antique frame can be charming. Oval frames from a variety store will give you more depth.

You may prefer to press the entire plant and frame a variety of herbs to be used as a grouping. You can also place your picture on a small easel on a table, where it can be easily changed.

APRIL — HERB-RELATED PRODUCTS

For a fresh outlook for spring, add a few new herb touches. There are many herb-related products on the market. Fabrics, dish towels, and paper towels are printed in herb designs. Herb prints, too, are available to be framed. China and pottery are decorated with herb designs.

Spruce up the bathroom with bowls of lavender and herb soaps.

Herb-scented candles can be made or bought. If making your own, simply add essential oils or stir crushed leaves into the paraffin.

Burn herb-scented incense to give your house a pleasing fragrance.

MAY — GARDENING IN CONTAINERS

Plan on growing some of your herbs in pots. They can be carried into the house and set in a basket or crock to fill a corner or to add a touch of color. Try putting some in hanging pots to hang over your kitchen sink. Wire chickens make delightful planters. Cover the complete form with sphagnum moss; then add soil and the plant.

A small strawberry jar filled with parsley is delightful to bring in on occasion to grace your kitchen work table.

Woody-stemmed oregano or rosemary can be trained to grow as a bonsai. Rosemary prostrata or myrtus communis can be shaped and pruned to grow around a wire form or into a topiary.

JUNE — HERB TERRARIUM

Herb plants are amenable to growing in a terrarium. A rectangular fish tank works especially well. Plants seem to grow better when left in the pots rather than when set directly in the soil.

Cover the tank bottom with perlite, then with decorative pebbles, arrange small pots of decorative herbs on the pebbles.

Artemisia, rosemary, lemon verbena, and a variety of thymes may be used. You may want to experiment with others.

More perlite or sphagnum moss may be added to hide the pots, if desired.

Cover the terrarium with a pane of glass or a sheet of clear plastic. Adequate light is essential, but do not place in direct sun, unless the terrarium is first uncovered. Artificial light may be used.

JULY — TUSSIE MUSSIES

A tussie mussie is a nosegay of fresh or dried herbs. Tussie mussies are carried for their scent and also used to send a message. Each herb or flower has its own interpretation. Books are available on the language of flowers.

Assemble a variety of herbs and flowers. Select a small flower, usually a rosebud, and surround it with a circle of thyme, rosemary, or any sweet smelling herb. A bit of baby's-breath adds a lovely touch, as do the silver leaves of artemisia. Add sprigs of herbs until you reach the desired size.

Tie the bunch with thread or wrap with florist's tape. Cut a hole in a paper doily and pull over the stems to surround the herbs. A bit of ribbon adds a finishing touch.

These may be used at individual places for a dinner party, shower, or luncheon, and they make lovely gifts. They are also stunning underneath a glass dome to be used as a centerpiece.

AUGUST — FRESH ARRANGEMENTS OF HERBS

An artistic arrangement using only herbs makes a lovely centerpiece. A pair of beribboned scissors placed nearby invites the guest to snip a few sprigs to accompany the meal.

Arrange your culinary herbs according to color, height, and texture. Calendula, nasturtiums, and borage flowers add a bit of color and may entice your guests into sprinkling a few petals on a salad.

SEPTEMBER — DISPLAYING THE HARVEST

September is harvest month. There is nothing as pleasing as seeing bundles of fresh herbs hanging in the kitchen. Simply tie a handful of fresh herbs and hang them upside down from a cuphook screwed into the ceiling. Hang away from direct sunlight and where air can circulate around them freely. Strands of red peppers and braided onions and garlic may also be hung.

Arrange your herb vinegar bottles on the kitchen windowsill so that the light shines through them. Attractive jars of jellies with personal labels may be covered with gingham. Store your herb teas in colorful containers. Your kitchen will take on an herbal air.

Dried flowers and herbs make lovely arrangements. Flowers, seedheads, and foliage may all be dried and incorporated into your design. Drying may be done by hanging or by using commercial drying mediums.

Freshly picked lavender may be tied into bundles. Pick lavender with long stems, arrange the heads evenly, and bind together with thread. Next, bend the stalks back and bring them over the flower heads. Weave satin ribbon through the stalks and finish with a bow. These are great for drawer sachets or for gracing a table.

OCTOBER — HERBS FOR HALLOWEEN

For a pleasing centerpiece for October, scoop out a pumpkin and insert a glass of water. Fill with a handful of fresh sage.

A large tureen of hot mulled cider with slices of floating, clove-studded oranges is very decorative. For added interest, set the tureen in the middle of an herb wreath covered with orange-colored rose hips.

Give a gift of a gallon of cider with your recipe and all the necessary spices attached to the handle. Sprigs of herbs and a colorful ribbon add a charming touch. It is as tasteful to observe as to imbibe.

NOVEMBER — HERB WREATHS

Two favorite herb wreaths are the bay and artemisia.

The artemisia is best made up when it is fresh and pliable. Use a wire wreath frame and encircle it with the artemisia. Attach with number 24 or 26 silver wire. After making a full base, add other dried herbs and flowers by wiring or gluing.

For a bay wreath, cover a Styrofoam wreath with velvet ribbon. Using straight pins, attach the bay leaves over the ribbon, overlapping to cover the pins. For a decorative finish, add a few dried peppers with a bow.

Wreaths may be hung or used to encircle a candle or punch bowl.

DECEMBER — AN HERBAL CHRISTMAS TREE

To end your herbal year, trim your Christmas tree with dried herbs. Select a live tree — Douglas fir works especially well — and gather together all your dried plant material.

If desired, small tiny white lights may be strung on the tree — first.

A filler material, such as baby's-breath, is needed for a background. Insert it between the branches. Next add your sprays of various artemisias and other dried plant material. Last of all, arrange yarrow, strawflowers, lavender, and other dried flowers strategically on the tree.

This may be done on a smaller scale for a tabletop tree.

FRAGRANCE FROM THE HERB GARDEN, WITH VERY LITTLE EFFORT AND NO EXPENSE

Rosella F. Mathieu, Copyright, 1979

While culinary herbs are the life of the herb garden, those grown primarily for fragrance are its glory. What can be more gratifying to the senses than the heady sweetness of lavender flowers, lemon verbena, rose geranium or citrus mint leaves, the last also called bergamot mint. These fragrant herbs are my personal favorites for their contribution to a simple, dry combination of pleasing scents, scents remaining alive and well long after summer is over.

Making a long-lasting classic potpourri is expensive and time-consuming. A satisfactory dry potpourri for an open bowl that will last at least a year can be achieved by the beginner, with no added expense, provided you have some of these herbs in your garden. After your materials are thoroughly dried — otherwise they may mold — combine equal quantities of any or all of the above for a desirable open-bowl potpourri. To release the fragrance, since herbs are 'fast of their smell,' leaves must be crushed slightly to release the cherished scent into the air, awakening and intensifying the perfumes of summer.

If you do not grow all of the above plants, they may be easily added to your garden. Each may be used for tea as well as fragrance. Some other herbs with desirable scents are: lemon thyme, sweet marjoram, spearmint, peppermint, dried heads of bergamot (beebalm), lemon balm, and German chamomile. Any of these may be added to the potpourri above. Or half a dozen handfuls of a single herb, the scent of which you enjoy, may be dried and then placed in an open bowl where it may be crushed in passing. Colorful flowers, even with no scent, add visual pleasure to any potpourri.

If you wish to use a closed container instead of an open bowl, your potpourri will last longer, but then the container needs an opening large enough for your hand to pass through in order to crush or stir the leaves.

For those who enjoy a spicy scent a teaspoon of ground cloves and one of cinnamon may be added to each two cups of dried material. This may cause a slightly dusty appearance. To reduce this, whole pounded cloves and broken pounded stick cinnamon may be added instead.

Following are two recipes for fascinating potpourri:

SUMMER IDYLL

1 cup rose geranium leaves
1 cup bergamot mint leaves
1 cup fragrant rose petals
1 cup lemon basil leaves
1 cup peony petals
½ cup yellow and orange marigold petals
½ cup red geranium petals
¼ cup star anise
2 tablespoons anise seed, cloves and allspice, crushed
1 cinnamon stick, broken into small bits

Combine all ingredients and store in covered container.

CUPBOARD FRESHENER (a woodsy, masculine scent)

1 cup balsam fir needles
1 cup bergamot mint
1 cup sweet woodruff thoroughly dried
½ cup patchouli leaves
6 large seed heads of red bergamot
2 tablespoons each fine sandlewood chips and crushed cloves
1 tablespoon styrax oil
1 teaspoon lavender oil
1 teaspoon bergamot

Combine dry ingredients. Mix oils in a bottle, shake well, and apply to dry mixture with an eye dropper, turning and stirring as you drop.

Rosella Mathieu's first book, THE HERB GROWER'S COMPLETE GUIDE, was an early source book. The publishing of this book in 1949 made her one of the pioneers in informing beginners on how to grow and use herbs. Through the book and her lectures, she was instrumental in encouraging the general use of herbs. Her articles have appeared in THE FARM QUARTERLY, THE JOURNAL OF THE BRONX BOTANICAL GARDENS, THE HERB QUARTERLY, AND THE HERBARIST, a publication of The Herb Society of America. Mrs. Mathieu is presently revising her book, THE COMPLETE HERB GUIDE, due to be released soon.

RECIPE INDEX

Page

RECIPE INDEX

RECIPE INDEX

Page

Page

RECIPE INDEX

Dill

Oregano

Parsley

Sweet Woodruff

Mint

Thyme

CULTIVATION AND COOKING

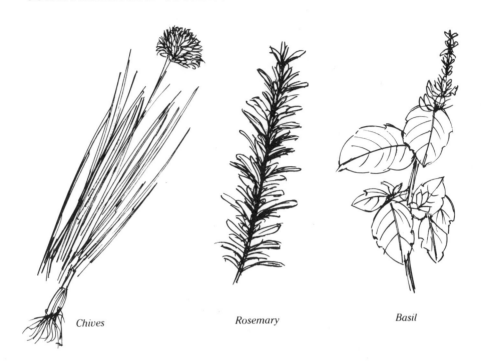

Chives   Rosemary   Basil

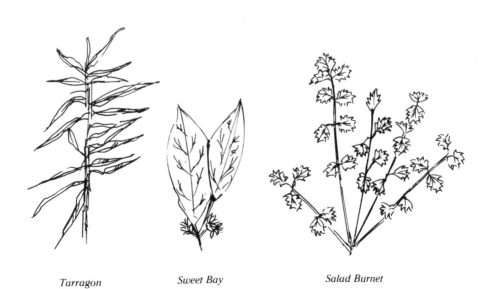

Tarragon   Sweet Bay   Salad Burnet

OUTDOOR PLANTING

There is no magic to growing herbs. Most of them are easily grown. The following herb cultivation chart gives you specific needs for individual herbs.

Select the herbs you personally like to use and follow the general instructions for those herbs. Growth habits and cultural requirements are quite different in the deep south or the far north. Our chart is based on the Southern Ohio area. You will find their needs vary, just as they do for flowers and vegetables. However they will adapt to less than ideal growing conditions.

As a general rule, most herbs prefer well-drained, alkaline, fairly lean soil and a sunny location. There are exceptions, which are noted in the chart. Your soil should be well-spaded and bone meal should be used at planting time. Cuttings are best made in the spring or summer.

CODE TO CHART THAT FOLLOWS:

* Can be grown indoors   H Hardy
# Best renewed every 3 years. P Perennial
A Annual   T Tender
B Biennial

Herb	Description	Culture & Comments	Light	Soil
Basil, sweet * Ocimum basilicum "The to-mato herb"	T.A. 12-30"	Easy from seed when soil is warm. Tamp soil firmly. Will root in water. Keep flower heads pinched off. Collapses with first frost. Subject to white fly. Many cultivars: O.b. 'Minimum' attractive pot plant amenable to topiary, O.b. 'Citriodorum', dainty, lemon-scented.	Full Sun	well-drained, humusy
Bay, sweet * Laurus nobilis	T.P. 2-10'	Cuttings are difficult, taking from 3 months to a year. Root stem cuttings in moist sphagnum and provide humidity or mist. For the first 2 years the plant grows slowly. Fertilize when in active growth. In cold climates it must be grown as a tub plant. In winter, put in a cool location; it does well under fluorescent light and will benefit by being summered outdoors in a protected location with filtered light.	Filtered light	rich well-drained
Borage Borago officinalis	H.A. 13-36"	Seeds germinate readily. Self-sows pro-lifically, resulting in very sturdy plants. Difficult to transplant, except when quite small. Cold enduring.	Full sun	lean
Chervil * Anthriscus cerefolium "Gourmet or French Parsley"	H.A. 8-15"	Sow seeds outdoors in early spring or late fall. It will perish in a hot, sunny location. To grow indoors, start new plants in the pots in which they will grow. Self-sows. Resents trans-planting. Cold enduring.	Partial shade	ordinary garden

INDOOR PLANTING

Many herbs can be successively grown indoors but since it is rather an unnatural environment, do not expect them to perform as well as they do in the garden. Obviously, the exception to this would be greenhouse cultivation.

For growing indoors, light is essential. Herbs should be placed at or near a sunny window or in a fluorescent light garden. Most herbs prefer a cool environment and they do not like to be crowded.

To control spider mites and white fly, give your plants an occasional dunking in soapy water, followed by a clear rinse. Insecticide sprays are not recommended for culinary herbs.

After a time, the soil will become depleted of nutrients and supplemental feedings should be given, periodically. Diluted fish emulsion is recommended.

Misting the foliage will add to the humidity and keep the plant leaves from drying out.

Water	Harvest	Decorative, ornamental, other
ample	Dry, freeze or microwave anytime. Difficult to air-dry. Make pesto in summer, omit cheese and nuts and freeze. Purple variety makes a lovely pink-to-red vinegar.	Clove-scented seed heads can be used in dried arrangements, on wreaths and in potpourri. Holy basil (O. Sanctum) has spicy foliage good for potpourri. "Dark Opal" (O. b. 'purpurascens') has purple foliage attractive in the ornamental garden.
moist	Use leaves, fresh or dry, after the plant begins to mature. To dry, press flat between newspapers or telephone directory.	Handsome house plant. Leaves used in tussie-mussies and on wreaths. Important ingredient in "bouquet garni."
dry	Use its cucumber-tasting leaves only when very young. Peeled stalks can be added to salads. Candy the flowers for confectionery. Float the star-shaped, clear blue flowers in summer drinks.	If flowers are carefully dried they may be used in potpourri. Widely cultivated to attract bees.
fairly moist	Harvest frequently to prevent its going to seed. Little taste when dried. Freezes beautifully. Good in vinegars. Important ingredient in fines herbes.	Pretty border plant. The lacy leaves make an attractive garnish.

Herb	Description	Culture & Comments	Light	Soil
Chives Allium Schoeno-prasum *	H.P. 18"	Root division easiest propagation. Can be grown from seed thickly sown, but takes a long time to produce an edible clump. Divide clump every 3 years. Prune after flowering to avoid self-sowing. For indoor culture, pot in fall, allow a period of dormancy and freezing before bringing indoors to bright light.	Full sun	rich in nitrogen
Chives, garlic or Chinese (also Oriental garlic) Allium tuberosum *	H.P. 15"			
Coriander; Coriandrum sativum (Spanish "Cilantro") (Chinese parsley)	A. 1-3'	Tamp down the seeds sown directly in the garden in a protected location in early spring. Make successive sowings, as they mature quickly. Self-sows.	Sun	ordinary garden
Dill; Anethum graveolens	A. 2-3'	Sow in shallow drills in early spring or fall. Will self-sow. Not easily transplanted. Make successive sowings, as it is short-lived and does not make new growth once it is cut. Do not plant near fennel, as it cross pollinates.	Full sun	fairly rich slightly acid
Fennel, common; Foeniculum vulgare	T.P. 3-5'	Usually grown as an annual. Sow in shallow furrow in early spring. May need staking. Successive sowings suggested. Fennels resent transplanting. Will self-sow. They cross-pollinate with dill.	Full sun	Alkaline, moderately rich — add compost
Fennel, Florence (Finocchio) — F.v. var. azoricum	A. 2"	Sow seeds midsummer. Don't allow it to flower. When the bulbous base begins to swell, mound the earth around it to blanch it. Harvest after frost.	Full sun	Same as Fennel, common.
Lemon verbena * Aloysai triphylla	T.P. 2-4'	Propagated by stem cuttings of new growth. A tender shrub, usually grown as a tub plant. It is more likely to bloom if grown in a pot than if planted in the ground. Not easily wintered over. Loses its leaves when it is dug and potted. Water it sparingly until February, then prune and give it more light and water. Highly susceptible to white fly and spider mites.	Full sun	moderately rich
Lovage; Levisticum officinale	H.P. 3-6'	Propagated by fresh seeds sown in spring or fall. Once established it requires little care. Keep yellowing foliage removed. Susceptible to leaf miner.	Sun or partial shade	fertile
Marjoram, Sweet Origanum majorana *	T.P. 12-15"	Grown as an annual in the northern states. In the southern states it is a perennial. Plant seeds in a sterile medium indoors. Transplant outdoors when the weather is settled. Can be divided or tip cuttings can be made. Dig a small specimen for indoor use and either keep it pruned for tidy growth in a pot or let its branches droop naturally in a hanging basket. It should have good light indoors and an occasional feeding of half-strength liquid fertilizer.	Full sun	rich chalky

232

Water	Harvest	Decorative, ornamental, other
fairly moist	Clip side leaves often. Snip into pieces to freeze. Purple flower heads of chives make an attractive rose-colored vinegar. Use flower heads of garlic chives as a salad garnish.	Dried seed heads of garlic chives are attractive in dried arrangements and on wreaths. Often used as an herb garden border.
average	Foliage often used in ethnic dishes. It freezes well. Dry seeds for baking.	Spicy seeds used in potpourri.
average	Frozen "weed" more flavorful than the dried. Can be preserved in salt. Frozen dill butter is excellent for basting fish. Seed heads, fresh or dried, can be used in vinegar. Dry seed heads in paper bags.	Flower heads and foliage attractive in flower arrangements.
fairly moist	Freeze foliage alone or in butter, which is a good media for absorbing its anise-like flavor. Harvest seeds when the fruiting umbels turn brown.	The cultivar 'Bronze' or 'Copper' is noted for its ornamental value. Seeds excellent for rolls, tea and butter. Use green seed heads and fernlike foliage in fresh flower arrangements.
fairly moist	In late fall, bulbs may be sliced and eaten raw or par boiled as a vegetable. Tender stems of Florence fennel can be frozen. Pleasant anise-like flavor.	Dried stalks on charcoal add excellent flavor when grilling fish. Use fresh leaves with fish dishes, seeds with breads.
average	Leaves dry quickly and are valued for their rich, lemon scent.	Well worth growing for its delightful odor. Fragrant in potpourri.
moist	It has a taste similar to, but stronger than, the leaves of celery. The outer leaves air dry quickly in a dark place and retain their taste. Leaves may also be frozen. Dried seeds may be used for seasoning.	Large, attractive background plant.
some moisture	It retains a great deal of flavor dried. Harvest it after the knotted flower buds form. Can be frozen. Makes an excellent butter.	Potpourri One of the most versatile of culinary herbs.

Herb	Description	Culture & Comments	Light	Soil
Mints Mentha: M.X. piperita peppermint M. spicata spearmint M. suaveolens * applemint M. piperita var. citrata bergamot, lemon, and orange mint	H.P. 2-3'	There are many species of mint, all very aromatic, each with a distinctive scent and appearance. The most popular are spearmint (for juleps, jellies, mint sauce); peppermint (for confections, peas and potatoes); applemint is good for tea and is one of the most attractive for fresh bouquets. It is also the best choice for indoor culture. They are propagated by cuttings (which will root in water) by division, or runners. Cutting before they bloom will eliminate cross-pollination. They tend to be invasive unless confined. Enrich the soil annually to keep them from dying out in the middle. Many are subject to mint rust. Mints tend to hybridize readily.	Semi-shade or more robust in sun	moderately rich, slightly acid
Oregano Origanum vulgare † wild oregano	H.P. 2-3'	One of the most perplexing herb families. There is considerable confusion about the nomenclature of the oregano species. Purchased dried "oregano" is often a blend of a variety of pungent aromatic herbs.	Full sun	lean, slightly alkaline
O. onites * Pot marjoram; O. heracleoticum * Winter, sweet marjoram	T.P. 1' T.P. 1' (trailing habit)	Oregano has a more robust flavor than sweet marjoram. Common wild oregano is too coarse and downy to have much value in cooking. A variety sometimes offered as "Greek" has a piquant flavor, sharper than that generally sold as O. onites. O. heracleoticum has a good, sharp bite. Most species are fairly easy to grow. Propagation by seed, division, stem cuttings and layering.		
Parsley, curly * Petroselinum crispum Parsley, Italian or flat leaved * P. crispum var. neapolitanum	H.B. 10-12" H.B. 12-18"	Usually grown as an annual. Seeds are slow to germinate, taking from 3-8 weeks. Soak the seeds overnight in tepid water. Cold treatment hastens germination. After planting the seeds, place the flat in your freezer or leave outdoors in freezing weather for at least a week before putting it in bright light; or sow them in ice cube trays with water, freeze, plant the ice cubes. Can also be sown outside in the fall or early spring, tamping them down firmly. Transplant only when quite small because of their deep tap root. To grow indoors, dig a small stocky plant in late summer or, better, start new seedings in mid summer. Give bright light.	Partial shade	rich in nitrogen

Water	Harvest	Decorative, ornamental, other
ample	At any time to make jelly, mint sauce or candy the leaves; air dry the leaves and flower heads. Make a base for mint juleps with fresh spearmint leaves and simple syrup; freeze into ice cubes for winter use. Air-dry leaves for tea.	Use fresh as a garnish and in flower arrangements. Dried flower heads are nice for wreaths. Use the citrus-scented dried leaves and flower heads of bergamot mint in potpourri.

| relatively dry | Easy to dry or freeze, the best flavor being obtained before blooming time. Dry the floral bracts of the wild and the white (O. v. Cv. 'Viride') for wreaths and bouquets. | Wild oregano is virtually indestructible and can be used to cover a bank where little else can be grown. Some, such as the cultivar 'Aureum' are very pretty in the ornamental border or in a rock garden. Some of the tender species, such as Dittany of Crete (O. dictamnus)* are pretty in hanging baskets and as a pot plant. |

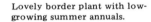

| moist | If dried in a barely warm oven, the bright green color will be retained. More nutritious frozen, either in packets or in ice cubes, which can be tossed into a pot of soup or stew. | Lovely border plant with low-growing summer annuals. Used in fines herbes and bouquet garni. |

Herb	Description	Culture & Comments	Light	Soil
Rosemary * Rosmarinus officinalis	T.P. 1-5'	Generally propagated by cuttings of new growth. They are easily layered but not easy to divide. Growing rosemary from seed is slow and unpredictable. Will root in water. In the summer the pot can be sunk in the ground. If it is unpotted and planted directly in the ground, it will grow rapidly but will be slow to adjust when it is dug up before frost. It is more likely to bloom, on previous year's growth, if slightly pot-bound. Never let your rosemary dry out! Place it in a cool bright spot in the winter and mist its foliage.	Full sun	sandy, alkaline well-drained
Sage, garden † Salvia officinalis	H.P. 1½-2½'	Propagated by stem cuttings, layering or division. Can be grown from seed, but germination is slow and spotty. Prune it severely in the spring to stimulate vigorous new growth. Prune again after flowering. Do not harvest after September.	Sun	alkaline
Salad Burnet Poterium sanguisorba	H.P. 1-2'	Almost an evergreen, it is up early in the spring and one of the last plants to be killed by a hard frost. It springs easily from seed sown in early spring or in autumn. Sturdy plants can be divided in the spring. Best to transplant when small. Will self-sow if seed heads are not removed. Do not cut out center of plant.	Sun or partial shade	Well-drained
Savory, summer Satureja hortensis "The bean herb"	T.A. 12-18"	Sow seeds outdoors when ground is warm. You may wish to mound soil around the base because of the slender, weak stems. Well-spaced plants are more compact. Make successive sowings as the leaves are small and do not yield much for harvest. It is sweeter than the winter variety.	Full sun	average garden
Savory, winter † Satureja montana	P. 12-18"	Is semi-evergreen, leaves turning reddish in winter. Generally started by tip cuttings in the spring, by division or by layering. It can be grown from seed, but they are slow to germinate and should be planted indoors. As it has a sprawling, spreading habit, it should be pruned diligently to keep it shapely. If planted in a wet location it will likely not survive. Mulch after the first hard freeze.	Full sun, partial shade	well-drained lean
Sweet Woodruff * Galium odoratum (German Waldmeister)	H.P. 6-10"	Common propagation is by division or stem cuttings. Spreads vigorously by creeping stolons. Can be grown from fresh seed, although germination is slow and erratic. By nature it is a woodland plant and will benefit by having leaf mold or peat moss incorporated into the soil. It does well as a house plant, especially in a terrarium. Self-sows.	Partial shade or shade	humusy, acid

Water	Harvest	Decorative, ornamental, other

moist Dry the leaves in a dark place so they will retain their color.

A beautiful and aromatic herb. Tuck sprigs in tussie-mussies or wreaths "for remembrance." Use sparingly in potpourri. Decorate pine-like foliage as a table top Christmas tree. Lends itself to bonsai technique; trailing variety (R.o. prostratus) is lovely in a hanging basket. Use dried twigs on your grill when barbecuing chicken.

---

dry Frequently to keep the plant shapely. Hang in bunches to dry.

Several of the ornamental and scented variants make attractive house plants and some make spectacular garnishes.

---

average Frequently for fresh use. The cucumber-flavored leaves can be infused in vinegar for a distinctive flavor.

One of the loveliest of garnishes. Its rounded, neat clumps of compound leaves make it a good candidate for the foreground of a flower or herb bed.

---

average Early, just before the flowers appear, hang in airy place to dry.

Attractive when grown in masses.

---

dry Air-dries quickly. Flavor is stronger if harvested before blooming. A few fresh sprigs may be harvested in winter.

Can be used in rock gardens and as a border plant, despite its sprawling habit.

---

moist Use the fresh foliage to make "Maibowle" in the spring when the scent is most intense. Strain it and set aside a bottle for winter use. Its coumarin scent is not released until it is dried. Air-dry it on screens in a dark place, then strip the foliage from the stems before storing.

Elegant ground cover which does well under shrubbery and trees. Appears early in the spring and is one of the last plants to be blackened by frost. Valuable ingredient in potpourri. Excellent garnish.

237

Herb	Description	Culture & Comments	Light	Soil
Tarragon † Artemisia dracunculus var. sativa (French "Estragon")	H.P. 3'	It is propagated only by cuttings or division, which are best done in spring. "French" tarragon is a sterile clone which does not set viable seed. If you buy tarragon seed it will be the inferior "Russian" variety. Add compost, bone meal or manure in spring. Good drainage is essential. It has a tendency to sprawl if not kept trimmed or staked. It does not do well in warm climates or indoors because it should have a period of dormancy and cold. Prune to ground after last harvest.	Full sun	well-drained friable, sweet
Thyme, Garden † French or English Thymus vulgaris	H.P. 9-18"	Of the hundreds of species of thymes, we shall mention only three commonly used for culinary purposes. Propagation is often accomplished by stem cuttings, layering or division. Seeds from many varieties germinate freely. For earliest growth start the tiny seeds indoors about February. Press them into a tray of shredded sphagnum moss which has been soaked in warm water. Germination is hastened by light and bottom heat. Can be sown in the open after the soil is warm; many varieties self-sow. As they are heavy feeders, bone meal should be added each spring. Prune the upright varieties in spring to keep them shapely and prune all varieties after they bloom. Do not prune upright thymes lower than 5 or 6 inches after early September. In harsh climates they may need a light mulch.	Full sun	Rich, sandy or stony, well-drained and well-limed
Thyme, Lemon † T.X. Citrio- dorus	H.P. 4-12"			
Thyme, Caraway T. Herba- barona	H.P. 2-5"			

Water	Harvest	Decorative, ornamental, other

dry

Fresh and often to keep it within bounds. It is far better frozen than dried, although the dried leaves do retain some of their anise-like flavor. Freeze it in butters to be used for basting poultry and fish. It is distinguished as a vinegar herb.

The gourmet herb, used in Bearnaise sauce, vinegars and many other Epicurean delights. Not recommended as a fore-ground plant in an ornamental garden.

dry

Best harvest is just before blooming. More than one harvest can be obtained in a season. As they are evergreens, light harvesting can be done in the dead of winter. It dehydrates quickly. Hang or spread the stems to dry and strip afterwards.

High ornamental value; many are shrubs, others are mat-forming variants of Mother-of-thyme. There is much variety in the color of the leaves, flowers, and scent. All are good rock garden plants, much-loved by the bees. Creeping thyme can be used as a ground cover in dry places and on barren slopes; it will grow between flag-stones, over rocks and down walls. Those with variegated foliage are not as hardy as the species. Both the foliage and flowers are used in potpourri.

HERB SEED AND PLANT SOURCES

There are far more sources across the country than we have listed. Many may be located in your area.

In the Greater Cincinnati area, one of the best sources is the annual Plant and Herb Sale held at the Civic Garden Center in the spring. It is a joint venture of the Garden Center and the Herb Society of Greater Cincinnati. For more information regarding this sale call (513) 221-0981.

W. Atlee Burpee Company
Warminster, PA 18974

Caprilands Herb Farm
534 Silver Street
N. Coventry, CT 06238

Hilltop Herb Farm, Inc.
P.O. Box 1734
Cleveland, TX 77327

Logee's Greenhouses
55 North Street
Danielson, CT 06239

Fox Hill Herb Farm
Box 7, 440 West Michigan Ave.
Parma, MI 49269

Faith Mountain Herbs
   & Antiques
Box 366
Sperryville, VA 22740

Hopewell Herbs
Manchester, OH 45144

Geo. Park Seed Co., Inc.
Greenwood, SC 29647

The Rosemary House
120 S. Market Street
Mechanicsburg, PA 17055

Sunnybrook Farm Nursery
9448 Mayfield Rd.
Chesterland, OH 44026

Taylor's Herb Garden, Inc.
1535 Lone Oak Road
Vista, CA 92083

Well Sweep Herb Farm
451 Mt. Bethel Road
Port Murray, NJ 07865

Lewis Mountain Herbs &
   Everlasting
2345 State Route 247
Manchester, OH 45144

Chalet Lodge Herb Farm
Delaware, OH 43015

Nichols Garden Nursery
1190 North Pacific Hwy.
Albany, OR 97321